THE
Picture Plus
Dictionary

SECOND EDITION

Virginia McKinney, Ph.D.

Illustrated by Rene Vega

Butte Publications, Inc.
Hillsboro, Oregon

Copyright © 1997, 2006 by Virginia McKinney

All rights reserved. No part of this publication may be reproduced in any form
or by any means, electronic or mechanical, including photocopying, without
permission in writing from the copyright owner.

Butte Publications, Inc.
P.O. Box 1328
Hillsboro, OR 97123-1328 USA

Publisher's Cataloging-in-Publication
(Provided by Quality Books, Inc.)

McKinney, Virginia.
    The picture plus dictionary / by Virginia McKinney ;
illustrated by Rene Vega. — 2nd ed.
    p. cm.
    SUMMARY: An English language dictionary, using sign
language illustrations as definitions.
    ISBN 978-1-884362-52-1
    ISBN 1-884362-52-4

    1. Picture dictionaries, English—Juvenile
literature. 2. English language—Dictionaries,
Juvenile. 3. Sign language—Dictionaries, Juvenile.
[1. Picture dictionaries. 2. English language—
Dictionaries. 3. Sign language—Dictionaries.
4. Vocabulary.]   I. Vega, Rene. II. Title.

PE1629.M36 2006   423'.17
                          QBI06-600050

INTRODUCTION

The Picture Plus Dictionary presents a basic functional vocabulary essential for the development of reading skills and face-to-face signed and/or spoken language. The 4500 + entries replace the traditional word/picture and word/sign format found in most picture dictionaries and sign language dictionaries with meaningful contextual settings that cover a wide range of subjects relating to life in the United States. Each frame presents the entry word used in a sentence, a sign language drawing, and a picture to help convey the word meaning as used in that sentence. The "Plus" in the publication title refers to the sign language drawings that form part of each entry. This dictionary was developed to assist hearing-impaired learners and second language learners master the use of a basic vocabulary as used in connected language structures. Many signs have an obvious conceptual base, and the sign drawings should enhance comprehension for both hearing-impaired and hearing learners.

Vocabulary Selection

The vocabulary in this dictionary was compiled over a period of years after an analysis of published word lists and language and reading materials involving a wide variety of subjects. Included in the list are the twenty-five function words compiled by Donald Moores from the Thorndike-Lorge Semantic Count that his analysis indicated accounted for one-third of the total words appearing in the printed material involved in the semantic count. Also included are the thirty-three function and content words identified by Jones and Wepman as accounting for more than fifty percent of all words uttered in their spoken word count. An impressive display of the importance of this small group of words may be obtained by circling each occurrence of the words as they appear on the front page of a newspaper.

Selection of additional vocabulary was influenced by relevance to everyday experiences such as home, work, employment, recreational activities, interpersonal relationships, citizenship, moral development, transportation, communication, etc.

Picture Selection

Some pictures depict a single object or action. Many pictures, however, depict a range of situation types involved in daily communicative interaction within our culture such as mother scolding a child, wife tending sick husband, careless pedestrian, efficient worker. Some of these situation pictures appear more than once throughout the dictionary to expose the learner to a constellation of verbal options associated with each situaton type.

The Sign Language Drawings

The signs presented in the dictionary reflect the author's observation of signs used by deaf adults, professionals in the area of deafness, and professional interpreters. More than one sign is included in many frames to expose the learner to a range of signs that might be encountered in signed communication. Signs that are used mostly in an educational setting have been marked with an asterisk (*). Many signs represent a concept rather than a single word, so the same sign may appear in more than one dictionary entry. In this situation the signs may be viewed as signalers of linguistic categories which provide the receiver with a closed set of alternatives from which to choose, the members of the set usually being distinguishable on the basis of gross lip movement differences.

Part-of-Speech Classification

Part-of-speech classification of two-word verbs and compound nouns follows Webster's International Dictionary classification.

All verb forms related to a simple present tense entry are provided for most verbs in the following order: pres. 3d sing. (s-form), past tense, present participle (-ing form), past participle (if different from the past tense form).

Comparative and superlative forms are listed for many adjectives.

Part-of-Speech Abbreviations

adj.	adjective	*pp.*	past participle
adv.	adverb	*prep.*	preposition
conj.	conjunction	*pres.*	present
contr.	contraction	*pron.*	pronoun
-ing form	present participle	*pt.*	past tense
interj.	interjection	*sing.*	singular
n.	noun	*s-form*	pres. 3d sing.
pl.	plural	*v.*	verb

References

Donald F. Moores, "Psycholinguistics and Deafness," <u>American Annals of the Deaf</u> 115 (January 1970): 44.

Lyle V. Jones and Joseph M. Wepman, <u>A spoken word count</u> (Chicago: Language Research Associates, 1966), p. 4.

ACKNOWLEDGEMENTS

Many people have contributed to the development of this version of the Picture Plus Dictionary and the much large data base of sign drawings. I am indebted to countless deaf adults, professionals in the area of deafness and professional interpreters I have worked with or associated with over the past thirty plus years for their input and encouragement. I wish to express particular appreciation to Julie DeSiderio, Diane Lessing, Sandra Vega and Anne Wallis, all teachers of the deaf, who read the text portion of the dictionary and made excellent suggestions.

I am also indebted to Diane Lessing for suggesting I explore the possibility of having Rene Vega do the artwork for the dictionary, and indebted to Rene for being such a talented and delightful person to work with.

The project in the early stages was partially funded by much appreciated generous gifts from Mary Lubisich and Rose Talbott, and might never have been completed without this initial assistance.

A very special thank you to Julie DeSiderio, Larry Fleischer, Etienne Harvey, Maree Jo Keller, Sharon Neumann Solow, Sandra Vega and Anne Wallis for their patience and hard work in reviewing all or part of the finished dictionary and for providing invaluable suggestions concerning signs, pictures and text.

I accept full responsibility for all errors and omissions.

Virginia McKinney

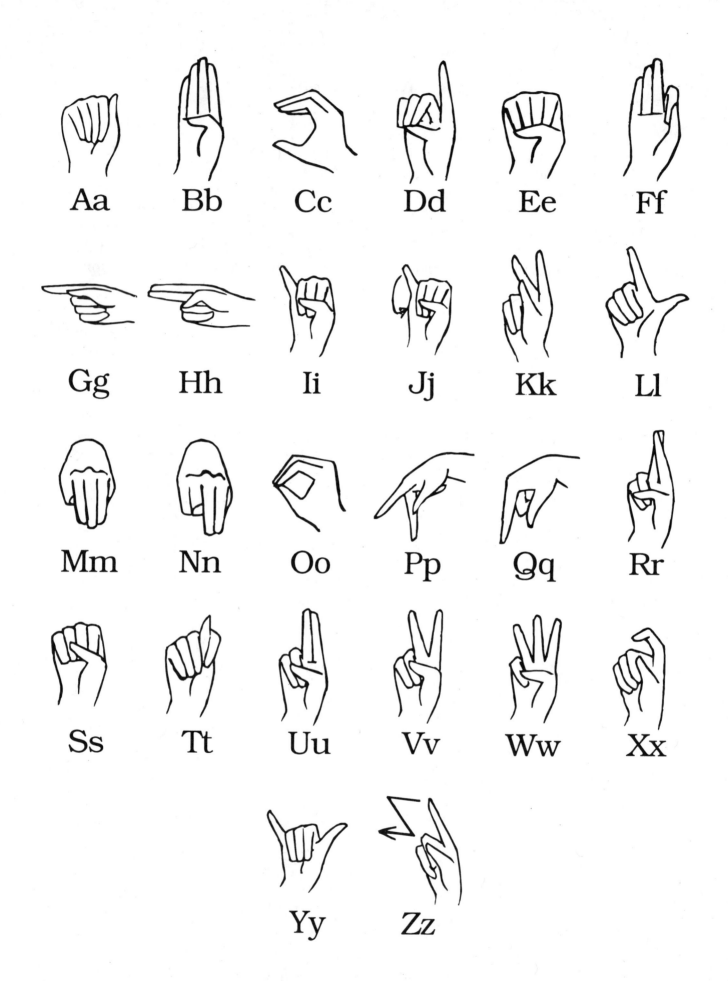

A a

a *indefinite article*

A boy and a girl went ice-skating.
The boy fell down.

able *adj.*

Mary <u>is able to</u> make her own lunch.
She <u>can</u> make her own lunch.

abandoned *adj.*

We saw an <u>abandoned</u> house.
We saw a <u>deserted</u> house.

not **able** *adj.* unable

He <u>is not able to</u> reach the cookies.
He <u>can't</u> reach the cookies.

ability *n.*

She <u>has the ability to</u> tie her shoes.
She <u>can</u> tie her own shoes.

abnormal *adj.*

A high temperature is <u>abnormal</u>.
It is <u>not normal</u>.

ability *n.*

He has great <u>ability</u> as a builder.
He has great <u>skill</u> as a builder.

aboard *prep.*

The men are <u>aboard</u> the ship.
They are <u>on</u> the ship.

2 about

about *adv.*

He has <u>about</u> finished planting the tree. He has <u>almost</u> finished.

above *prep.*

The fixture is <u>above</u> the table.
It is <u>over</u> the table.

about *prep.*

It is <u>about</u> 8:30.
It's <u>almost</u> 8.30.

abrupt *adj.*

The car made an <u>abrupt</u> stop.
It made a <u>sudden</u> stop.

about *prep.*

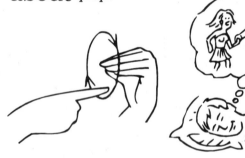

Bill is dreaming <u>about</u> the dance.
He is dreaming <u>of</u> the dance.

absent *adj.*

One student is <u>absent</u>.
One student is <u>not here</u> today.

above *adv.*

The clouds are <u>above</u>.
They are <u>overhead</u>.

absolutely *adv.*

I am <u>absolutely</u> innocent.
I'm <u>completely</u> innocent.

accompany 3

abuse *v.* mistreat

She should not abuse her toys.
abuses abused abusing

accident *n.* collision

The woman saw an accident.
accident   accidents

accept *v.*

or

The boy will <u>accept</u> the trophy.
He will <u>take</u> the trophy.

accident *n.*

It was an accident. I didn't
break the window on purpose.

acceptable *adj.*

His grades are <u>acceptable</u>.
They are <u>all right</u>.

accidentally *adv.*

or

He broke the window accidentally.
He didn't mean to break it.

not **acceptable** *adj.*

His behavior is <u>not acceptable</u>.
It is <u>not all right</u>.

accompany *v.*

Bob's girlfriend will accompany him.
She will go with him.

4   accordion

accordion *n. musical instrument*

Can you play an accordion?
accordion accordions

account *v.*

He can't <u>account for</u> the missing candy. He can't <u>explain</u> it.

account *n.*

or

She has an account at this store.
account   accounts

accurate *adj.*

She gave an <u>accurate</u> account of the accident. She gave an <u>exact</u> account.

account *n.*

We can't play <u>on account of</u> the rain.
We can't play <u>because of</u> the rain.

accuse *v.*

I accuse you of taking the candy.
I blame you.

account *n.*

or

Each man gave a different <u>account</u>.
Each gave a different <u>explanation</u>.

accuse *v.*

Don't accuse me of taking the candy.
Don't blame me.

act 5

ache *v.*

Does your shoulder ache?
Does it hurt?

across *prep.*

He lives across the street. He lives on the other side of the street.

acorn *n. nut*

Acorns grow on oak trees.
acorn   acorns

across *prep.*

Tijuana is across the border.
It is beyond the border.

acrobat *n.*

We watched the acrobat.
acrobat   acrobats

across *prep.*

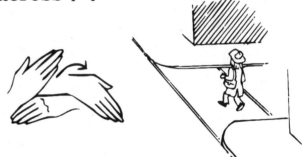

She is walking across the street.
She's crossing the street.

come across *v.*

Did he come across his ball?
Did he find it?

act *n. informal*

He is not really honest and friendly.
He's just putting on an act.

6 act

act n.
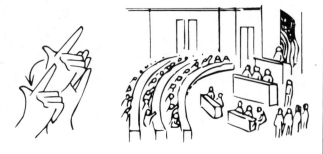
The Senate voted on the <u>act</u>.
The Senate voted on the <u>law</u>.

active adj.

Their children are very <u>active</u>.
They are very <u>lively</u>.

act v.

He should not act silly.
He shouldn't do silly things.

actor n.

Who is your favorite actor?
actor   actors

act v.
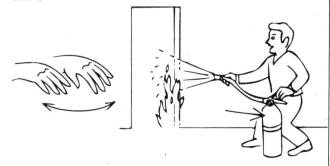
You must act fast when you see a fire. You must do something.

actress n. female actor

Who is your favorite actress?
actress   actresses

action n.

His quick action saved the house.
action   actions

actual adj.

The woman's <u>actual</u> weight is 160.
Her <u>real</u> weight is 160.

address 7

ad *n.*

Check the ads for bargains.
Check the advertisements.

addicted *adj.*

He is addicted to drugs.

add *v.*

Add 1 and 1 and you have 2.
The sum of 1 and 1 is 2.

addition *n.*

The boy is learning addition.
He is learning how to add.

add *v.*

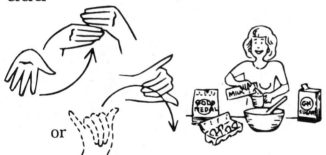

I must add milk to the batter.
adds   added   adding

address *n.*

I wrote the address on the envelope.
address   addresses

add *v.*

The boy has to add the numbers.

address *v.*

I must address the envelope.
addresses addressed addressing

8 adhesive tape

adhesive tape n.

Adhesive tape is hard to remove.

advance v.

The soldiers will <u>advance</u>.
They will <u>move forward</u>.

adjective n.

 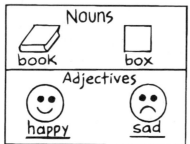

The underlined words are adjectives.
adjective   adjectives

advance v.

The army will <u>advance</u> him in rank.
The army will <u>promote</u> him.

adjust v.

I always have to adjust the antenna.
adjusts   adjusted   adjusting

adventure n.

The boy dreams of adventures at sea.
He dreams of an exciting life at sea.

adult n.

He is an <u>adult.</u> He is not a child.
He's <u>of age</u>. He's <u>a grown-up</u>.

affect v.

Smoking can affect your health.
affects   affected   affecting

again 9

afford *v.*

He can't afford to buy the candy.
He doesn't have enough money.

run after *v.*

Does the dog always <u>run after</u> that cat?
Does the dog always <u>chase</u> it?

afraid *adj.*

The girl is <u>afraid</u> of the mouse.
She is <u>scared</u> of it.

after *prep.*

It is twenty-two minutes after 8.
It's eight twenty-two.

Africa *n. continent*
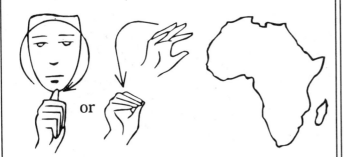
Africa is south of Europe.

afternoon *n. noon till sunset*

I lost my ball yesterday <u>afternoon</u>.
I lost it <u>between noon and evening</u>.

come after

Does the lady <u>come after</u> the tall man?
Is she <u>behind</u> him?

again *adv.*
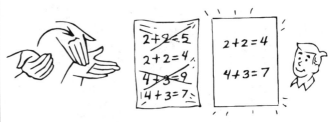
I did the paper again.
I did it once more. I did it over.

10 against

against *prep.*

The candidate is <u>against</u> war.
He is <u>opposed to</u> it.

ago *adv.*

or

<u>Long ago</u>, ships used sails.
<u>In the past</u>, they used sails.

against *prep.*

The ladder is leaning <u>against</u> the house. It's leaning <u>upon</u> the house.

agree *v.*

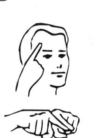

Did they agree on a price?
agrees agreed agreeing

against the law illegal

Stealing is against the law.

ahead *adv.*

He moved his wheelchair <u>ahead</u>.
He moved it <u>forward</u>.

age *n.*

The girl is six years of age.
She is six years old.

ahead *adv.*

A tall man is <u>ahead of</u> the woman.
He is <u>in front of</u> her.

aisle 11

aim v.

You must <u>aim</u> the dart at the target.
You must <u>point the dart</u> at it.

Air Force n.
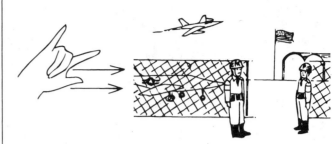
He will join the Air Force.

air n.

I opened the window
to let in some air.

airplane n.

Our airplane landed on time.
airplane   airplanes

air n.

They <u>traveled by air</u>.
They <u>flew</u>. They <u>took a plane</u>.

airport n.
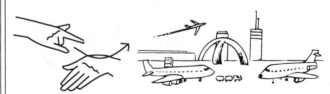
The plane landed at the airport.
airport   airports

air conditioner n.
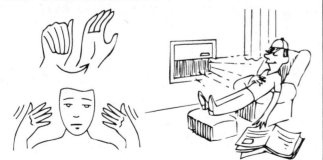
The air conditioner cools the air.
air conditioner   air conditioners

aisle n.

Canned goods are in aisle 4.
aisle   aisles

12 alarm

alarm n.
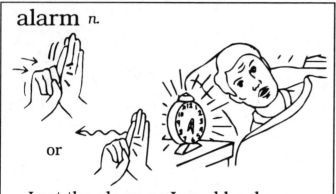
I set the alarm so I would wake up.
The alarm went off at 6:30.

alcohol n.
I set the alarm so I would wake up.
Alcohol ruined his life.
Liquor ruined his life.

Alaska n. state: AK
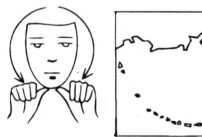
Alaska became a state in 1959.

alcoholic n.

The man is an alcoholic.
He is not able to stop drinking.

album n.
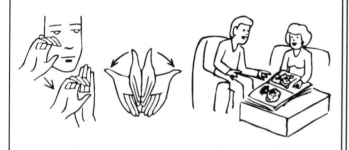
I put the picture in my album.
album   albums

alike adj.

The twins look alike.
They look the same.

alcohol n.
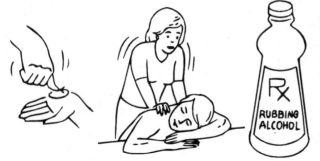
She rubbed his back with alcohol.

alive adj.
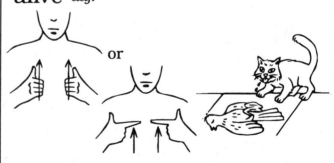
The cat is alive. The bird is dead.
The bird is not alive.

alligator 13

all *adj.*

He ate <u>all</u> the donuts.
He ate <u>every one of</u> them.

all right *adv.* OK

I asked if I could go out, and she said, "All right." She said, "Yes."

all *pron.*

<u>All of us</u> are going to the beach.
<u>Everyone</u> is going to the beach.

all right *adv.* OK

or

He did all right in art –
not good, not bad.

all at once

or

<u>All at once</u>, it started to rain.
<u>Suddenly</u>, it started to rain.

alley *n.*

or

*

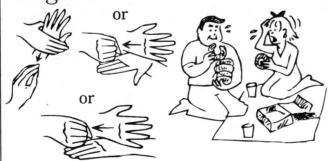

The trash cans are in the alley.
alley   alleys

all gone

or

or

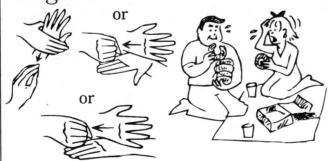

The donuts are all gone.
There are no donuts left in the box.

alligator *n. reptile*

The alligator has thick skin.
alligator   alligators

14 allow

allow v.

The sign doesn't <u>allow</u> hunting here.
It doesn't <u>permit</u> hunting here.

almost adv.

He <u>almost</u> missed the bus.
He <u>nearly</u> missed it.

allow v.

Why did she <u>allow</u> the meat to burn?
Why did she <u>let</u> the meat burn?

alone adj.

The man is alone on the island.
He is all by himself.

allowance n.

My allowance is $3.00 a week.
I get $3.00 a week for spending money.

along adv.

Bob went for a walk and took his son along. Bob took his son with him.

almost adv.

It is <u>almost</u> 8:30.
It's <u>nearly</u> 8:30.

run **along** v.

He told the children to <u>run along</u>.
He told them to <u>leave</u>.

am 15

along *prep.*

They walked along the beach.
They walked the length of the beach.

altogether *adv.*
He has three cents <u>altogether</u>.
He has three cents <u>in all</u>.

alphabet *n.*
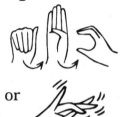
abcdefghijklm
nopqrstuvwxyz
The English alphabet has twenty-six letters in it.

aluminum *n. metal*

The pie pan and foil are made of aluminum.

already *adv.*
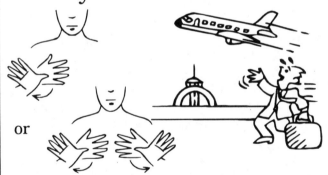
The plane had already left.

always *adv.*

The sun always rises.
It rises every morning.

also *adv.*

He hates carrots. He hates peas, <u>also</u>.
He hates peas, <u>too</u>.

am *v. pres. 1st sing. of* **be**
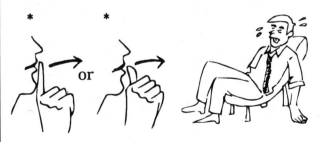
I am very tired.
I'm exhausted.

16 am going to

am going to
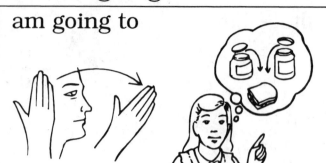
I am going to make a sandwich.
I will make a sandwich.

amount *n. total*

The amount of the bill shocked him.
The total cost shocked him.

ambulance *v. vehicle*

Someone called an ambulance.
ambulance   ambulances

an *indefinite article*

Use 'an' instead of 'a' before vowels. I ate an apple.

America *n. country*

I was born in America.
I was born in the United States.

ancestors *n.*

He pointed to a picture of his ancestors.

American *n.*

He was an American. He was a citizen of the United States.

anchor *n.*

He dropped the anchor into the water.
anchor   anchors

answer 17

and *conj.*

We had dinner and went to a movie.

ankle *n. body part*

He hurt his ankle.
ankle   ankles

angel *n.*

The angel has wings.
angel   angels

annoy *v.*

Why does he always <u>annoy</u> that girl?
Why does he always <u>bother</u> her?

angry *adj.*

The women are <u>angry</u>. They are <u>mad</u>.
angrier   angriest

another *adj.*

The boy wants another cookie.
He wants one more cookie.

animal *n.*

Do you like animals?
animal   animals

answer *n.*

The boy gave the right answer.
answer   answers

18 answer

answer *v.*

The woman must answer the question.
answers   answered   answering

antique *n.*

The car is an antique.
It's old and valuable.

ant *n. insect*

or
There are ants on the counter.
ant   ants

antler *n. animal body part*

Deer, elk, and moose have antlers.
antler   antlers

antelope *n. animal*

The antelope has long horns.
antelope   antelopes

any *adj.*

The girl isn't wearing any clothes.
She doesn't have any clothes on.

antidote *n. remedy*

The doctor gave him an antidote
to counteract the poison.

any *pron.*
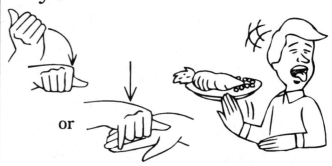
or
Mother asked him to eat some peas
and carrots. But he didn't want any.

appear 19

anybody *pron.*

Has <u>anybody</u> seen my baseball?
Has <u>anyone</u> seen it?

apartment *n.*

My apartment is on the third floor.
apartment   apartments

anyone *pron.*

Does <u>anyone</u> want a cookie?
Does <u>anybody</u> want one?

ape *n. animal*

The ape has long arms.
ape   apes

anything *pron.*

The man doesn't have anything in
his pockets. His pockets are empty.

apologize *v.*

Did he apologize for breaking the
window? Did he say he was sorry?

apart *adv.*

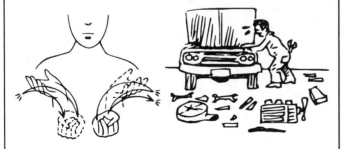

He took the car <u>apart</u>.
He took the car <u>to pieces</u>.

appear *v.*

Does it <u>appear that</u> it may rain?
Does it <u>look like</u> it may rain?

20 appear

appear *v.*

The woman does <u>appear</u> to be angry.
She does <u>seem</u> to be angry.

apply *v.*
He will apply for a job.
applies   applied   applying

appear *v.*

Did a vase suddenly appear?
appears   appeared   appearing

appointment *n.*

He has an appointment with the doctor.
appointment   appointments

apple *n. fruit*

Bob eats an apple every day.
apple   apples

appreciate *v.*

I appreciate the nurse's help.
appreciates   appreciated   appreciating

application *n.*

The man is filling out an
application for a loan.

approach *v.*

The woman will <u>approach</u> the door.
She will <u>walk toward</u> the door.

are going to 21

appropriate *adj.*

His behavior is always <u>appropriate</u>.
His behavior is always <u>acceptable</u>.

aquarium *n.*

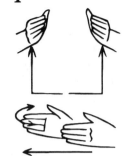

An aquarium is a large tank or bowl for fish.

apricot *n. fruit*

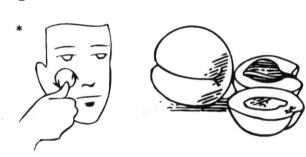

Apricots grow on trees.
apricot apricots

Arctic *n.*

The Arctic is the area around the North Pole.

April *n. month*

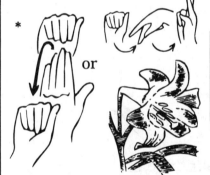

Easter sometimes comes in April.

are *v. pres. pl. & 2nd sing. of* **be**

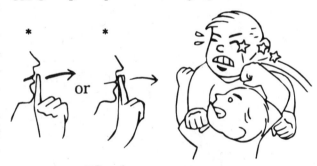

The boys are angry.
They are fighting.

apron *n. clothing*

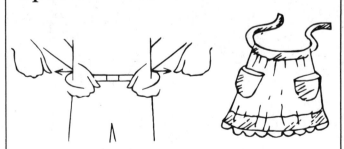

An apron will protect your clothes.
apron aprons

are going to

They <u>are going to</u> take a trip.
They <u>will</u> take a trip.

22 area

area *n.* space

The area in front of the theater is crowded with people.

arithmetic *n.* math

The boy got an A in arithmetic.

area code *n.*

My phone number is 555-0794
My area code is 213.

Arizona *n.* state: AZ

Arizona became a state in 1912.

aren't *contr. of* **are not**

His grades <u>aren't</u> good.
They <u>are not</u> good.

arm *n.* body part

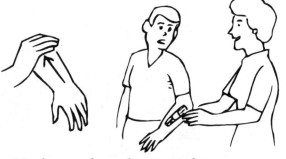

He has a bandage on his arm.
arm   arms

argue *v.* quarrel

They always argue about the dog.
argues   argued   arguing

arm *n.* chair part

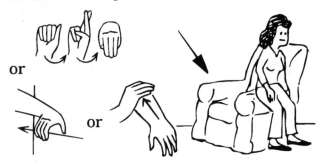

She sat on the arm of the chair.

arrow 23

army n.

Her son joined the army.
army   armies

arrange v.

I must arrange the books.
arranges   arranged   arranging

around prep.

The girl walked around the chair.

arrest v.
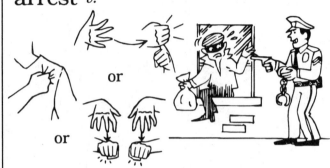
The officer will arrest the burglar.
arrests   arrested   arresting

look around v.

I have to <u>look around</u> for my ball.
I have to <u>search for</u> it.

arrive v.

When did she <u>arrive</u> home?
When did she <u>come</u> home?

turn around v.

Why did he turn around?

arrow n. weapon
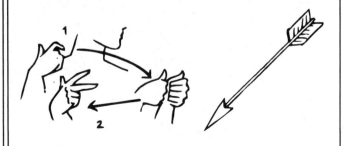
The arrow has a sharp point.
arrow   arrows

24 art

art n.

She in studying art.

artificial adj.

These flowers are artificial. They are not real. They're made of paper.

artichoke n. vegetable

Do you like artichokes?
artichoke   artichokes

artist n.

The artist is painting a picture.
artist   artists

article n.

I read an article about the fire.
I read a story about it.

as conj. while

It began to rain as I was hanging up the clothes.

article n.

She bought a few articles.
She bought a few things.

as a rule
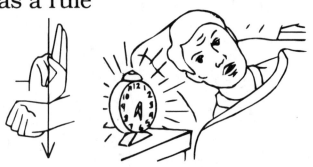
As a rule, he gets up at 6:30.
He usually gets up then.

assemble 25

ashamed *adj.*

The dog is ashamed of itself.

asleep *adj.*

The man is asleep. He is sleeping.

ashtray *n.*

The ashtray is made of glass.
ashtray   ashtrays

asparagus *n. vegetable*

I bought some asparagus for dinner.
Asparagus costs 99 cents a bunch.

Asia *n. continent*

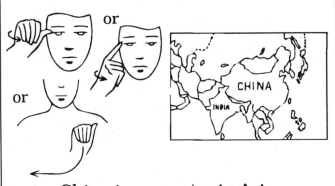

China is a country in Asia.

aspirin *n.*

He took an aspirin for his headache.

ask *v.*

Did the lawyer ask a question?
asks   asked   asking

assemble *v.*

I can assemble model planes.
I can put them together.

26 assign

assign v.

What did the teacher assign?
What did she tell us to read?

at prep.

She is <u>at</u> the grocery store.
She is <u>in</u> the grocery store.

associate v.

Does he associate with bad companions?
Is he friendly with bad boys?

at prep.

Father pointed <u>at</u> the dog.
He pointed <u>toward</u> the dog.

astronaut n.
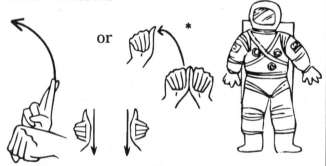
The astronaut flew to the moon.
astronaut   astronauts

at last adv.

<u>At last</u> she finished her work.
She <u>finally</u> finished it.

at prep.

Someone is <u>at</u> the door.
Someone is <u>by</u> the door.

at once adv.
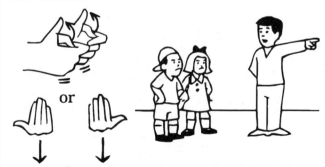
I want you to go <u>at once</u>.
I want you to go <u>immediately</u>.

attention 27

ate pt. of eat

The boy ate an apple.

attach v. connect

He must attach the hose.
attaches attached attaching

athlete n.
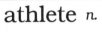
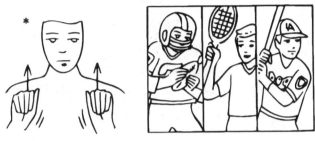
He is a good athlete.
athlete   athletes

attack v.
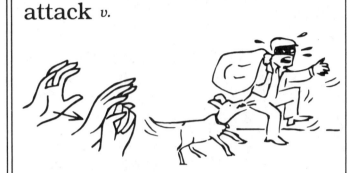
Why did the dog attack the man?
attacks attacked attacking

atmosphere n.

Air is part of the atmosphere that surrounds Earth.

attend v.

I attend school.
I go to school.

atomic bomb n.

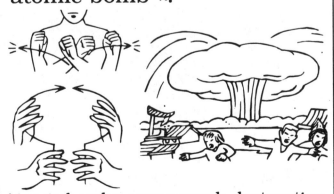
Atomic bombs cause much destruction.

attention n.

Her attention is on her book. She's not paying attention to her cooking.

28 attic

attic n.

The attic is below the roof.

August n. month

He takes his vacation in August.

attitude n. feeling
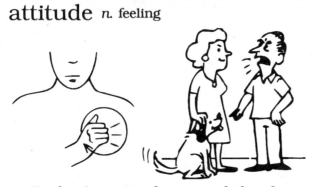
Father's attitude toward the dog never seems to change.

aunt n. female relative

That woman is my aunt. She is my mother's sister.

audience n.

The audience enjoyed the performance.
audience   audiences

Australia n. country
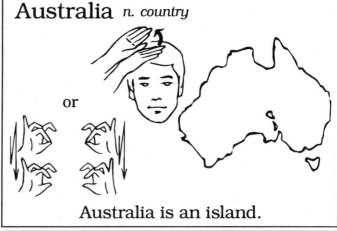
Australia is an island.

auditorium n.

The auditorium is empty.
auditorium   auditoriums

author n. writer

Daniel Defoe was the author of *Robinson Crusoe*. He wrote the book.

avoid 29

authority n. power

A policeman has the authority to arrest people for crimes.

available adj.

The doctor is not available.
The doctor is not in the office.

automatic teller n.

He is using an automatic teller.
automatic teller   automatic tellers

avenue n.

We walked along the avenue.
We walked along the wide street.

automobile n. car, auto

He bought a new automobile.
automobile   automobiles

avocado n. fruit

Avocados grow on trees.
avocado   avocados

autumn n. season

<u>Autumn</u> is between summer and winter.
<u>Fall</u> is between summer and winter.

avoid v.

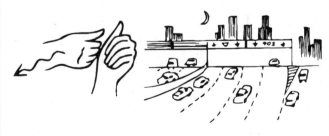

I avoid traffic by leaving early.
avoids   avoided   avoiding

30 awake

awake *adj.*

Bill is awake. He is not asleep.

away *adv.*

or

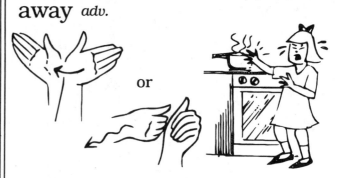

Children should stay away from hot stoves.

award *n.*

or

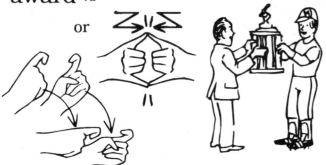

The boy is accepting the award.
He is accepting the trophy.

awful *adj.*

or

The man has an awful headache.
He has a terrible headache.

aware *adj.*

She is not aware of the danger.
She's not conscious of it.

awkward *adj.*

Penguins are awkward on land.
They are clumsy on land.

away *adj.*

The family will be away for a week.
They will not be at home.

ax/axe *n. tool*

He used an ax to cut down the tree.
    ax   axes

B b

baby *n.* infant

The baby is happy.
baby   babies

backache *n.*

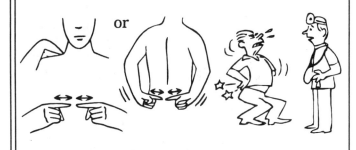

The man's back hurts.
He has a backache.

back *adj.*

We sat in the back seat.
We sat in the rear seat.

backpack *n.*

The backpack is very heavy.
backpack   backpacks

back *n. body part*

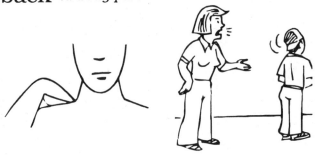

I was looking at the boy's back.
back   backs

backward *adj.* backwards

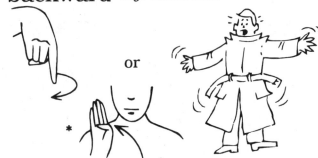

He put the coat on backward.
He put it on the wrong way.

back and forth

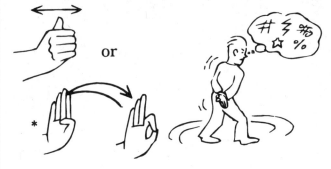

The angry man walked back and forth.

backward *adj.*

He counted backward.
He counted in reverse order.

31

32 bacon

bacon *n. meat*

He had bacon with his eggs.

bag *n. container*

The bag is empty.
The sack is empty.

bad *adj. not good*

The girl did a bad thing.
She didn't control her temper.

bag *n.*
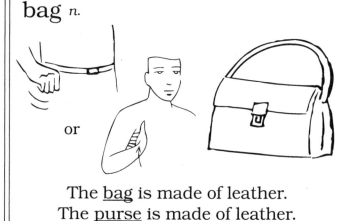
or
The bag is made of leather.
The purse is made of leather.

badge *n.*

or
The policeman wears a badge.
badge   badges

bag *n.*

The bellboy carried our bags.
He carried our suitcases.

badminton *n.*
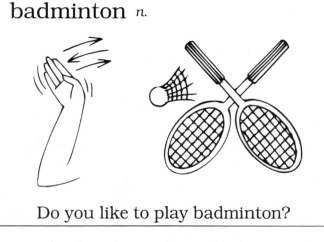
Do you like to play badminton?

bake *v.*

She will bake the cake.
bakes baked baking

balloon 33

baker n. worker
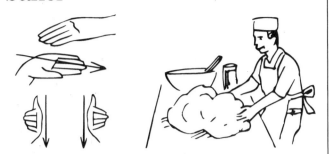
The baker is kneading the dough.
baker   bakers

ball n. toy
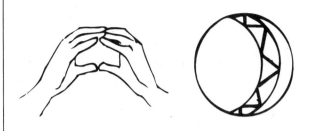
The ball is round.
ball   balls

bakery n.

The woman went to the bakery.
bakery   bakeries

ball n.

Cinderella went to the <u>ball</u>.
She went to the <u>dance</u>.

balance n.

He held out his arms to keep his balance.

ballet n.

We enjoyed the ballet.

balance n. informal: remainder

She ate one donut, and he ate the <u>balance</u>.
She ate one, and he ate the <u>rest</u>.

balloon n. toy

The girl has a balloon.
balloon   balloons

34 ballot

ballot n.

The man is marking his ballot.
ballot   ballots

band-aid n.
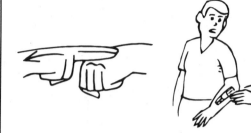
Mother put a band-aid on my arm.
band-aid   band-aids

banana n. *fruit*

or

Bananas grow on trees.
banana   bananas

bandanna, bandana n. *clothing*
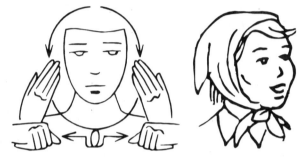
She is wearing a bandanna.
bandanna   bandannas

band n.

The band played my favorite song.

bang v.

or

Why did he <u>bang</u> on the door?
Why did he <u>pound</u> on it?

bandage n.
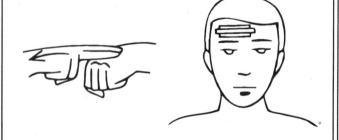
He has a bandage on his forehead.
bandage   bandages

bangs n.

Her bangs cover her forehead.

barge 35

banjo *n. musical instrument*

He can play the banjo.
banjo   banjos/banjoes

barber *n. worker*

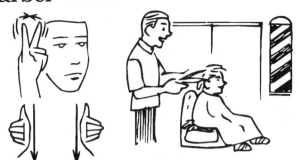

The barber is cutting Bob's hair.
barber   barbers

bank *n.*

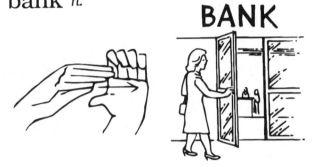

The woman went to the bank.
bank   banks

bare *adj.*

The cupboard is bare.
It is empty.

banner *n.*

The students are carrying a banner.
banner   banners

bargain *n.*

The dress was a bargain.
It was inexpensive.

barbecue *n. barbeque*

The family is having a barbecue.
barbecue   barbecues

barge *n.*

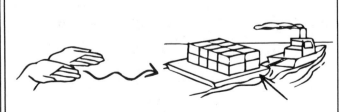

The barge has a flat bottom.
barge   barges

36 bark

bark v.

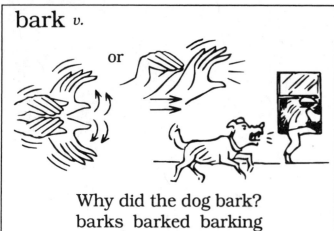

Why did the dog bark?
barks barked barking

base n.

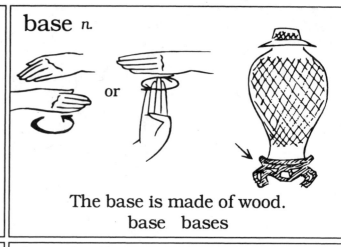

The base is made of wood.
base   bases

barn n. building

The cows sleep in the barn.
barn   barns

baseball n. game

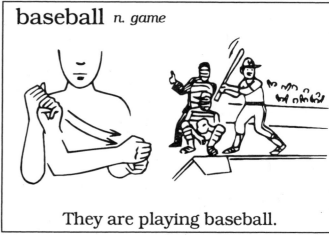

They are playing baseball.

barrel n.

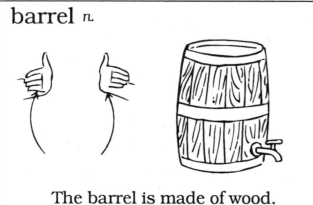

The barrel is made of wood.
barrel   barrels

basement n.

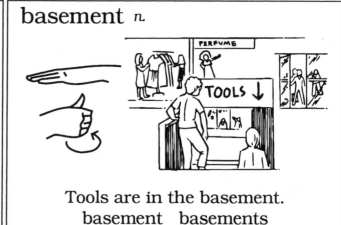

Tools are in the basement.
basement   basements

base n.

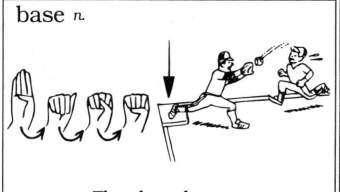

The player has one
foot on the base.

bashful adj.

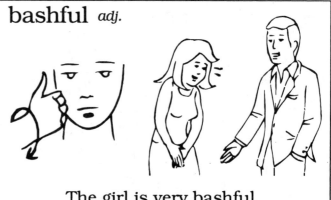

The girl is very bashful.
She's very shy.

bathroom 37

basket n. container

The basket is full of groceries.
basket   baskets

bath n.
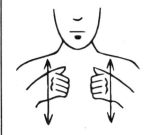
The boy is taking a bath.
bath   baths

basketball n.

They are playing basketball.

bathing suit n.

She is wearing a bathing suit.
bathing suit   bathing suits

bat n. animal
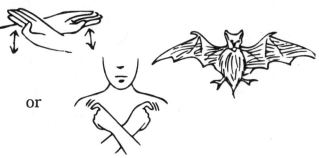
or
Bats fly at night.
bat   bats

bathrobe n. clothing
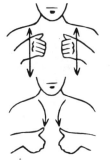 
Father is wearing a bathrobe.
bathrobe   bathrobes

bat n.
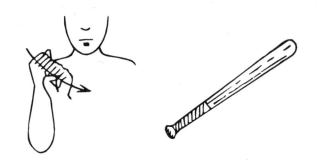
The bat is made of wood.

bathroom n.
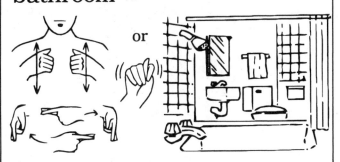
My apartment has one bathroom.
bathroom   bathrooms

38 bath towel

bath towel n.
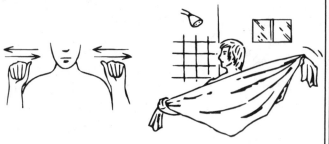
The man is using a bath towel.
bath towel   bath towels

bay n.
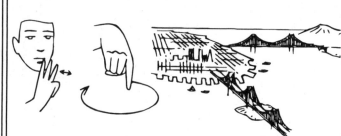
They built a bridge across the bay.
bay   bays

bathtub n.
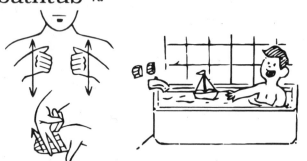
The boy is in the bathtub.
bathtub   bathtubs

be v.
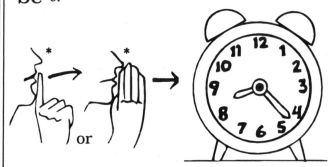
It will soon be 8:30.

battery n.

The flashlight needs new batteries.
battery   batteries

beach n. shore

They walked along the beach.
beach   beaches

bawl out v. informal

Why did she bawl him out?
Why did she scold him?

bead n. jewelry

She is wearing a string of beads.
bead   beads

beat 39

beak *n. animal body part*

The bird has a long beak.
beak   beaks

bear *v. stand, endure*

Father can't bear the noise.
bears   bore   bearing   borne

bean *n. vegetable*

We had green beans for dinner.
bean   beans

beard *n. body part*

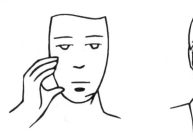

The man grew a beard.
beard   beards

bean *n. vegetable*

Mother will fix beans for dinner.

beat *v.*

He likes to beat the drum.
beats   beat   beating   beaten/beat

bear *n. animal*

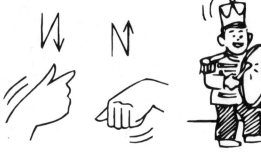

I saw a brown bear at the zoo.
bear   bears

beat *v.*

Why did he beat on the door?
Why did he bang on it?

40 beat

beat adj. informal
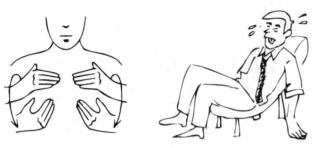
The man is beat.
He is completely exhausted.

beautiful adj. pretty

She is a beautiful woman.
more beautiful   most beautiful

beat v.
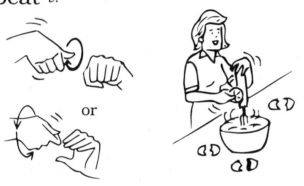
I have to beat the eggs.

beauty parlor n. beauty shop
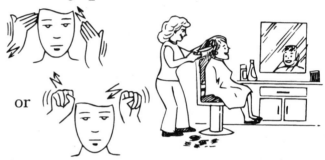
The woman is at the beauty parlor.
beauty parlor   beauty parlors

beat v.

Did the Giants beat the Pirates?
Did they win the game?

beaver n. animal

The beaver has strong teeth.
beaver   beavers

beaten pp. of beat

The Giants have beaten the Pirates.

became pt. of become
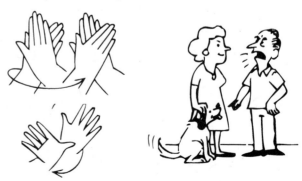
He became angry when he saw the dog..

beehive 41

because *conj.*

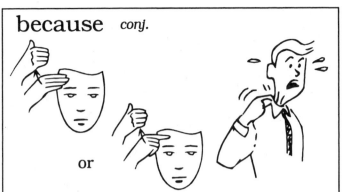

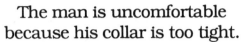

The man is uncomfortable because his collar is too tight.

bedroom *n.*

I have a large bedroom.
bedroom   bedrooms

become *v.*

I become angry when I see the dog.
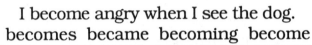
becomes   became   becoming   become

bee *n. insect*

Bees make honey.
bee   bees

become *pp. of* **become**

What has <u>become of</u> my clothes?
What has <u>happened to</u> them?

beef *n. meat*

I prefer beef to pork and veal.

bed *n. furniture*

My bed is comfortable.
bed   beds

beehive *n.*

Bees live in beehives.
beehive   beehives

42 beep

beep v. honk

The man is beeping his horn.
He's honking his horn.

before prep.

The lawyer stood <u>before</u> the witness.
He stood <u>facing</u> the witness.

beet n. vegetable

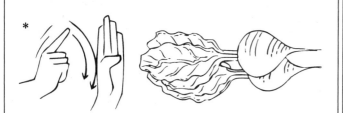

Beets are red and have green leaves.
beet   beets

beg v.

Why does he beg for money?
begs   begged   begging

beetle n. insect

I saw a beetle in the yard.
beetle   beetles

began pt. of **begin**

It <u>began</u> to rain.
It <u>started</u> to rain.

before prep.

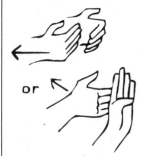 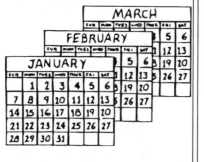

January <u>comes before</u> February.
January <u>is earlier than</u> February.

beggar n.

The beggar was old and poor.
beggar   beggars

bell 43

begin *v.* start

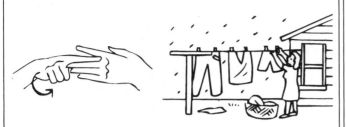

I just knew it would begin to rain.
begins   began   beginning   begun

behind *prep.*

The woman is <u>behind</u> the tall man.
She is <u>in back of</u> him.

begun *pp. of* **begin**

It has <u>begun</u> to rain.
It has <u>started</u> to rain.

believe *v.*

Do you believe that's real gold?
believe   believed   believing

behave *v.*

I want you to learn to behave. Let's try time-out so you can think about it.

bell *n.*

The bell is ringing.
bell   bells

behind *prep.*

The window is <u>behind</u> the desk.
It is <u>in back of</u> the desk.

bell *n.*

The mailman rang the <u>bell</u>.
He rang the <u>doorbell</u>.

44 bell

bell n.

The cow has a bell around its neck.

bench n.

We saw an old bench in the park.
bench   benches

belong v.

Does this book belong to Mary?
Is this Mary's book?

bend v.

How did you bend the fork?
bends   bent   bending

below prep.

The clock is below the picture.
It is under the picture.

bend over

She had to bend over
to pick up the clothes.

belt n. clothing
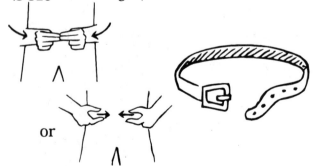
The belt is made of leather.
belt   belts

berry n. food

The berries are sweet.
berry   berries

beware 45

beside *prep.*

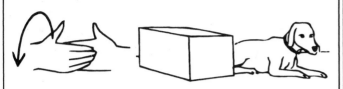

The dog is <u>beside</u> the box.
The dog is <u>near</u> the box.

better *adj.*

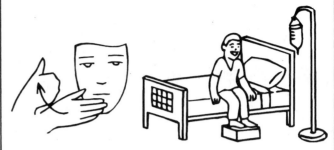

The man is better.
His health has improved.

best *adj.*

The boy's best grade was in math.
He did best in math.

between *prep.*

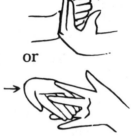
or
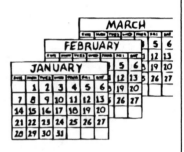

The month of February is
between January and March.

bet *v.*

I always <u>bet</u> my money and lose.
I always <u>wager</u> my money and lose.

beverage *n. liquid drink*

Do you want a beverage?
Do you want something to drink?

better *adj.*

The boy did better in math
than he did in English.

beware *v.*

You must beware of skating on thin
ice. You must be very careful.

46 beyond

beyond *prep.*

Tijuana is <u>beyond</u> the border.
It's <u>across</u> the border.

big *adj.* large

One bear is big.
bigger   biggest

bib *n. clothing*

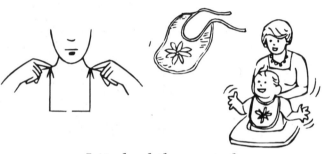

I tied a bib around
the baby's neck.

bike *n. informal:* bicycle

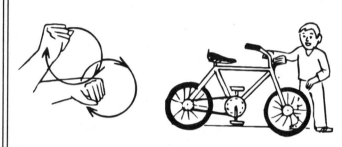

This is my <u>bike</u>.
This is my <u>bicycle</u>.

Bible *n.*

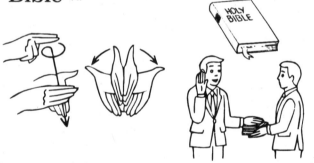

He placed his hand on the Bible.
Bible   Bibles

bill *n.*

The waiter handed the man the bill.
The bill was $75.00.

bicycle *n. vehicle*

The boy has a bicycle.
bicycle   bicycles

bill *n.*

This is a one dollar bill.
bill   bills

birth 47

bill n. animal body part

The bird has a long bill.
It has a long beak.

binder paper n.
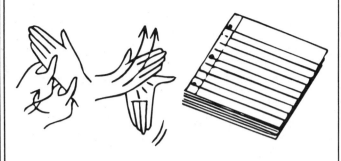
The binder paper has three holes.

billfold n.

I keep my license in my billfold.
I keep it in my wallet.

bird n.

The bird is in the cage.
bird   birds

bind v.

I must bind these old papers.
I must tie up these old papers.

birdhouse n.
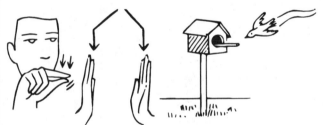
The bird flew into the birdhouse.
birdhouse   birdhouses

binder n. notebook

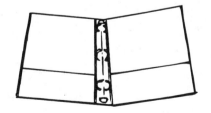
I need paper for my binder.
binder   binders

birth n.
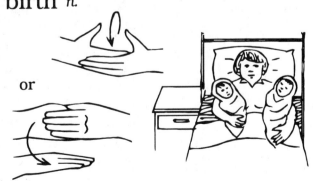
or

The birth of the twins pleased her.

48 birth certificate

birth certificate n.
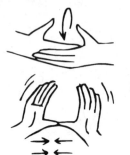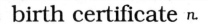
Do you have a copy of your birth certificate?

bit pt. of **bite**

The dog bit the man.

birthday n.

Today is her birthday.
birthday birthdays

bite v.

Why did the dog bite the man?
bites bit biting bitten

biscuit n. food
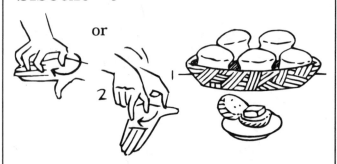
I made biscuits for dinner.
biscuit biscuits

bitten pp. of **bite**

The dog has bitten the man.

bit n.

She ate a <u>bit</u> of the cake.
She ate a <u>little piece</u> of the cake.

bitter adj.

The medicine was bitter.
more bitter   most bitter

blank 49

black *adj. color*	**blade** *n.*
  He wore a black tie. blacker blackest	The knife has a long blade. blade blades
blackberry *n. fruit*	**blame** *v.*
 Blackberries are sweet and juicy. blackberry blackberries	 I blame you. I think you took the candy.
blackboard *n. board*	**blank** *adj.*
 The teacher pointed to the blackboard.	 Sign your name on the <u>blank</u> line. Sign your name on the <u>empty</u> line.
blacksmith *n. worker*	**blank** *n.*
 The blacksmith is fixing the horseshoe.	  His <u>mind is blank</u>. He can't remember what happened to his money.

50 blanket

blanket *n.*

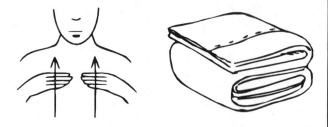

I have warm <u>blankets</u> on my bed.
I have warm <u>covers</u> on my bed.

blimp *n.*

A blimp flew over the city.
blimp   blimps

bleed *v.*

Did the boy's hand bleed?
bleeds   bled   bleeding

blind *adj.*

The man is blind. He can't see.
He is a blind man.

blender *n.*

Do you have a blender?
blender   blenders

blind *n. window cover*

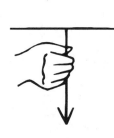 

The woman <u>pulled down the blind</u>.
She <u>pulled down the shade</u>.

blew *pt. of* **blow**

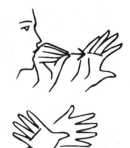 

The boy blew some bubbles.

blind *n. window cover*

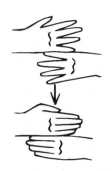 

The woman <u>closed the blinds</u>.

blindfold *n.*

Mother tied the blindfold. Now the girl must try to pin the tail on the donkey.

blink *v.*

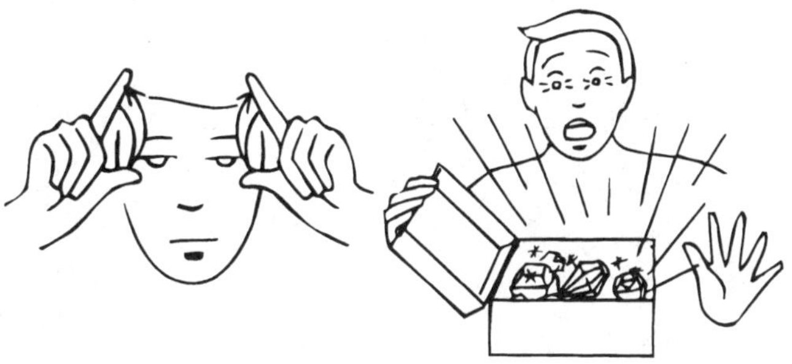

I had to blink my eyes in surprise. I opened and closed them rapidly.

blister *n.*

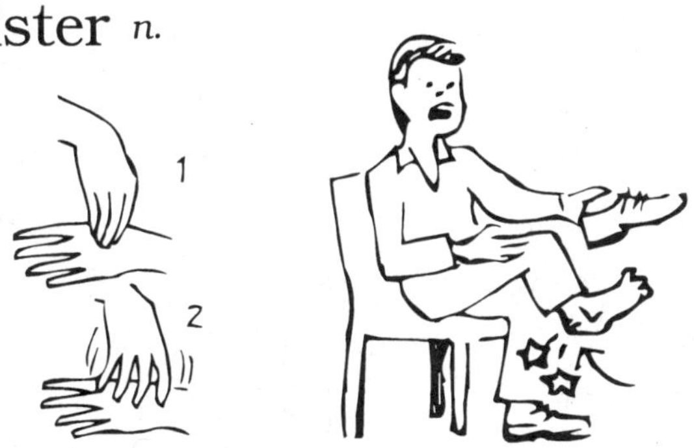

He has a blister on his heel.
blister blisters

block *n. toy*

The baby likes to play with blocks.
block blocks

block *n.*

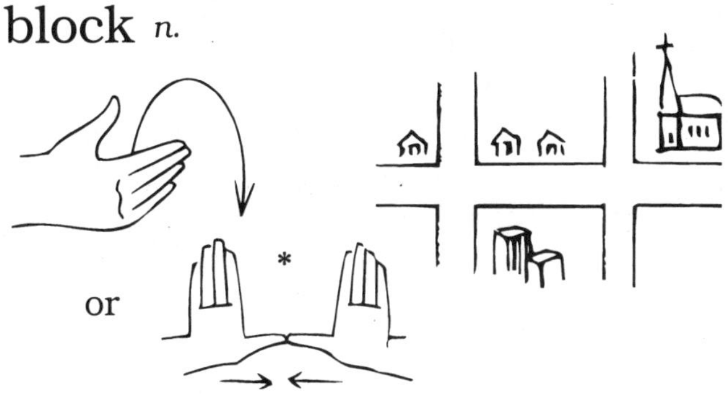

The church is only a block from her home.

blood *n.*

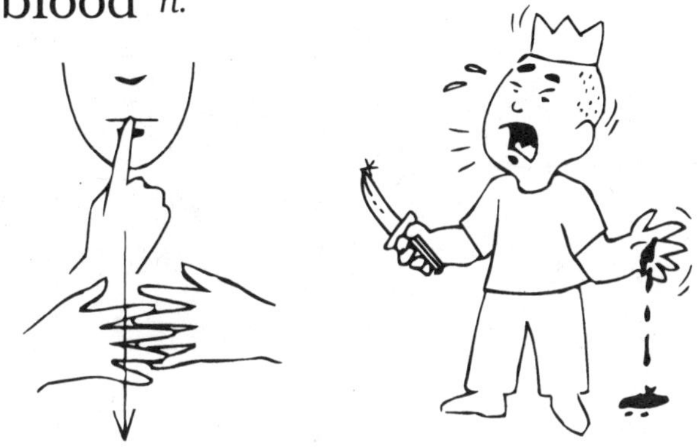

He cried when he saw the blood.

blood pressure *n.*

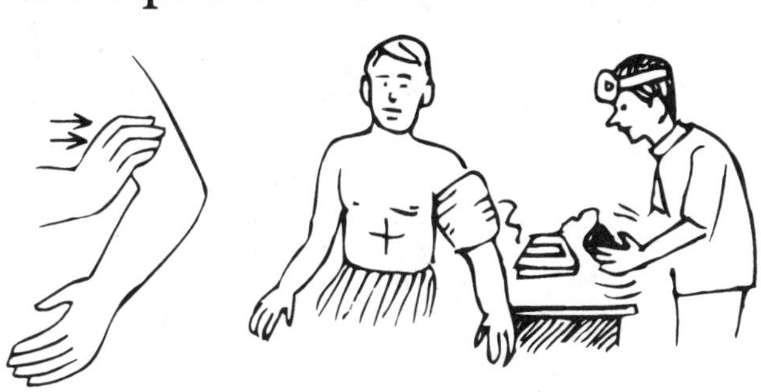

The doctor is taking his blood pressure.

blossom *n. flower*

The branch is covered with blossoms.
blossom blossoms

52 blouse

blouse *n. clothing*

The blouse has short sleeves.
blouse   blouses

blow up *v.*

I always <u>blow up</u> when I see the dog. I always <u>become very angry</u>.

blow *n. shock*

The amount of the bill was a blow.
The high cost was a shock to him.

blown up *pp. of* **blow up**

The girl has blown up the balloon..

blow *v.*

Did the wind blow today?
blows blew blowing blown

blue *adj. color*

The sky is blue.
bluer bluest

blow *v.*

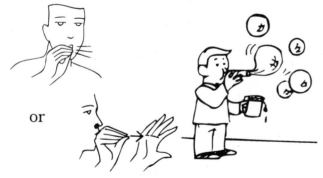

He can blow bubbles.

blueberry *n. fruit*

Blueberries are round and sweet.
blueberry   blueberries

boil 53

blush *v.*

I blush when he winks at me.
blushes blushed blushing

boast *v.*

Did he boast about his big fish?
Did he brag about it?

board *n.*

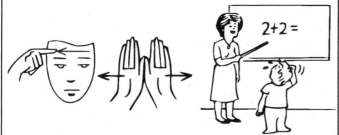

She pointed to the board.
She pointed to the blackboard.

boat *n.*

We went fishing in a small boat.
boat   boats

board *n.*

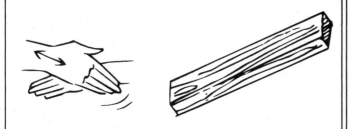

This is a board.
This is a piece of wood.

body *n.*

The man has a strong body.
body   bodies

board *v.*

He will board the train.
He'll get on the train.

boil *v.*

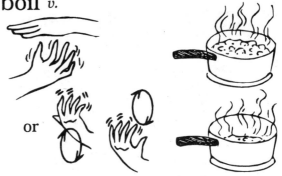

The water may boil away.
boils boiled boiling

54 boil over

boil over v.

If the heat is too high, the pot will boil over.

bonnet n. clothing

She is wearing a bonnet.
bonnet   bonnets

bologna n. food

We had bologna sandwiches for lunch.

Boo! interjection

"Boo!" cried the boy.
He tried to scare the girl.

bomb v.

Did they bomb the fire with water?
Did they drop water on the fire?

book n.

This is a book.
book   books

bone n. body part

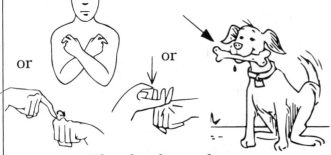

The dog has a bone.
bone   bones

bookcase n. furniture

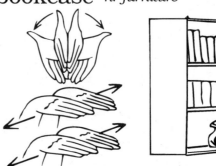

I have a bookcase in my room.
bookcase   bookcases

borrow 55

boost n.
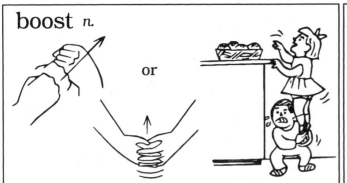
He gave the girl a boost so she could reach the cookies.

bored adj.

The woman is bored.
The speech is not interesting.

boot n. clothing

He is wearing rubber boots.
boot   boots

boring adj.
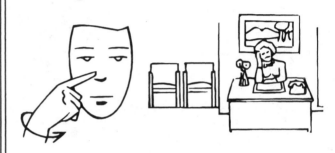
The woman has a boring job.
She has a dull job.

boot v.

He can boot the ball far.
He can kick it far.

born pp. of bear

The baby was born in the hospital.

booth n.
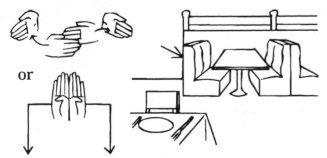
Do you prefer a booth or a table?
booth   booths

borrow v.
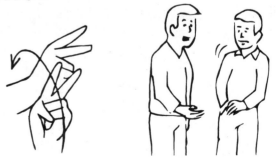
May I borrow some money?
borrows   borrowed   borrowing

56 boss

boss n.

The boss is not happy with her work.
boss   bosses

bottom adj.
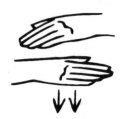
There are no books on the bottom shelf.

both pron.

He hates peas. He hates carrots. He hates both.

bought pt. of buy

The woman bought a vacuum cleaner.

bother v.

Why does he always <u>bother</u> that girl?
Why does he always <u>annoy</u> her?

bounce v.

He likes to bounce his ball.
bounces   bounced   bouncing

bottle n. container
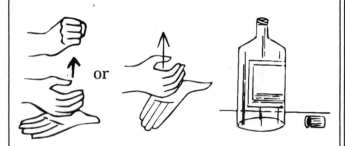
The bottle is empty.
bottle   bottles

bow n. clothing

She has a bow in her hair.
bow   bows

boy 57

bow n. weapon

You need a bow to shoot an arrow.

bow-wow
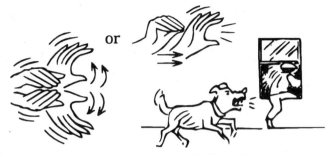
"Bow-wow!" said the dog.
The dog barked.

bowel movement n.
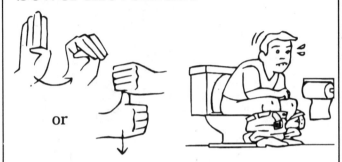
The boy is having a bowel movement.
bowel movement   bowel movements

box n. container
 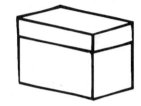
The box has a lid.
box   boxes

bowl n.
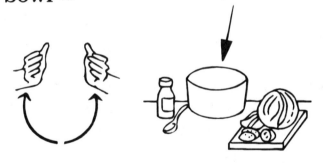
I need a bowl for the salad.
bowl   bowls

box v.

The men often box.
boxes   boxed   boxing

bowl v. game

I bowl every Friday.
bowls   bowled   bowling

boy n. male child

The boy has a football.
boy   boys

58 boyfriend

boyfriend n.

She broke up with her <u>boyfriend</u>.
She broke up with her <u>sweetheart</u>.

brag v. boast
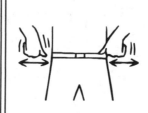
He will brag about his big fish.
brags   bragged   bragging

boy scout n.

The boy scouts went on a hike.
boy scout   boy scouts

braid v.

I will braid your hair.
braids   braided   braiding

bra n. brassiere
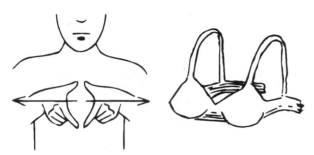
A bra is an undergarment.
A bra is a piece of underwear.

brain n. body part
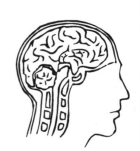
The brain is protected by the skull.
brain   brains

bracelet n. jewelry
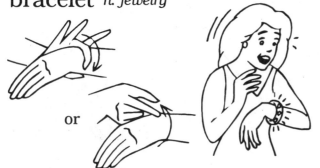
She got a bracelet for Christmas.
bracelet   bracelets

brake n. auto part

He applied the brakes.
He stepped on the brake pedal.

break 59

branch n. tree limb

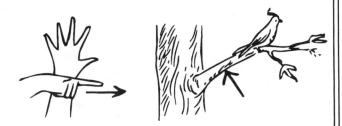

The bird is on the branch.
branch   branches

brat n.

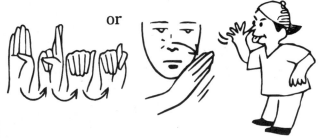

He is an awful brat.
He is a very annoying child.

brand n.

Which brand do you like best?
brand   brands

brave adj.

The boy is brave.
He is not afraid.

brand v.

They must brand the cattle.
brands   branded   branding

bread n. food

I have one loaf of bread.
I need two loaves of bread.

brass n. metal

The fire screen is made of brass.

break n.

He took a short break.
He stopped working for a short time.

60 break

break *v.*

Did the girl break her doll?
breaks   broke   breaking   broken

breeze *n.*

A gentle breeze was blowing.
A slight wind was blowing.

breakfast *n.*

I had bacon and eggs for breakfast this morning.

brick *n. building material*

Bricks are made of clay.
brick   bricks

breath *n.*

The man drew in a breath.
He inhaled.

bride *n.*

The bride wore a long veil.
bride   brides

breathe *v. inhale & exhale*

 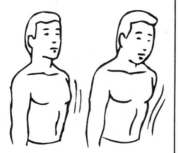

We must breathe to live.
breathes   breathed   breathing

bridegroom *n.*

The bridegroom is very handsome.
bridegroom   bridegrooms

broil 61

bridge n.

They built a bridge across the bay.
bridge   bridges

brightly adv.

The sun is shining brightly.

bridge n.

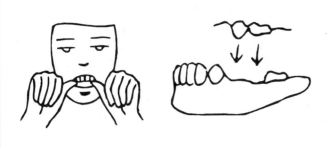

She wears a bridge.

bring v. carry

I bring my lunch to school.
brings   brought   bringing

bright adj.

or

The sun is very bright today.
brighter   brightest

broccoli n. vegetable

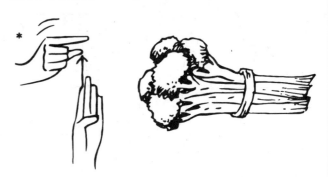

Broccoli is my favorite vegetable.

bright adj.

The boy is very bright.
He is very smart.

broil v.

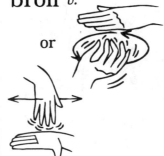

or

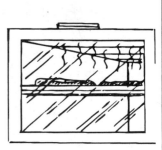

I will broil steaks for dinner.
broils   broiled   broiling

62 broke

broke *adj. slang*

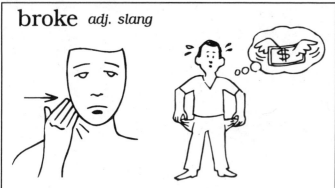

The man is broke.
He doesn't have any money.

broken *pp. of* **break**

The girl has broken her doll.

broke *pt. of* **break**

Someone broke the window.

brooch *n. jewelry*

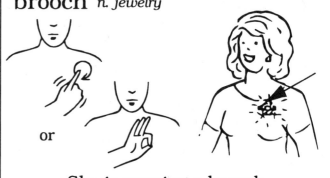

or

She is wearing a brooch.
brooch   brooches

broken *adj.*

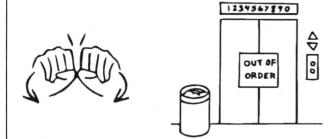

The elevator is broken.
It is not working.

brook *n. creek*

A brook is smaller than a river.
brook   brooks

broken *adj.*

The window is broken.
The window is in pieces.

broom *n.*

 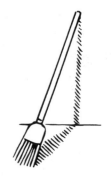

I need a broom to sweep the floor.
broom   brooms

bucket 63

broth n.

I had a bowl of broth.
I had a bowl of thin soup.

brush n.

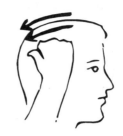

The brush has a wooden handle.
brush   brushes

brother n.

The girl has only one brother.
brother   brothers

brush v.

I must brush my coat.
brushes brushed brushing

brought pt. of bring

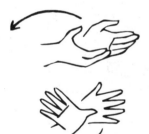

She brought the roast to the table.

bubble n.

The boy is blowing bubbles.
bubble   bubbles

brown adj. color

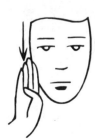

The bear is brown.
browner   brownest

bucket n. container

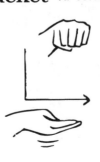

The bucket is empty.
bucket   buckets

64 buckle

buckle n.

The belt has a metal buckle.
buckle   buckles

bug n. insect

I saw many bugs in the garden.
bug   bugs

bud n.
or or

A bud is a partly opened flower.
bud   buds

buggy n.

She put the baby in the buggy.
buggy   buggies

budget n.
or
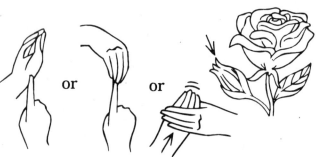

He must make a new budget.
budget   budgets

buggy n.

The horse is pulling the buggy.

buffalo n. animal
or
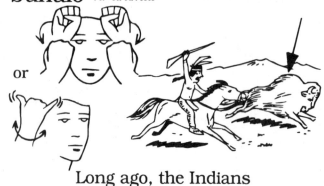

Long ago, the Indians hunted buffalo.

bugler n. worker

The bugler is blowing his bugle.
bugler   buglers

bulletin board 65

build v.

He will build a house.
builds   built   building

bull n. animal

The bull is worth $1000.
bull   bulls

building n.
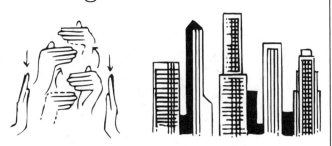
The city has many tall buildings.
building   buildings

bulldozer n.

The man is driving a bulldozer.
bulldozer   bulldozers

built pt. of build

The man built a house last year.

budge n. move

The horse refused to budge.
The horse refused to move.

bulb n.

I need a new bulb for the lamp.
bulb   bulbs

bulletin board n.

I saw a notice on the bulletin board.
bulletin board   bulletin boards

66 bullfight

bullfight n.

We watched the bullfight.
bullfight bullfights

bunch n.

A bunch of asparagus costs 99 cents.
bunch bunches

bump n.

There was a <u>bump</u> in the road.
There was a <u>hump</u> in the road.

bunch n.

This is a bunch of grapes.

bump v.

Ouch! I always bump my head when I leave that door open.

bundle n.

She has a <u>bundle</u> under her arm.
She has a <u>package</u> under her arm.

bun n. food

I put a hot dog in the bun.
bun buns

bunk n.
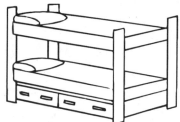
He sleeps in the upper bunk.
bunk bunks

burn 67

bunny n.

The <u>bunny</u> has soft fur.
The <u>baby rabbit</u> has soft fur.

buried pt. of **bury**

The pirate buried the chest.

burden n.

His debts are a heavy burden.
They are a big responsibility.

burn v.

or

I must burn these leaves.
burns   burned/burnt   burning

burger n. informal

He ate a <u>burger</u>.
He ate a <u>hamburger</u>.

burn v.

The meat will burn.

burglar n.

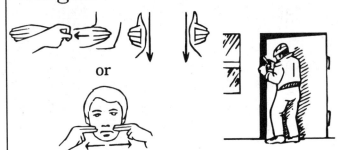

or

The burglar broke into the house.
burglar   burglars

burn v.

Sometimes I burn with anger.

68 burp

burp *v.*

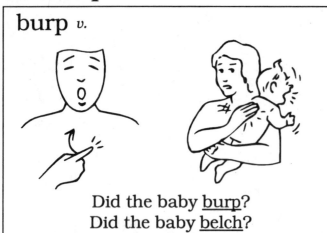

Did the baby burp?
Did the baby belch?

bury *v.*

or

The man will bury the casket.

burrito *n. food*

He had a burrito for lunch.
burrito   burritos

bus *n. vehicle*

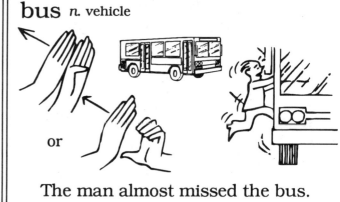

or

The man almost missed the bus.
bus   buses or busses

burro *n. animal*

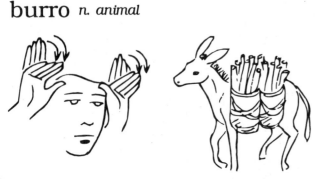

The burro can carry heavy loads.
The donkey can carry heavy loads.

bush *n.*

A bush is smaller than a tree.
bush   bushes

bury *v.*

Will the dog bury the bone?
buries   buried   burying

business *n.*

or

He is in the building business.

butt in 69

busy *adj.*

or
She is busy right now.
She's working right now.

butter *v.*

or
She will butter the bread.
She'll spread butter on the bread.

but *conj.*

The boy wants a cookie, but he cannot reach the cookie jar.

buttercup *n. flower*
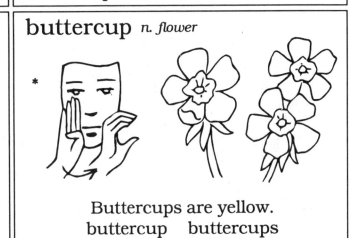
Buttercups are yellow.
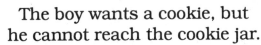
buttercup   buttercups

butcher *n. worker*

The butcher is cutting the meat.
butcher   butchers

butterfly *n. insect*
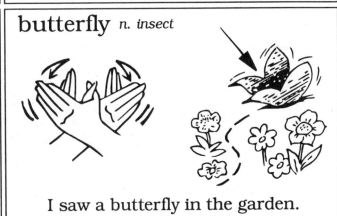
I saw a butterfly in the garden.
butterfly   butterflies

butter *n. food*

I have one cube of butter.
I need two cubes of butter.

butt in *v. slang*

or
Why did she butt in?
Why did she interrupt us?

70 button

button *n.*

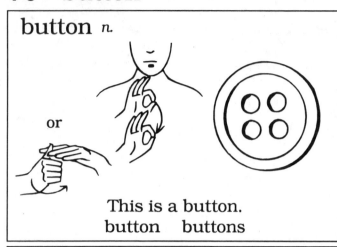

This is a button.
button   buttons

buzz *v.*

He must buzz for his secretary.

button *v.*

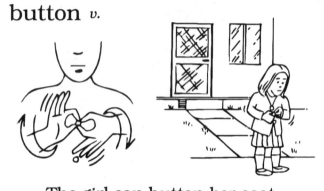

The girl can button her coat.
buttons   buttoned   buttoning

by *prep.*

The dog is <u>by</u> the box.
The dog is <u>near</u> it.

buy *v.*

The woman will buy a cake.
buys   bought   buying

by and by *adv.*

I'll file the letters <u>by and by</u>.
I'll file them <u>later</u>.

buzz *v.*

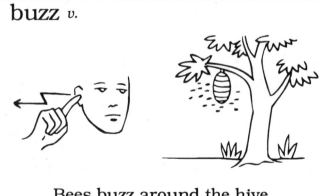

Bees buzz around the hive.
buzzes   buzzed   buzzing

bye-bye *interjection:* by-by

The boy waved bye-bye
to his grandparents.

C c

cab n. taxi

He took a cab to the airport.
cab   cabs

cactus n. plant

The cactus plant is pretty.
cactus   cactuses or cacti

cabbage n. vegetable

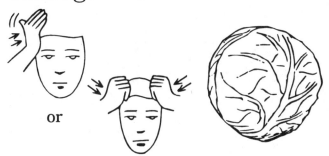

This is a head of cabbage.
one head   two heads

cafe n.

They ate at a <u>cafe</u>.
They ate at a <u>small restaurant</u>.

cabin n. cottage

They have a cabin in the mountains.
cabin   cabins

cafeteria n.

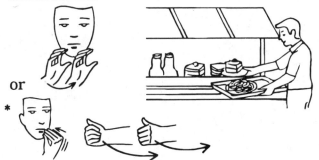

In a cafeteria you get your own food.
cafeteria   cafeterias

cabinet n.

The dishes are in the cabinet.
cabinet   cabinets

cage n.

The bird is in the cage.
cage   cages

72 cake

cake *n.* food

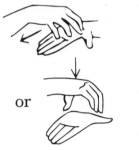
or
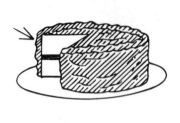

The cake has chocolate frosting.
cake   cakes

California *n.* state: CA

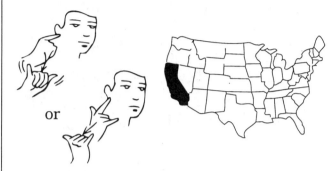

California became a state in 1850.

calculator *n.*

I can use a calculator.
calculator   calculators

call *v.*

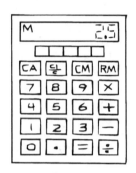
or

I must call the children.
calls   called   calling

calendar *n.*

I hung the calendar on the wall.
calendar   calendars

call *v.*

I will <u>call</u> my parrot "Poll."
I'll <u>name</u> my parrot "Poll."

calf *n.*

 or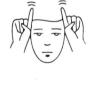

A calf is a young cow.
calf   calves

call *v.*

I <u>call</u> my mother every day.
I <u>telephone</u> her every day.

Canada 73

call *v.*

I call my friend on the TDD.

camp *v.*

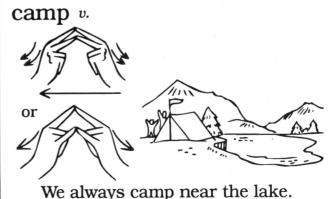

We always camp near the lake.
camps   camped   camping

came *pt. of* **come**

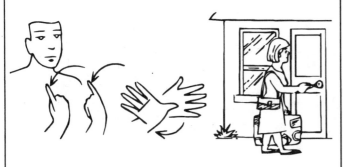

The woman came home last night.

can *n. container*

I opened a can of soup.
can   cans

camel *n. animal*

The camel has two humps.
camel   camels

can *v.*

Mary <u>can</u> make her own lunch.
She <u>is able to</u> make her own lunch.

camera *n.*

I took pictures with my camera.
camera   cameras

Canada *n. country*

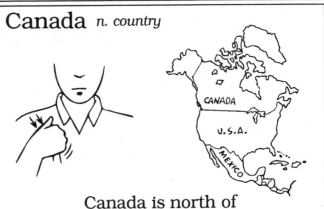

Canada is north of
the United States.

74 canary

canary n. bird

The canary is yellow.
canary   canaries

candy cane n.

We usually hang some candy
canes on our Christmas tree.

candidate n.

The candidate wants people
to vote for him.

cane n.

or

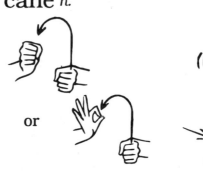

The man uses a cane.
cane   canes

candle n.

The girl is blowing out the candles.
candle   candles

canned adj.

These are canned tomatoes.
They are not fresh.

candy n.

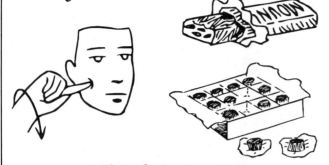

Candy is sweet.
candy   candies

cannon n. weapon

or

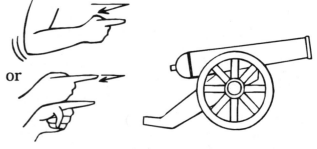

The cannon is mounted on wheels.
cannon   cannons

capital 75

cannot v.

The boy cannot reach the cookie jar.
He can't reach it.

cap n. clothing

The boy is wearing a cap.
cap   caps

canoe n. light boat

The canoe is on the beach.
canoe   canoes

cap n. lid

He put the cap on the bottle.
He put the lid on the bottle.

can't contr. of can not
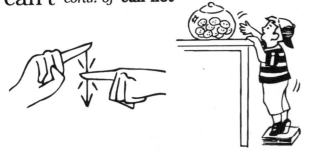
The boy wants a cookie, but he
can't reach the cookie jar.

cape n. clothing
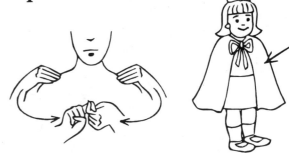
She is wearing a cape.
cape   capes

cantaloupe n. fruit

The cantaloupe is sweet.
cantaloupe   cantaloupes

capital n.
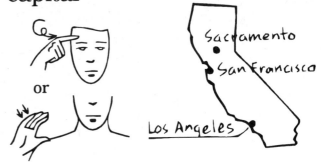
Sacramento is the capital
of the state of California.

76 capital

capital *adj.*

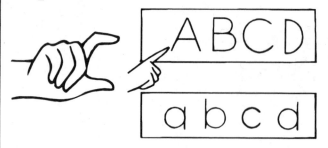

You should begin your sentences with a capital letter.

capture *v.*

Pirates will capture the ship. They will take it by force.

Capitol *n.*

Congress meets in the Capitol.

car *n. vehicle*

He bought a new car.
car   cars

captain *n. leader*

The captain is the boss on a ship.
captain   captains

card *n.*

I received a birthday card.
card   cards

caption *n.*

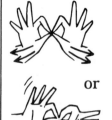 or

The film has captions.
caption   captions

card *n.*

He drew a card from the deck.

cardboard n.

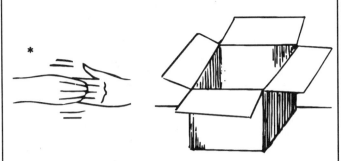

The box is made of cardboard.

care v.

I care for the child.
I take care of the child.

cards n. game

They are playing cards.

careful adj.

You must be careful around a stove.
more careful   most careful

care n.

You should always drive with care.
You should always drive carefully.

careful adj.

The girl is being careful
with the eggs.

care v. cherish

They care for each other.
cares   cared   caring

careless adj.

The man was careless.
He was not careful.

78 carnival

carnival n.

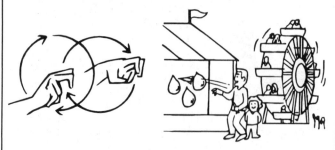

We enjoyed the carnival.
carnival   carnivals

carried pt. of **carry**

She carried the tray to the table.

carpenter n. worker

The carpenter is sawing
a piece of wood.

carrot n. vegetable

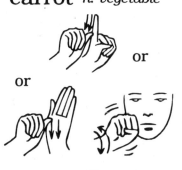 

Carrots are orange
and have green tops.

carpet n. floor covering

The man is laying the carpet.
carpet   carpets

carry v.

He can carry heavy boxes.
carries   carried   carrying

carriage n. vehicle

She rode in an open carriage.
carriage   carriages

cart n. vehicle

The man is pushing a small cart.
cart   carts

catch 79

cash n. coins & bills

She paid for the cake in cash.
She paid with bills and coins.

castle n.

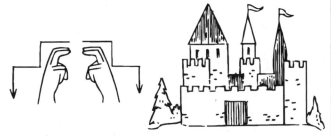

The castle has thick walls.
castle   castles

cashier n. worker

The cashier took my money.
cashier   cashiers

cat n. animal

The cat is very small.
cat   cats

casserole n.

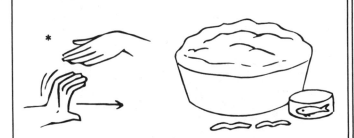

I made a tuna casserole.
casserole   casseroles

catalog n.

He looked through the catalog.
catalog   catalogs

cast n.

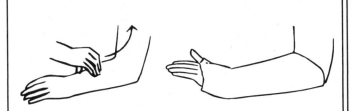

He has a cast on his arm.
cast   casts

catch v.

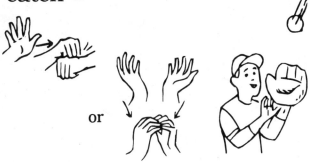

The boy will catch the ball.
catches   caught   catching

80 catcher

catcher n.

The catcher is wearing a mitt.
catcher   catchers

caught pt. of catch
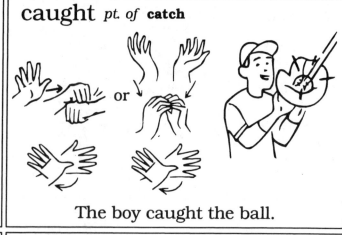
The boy caught the ball.

caterpillar n.
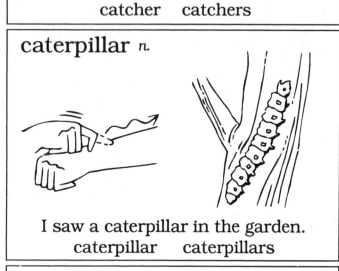
I saw a caterpillar in the garden.
caterpillar   caterpillars

cauliflower n. vegetable
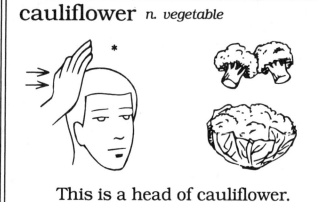
This is a head of cauliflower.
one head   two heads

catsup n. food
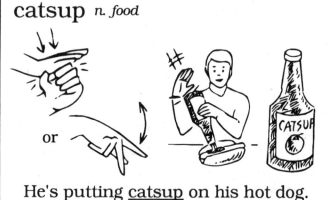
He's putting catsup on his hot dog.
He's putting ketchup on it.

cause v.

A tight collar can cause discomfort.
causes   caused   causing

cattle n. food animals
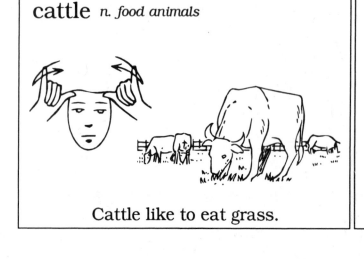
Cattle like to eat grass.

caution v. warn

Someone should caution that girl to stay away from the hot stove.

center 81

cave n.
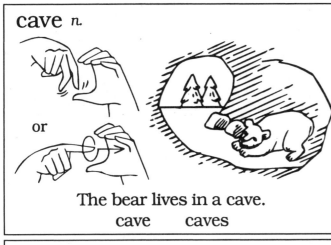
or

The bear lives in a cave.
cave   caves

celery n. vegetable

or

I put some celery in the salad.

cavity n.
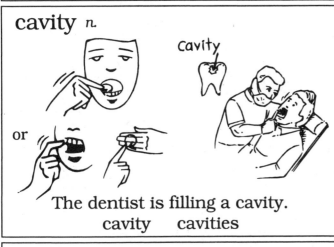
or

The dentist is filling a cavity.
cavity   cavities

cellar n.
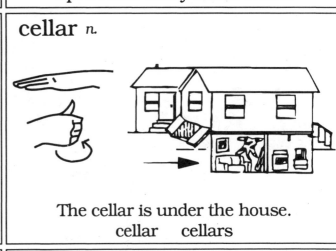

The cellar is under the house.
cellar   cellars

ceiling n.
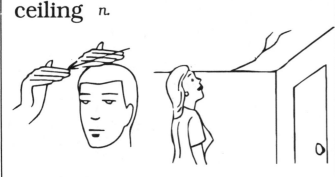

There is a crack in the ceiling.
ceiling   ceilings

cent n.
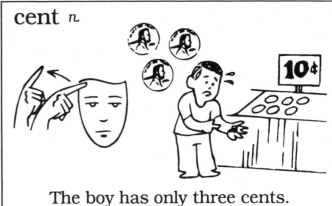

The boy has only three cents.
He has only three pennies.

celebrate v.

They will celebrate New Year's eve.
celebrates   celebrated   celebrating

center n. middle
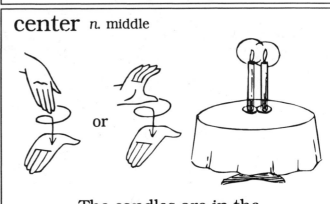
or

The candles are in the
center of the table.

82 center

center n.
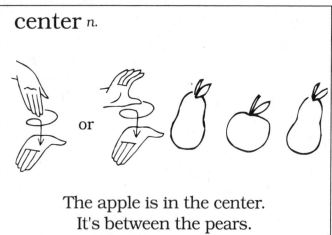
The apple is in the center.
It's between the pears.

chair n.
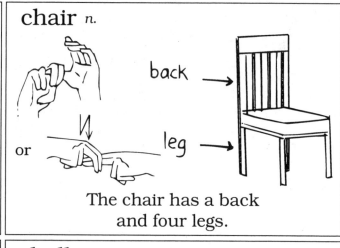
The chair has a back
and four legs.

cereal n. food

He ate a bowl of cereal.

chalk n.

I need some chalk to write
on the blackboard.

certain adj.

I am certain you took the candy.
I'm sure you took it.

challenge v.

He challenged me
to a game of chess.

chain n.
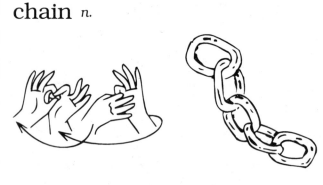
There are 5 links in the chain.
chain   chains

champion n.

He is the champion.
He won first place.

character 83

chance n. opportunity

or

He had a chance to steal a cookie.
chance   chances

channel n.

Which channel do you want to watch?
channel   channels

chance n.

or

She took a chance
and won the jackpot.

Chanukah n.

They are celebrating Chanukah.
They're celebrating Hanukkah.

change n. money

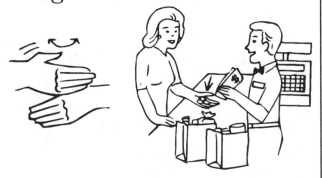

The cashier gave me my change.

chapter n. book section

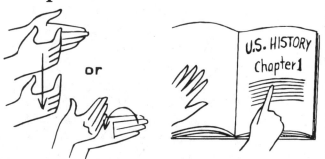

or

He is reading the first chapter.
chapter   chapters

change v.

or

He has to change the tire.
changes   changed   changing

character n.

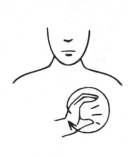 

Friday is one of the characters in
the story of Robinson Crusoe.

84 charcoal

charcoal n.

She opened a bag of charcoal.

chase v.

Did the dog chase the cat?
chases chased chasing

charge v.

She will charge the lamp.
charges charged charging

chase v.
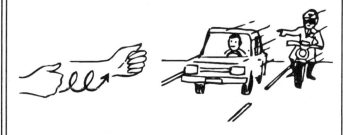
The officer will <u>chase</u> the car.
He will <u>try to catch</u> it.

charge v.

How much do they charge
for a bunch of asparagus?

chat v. talk
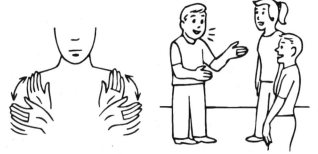
I often chat with my friends.
chats chatted chatting

chart n.
or

The doctor pointed to the chart.
chart charts

cheap adj.

The dress is cheap.
It is not expensive.

cheerleader 85

cheat v.

Did the winner cheat?
cheats cheated cheating

checkup n.

He went to the doctor for a <u>checkup</u>.
He went for a <u>physical examination</u>.

check n.
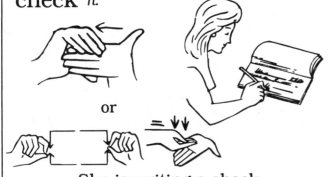
She is writing a check.
check   checks

cheek n. body part

Mother kissed the baby's cheek.
cheek   cheeks

check v.

I will <u>check</u> the paper.
I'll <u>correct</u> the paper.

cheer v.
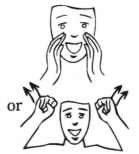

Why did the people <u>cheer</u>?
Why did they <u>shout</u>?

check in v.

We must check in. When we arrive at the hotel we must register.

cheerleader n.

The cheerleader is wearing boots.
cheerleader   cheerleaders

86 cheese

cheese n. food

Mice like to eat cheese.
cheese   cheeses

chest n. furniture

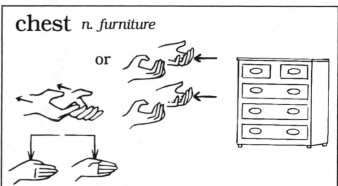

The chest has five drawers.
chest   chests

chef n. worker

The chef is tasting the soup.
chef   chefs

chest n. body part

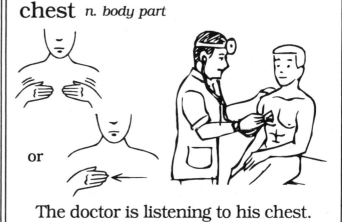

The doctor is listening to his chest.

chemistry n.

He is studying chemistry.

chest n. box, trunk

The pirate is burying a chest.

cherry n. fruit

Cherries grow on trees.
cherry   cherries

chew v.

I always chew gum.
chews   chewed   chewing

chilly 87

chewing gum n.
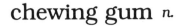
or

This is a stick of chewing gum.
one stick   two sticks

chief n. leader
The Indian chief is wearing a feather headdress.

chick n. baby chicken
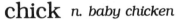
or

The chicks are cute.
chick   chicks

child n.

She is a cute child.
child   children

chicken n.
or

They raise chickens on the farm.
chicken   chickens

children n. plural of child

They have two children.
child   children

chief adj. main
or

The chief ingredient of catsup is tomatoes.

chilly adj.

It is <u>chilly</u> outside.
It's <u>cold</u> outside.

88 chimney

chimney n.
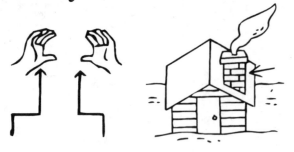
The chimney comes through the roof.
chimney   chimneys

chipmunk n. animal
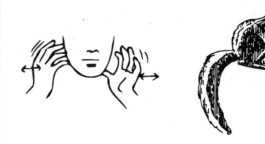
The chipmunk has soft fur.
chipmunk   chipmunks

chin n. body part
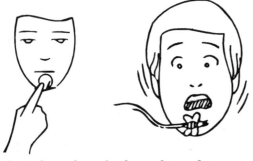
A bee landed on his chin.
chin   chins

chocolate n.

I drank some hot chocolate before I went to bed.

China n. country
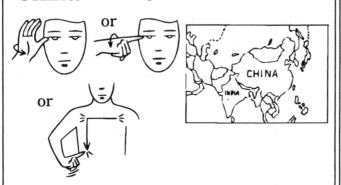
China is a country in Asia.

chocolate n.

Someone gave me a box of chocolates.
chocolate   chocolates

chip n.
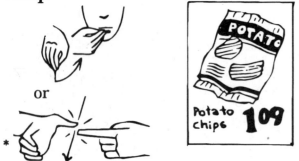
I bought a bag of potato chips.
chip   chips

choice n.

He has to make a choice.
choice   choices

chore 89

choir *n.*

The choir sang a song.
choir   choirs

choose *v.*
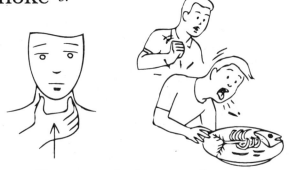
I must <u>choose</u> a dress.
I must <u>select</u> one.

choke *v.*
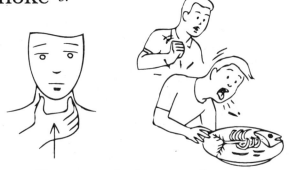
You can choke on a bone.
chokes choked choking

chop *v.*

He will chop some wood.
chops chopped chopping

choke up

I choke up when I think of my parents.
I feel sad and start to cry.

chop *v.*
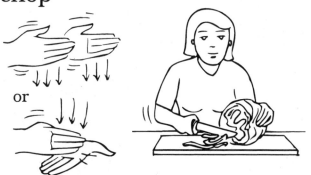
I have to chop the cabbage.

choose *v.* pick out

What should I choose for dessert?
chooses   chose   choosing   chosen

chore *n.*

She has some <u>chores</u> to do.
She has some <u>small tasks</u> to do.

90 chose

chose pt. of choose

The woman chose a dress.

church n.

They go to church regularly.
church   churches

chosen pp. of choose

She has chosen a cake.

cider n. beverage

We drank a glass of apple cider.

Christmas n.

Christmas is the 25th of December.
Christmas   Christmases

cigar n.

The man is smoking a cigar.
cigar   cigars

Christmas tree n.

We like our Christmas tree.
Christmas tree   Christmas trees

cigarette n.

You must stop smoking cigarettes.
cigarette   cigarettes

clap 91

Cinderella n.

Cinderella lost her slipper.

city n.
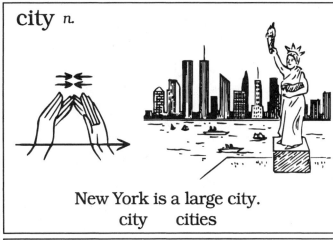
New York is a large city.
city   cities

circle n.

The children formed a circle.
circle   circles

Civil War n.
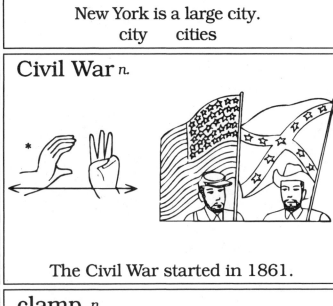
The Civil War started in 1861.

circle v.
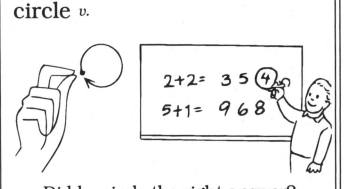
Did he circle the right answer?
circle   circled   circling

clamp n.
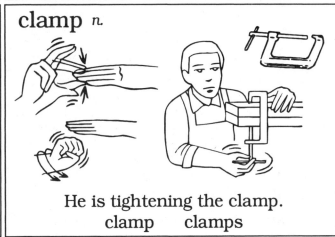
He is tightening the clamp.
clamp   clamps

circus n.

The children enjoyed the circus.
circus   circuses

clap v.

Why did she clap her hands?
claps   clapping   clapped

92 class

class *n. group*

The class is studying history.
class   classes

clean *v.*

I must clean the bathtub.
cleans cleaned cleaning

claw *n. animal body part*

or

The tiger has sharp claws.
claw   claws

cleaners *n.*

I took some clothes to the cleaners.

clay *n.*

or

The boy is molding the clay.

clear *adj.*

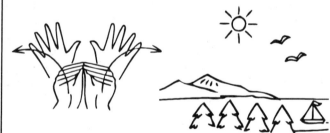

It is a clear day today.
clearer   clearest

clean *adj.*

The girl's face is clean.
cleaner   cleanest

clear *v.*

He will clear the table.
He'll remove the dirty dishes.

close 93

clerk n.

The clerk is waiting on the woman.
clerk   clerks

clippers n. tool

He is using a pair of clippers to trim the hedge.

client n.

The lawyer talked to his client.
client   clients

clock n.

I have a clock in my bedroom.
clock   clocks

climb v. go up
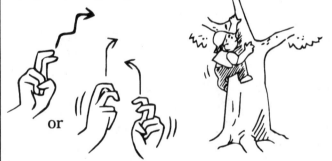
The boy can climb the tree.
climbs   climbed   climbing

close adj.

He lives <u>close to</u> the school.
He lives <u>near</u> the school.

clinic n.

She took her son to the clinic.
clinic   clinics

close v. shut

He will close the door.
closes   closed   closing

94 closet

closet n.

He hung his clothes in the closet.
closet   closets

clothes hamper n.

The dirty clothes are in the clothes hamper.

cloth n.

or
I bought some cloth. I bought some fabric. I bought some material.

clothesline n.

or
The clothesline broke.
clothesline   clotheslines

clothes n.

I need some new clothes.

clothespin n.

You fasten the clothes to the clothesline with clothespins.

clothesbrush n.

He's using a clothesbrush.
clothesbrush   clothesbrushes

cloud n.

or
The clouds are in the sky.
cloud   clouds

coal 95

clover n.

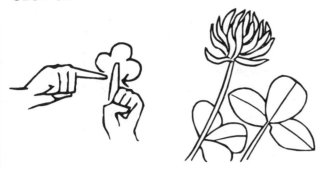
Horses like to eat clover.

clue n.

The policeman found a clue.
He found some evidence.

clown n.

The clowns made the children laugh.
clown   clowns

coach n. worker
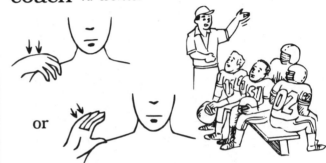
The coach talked to the team.
coach   coaches

club n. social group

Do you belong to any clubs?
club   clubs

coach v.

I coach my brother in math.
I help him learn math.

club n. weapon

The caveman is carrying a club.

coal n. mineral
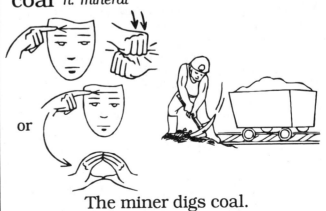
The miner digs coal.

96 coast

coast n. seashore

They walked along the coast.
They walked along the shore.

cobweb n. spider web

She saw cobwebs in the attic.
cobweb   cobwebs

coast v.

or

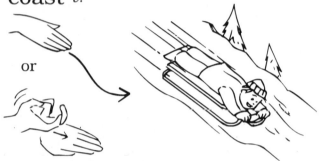

I will coast down the hill.
coasts   coasted   coasting

Coca-Cola n. beverage

He had a Coca-Cola
with his hamburger.

coat n. clothing

The man is wearing a coat.
coat   coats

coconut n. fruit

Coconuts have very hard shells.
coconut   coconuts

coax v. persuade

or

He tried to coax her into the car.
She should run away.

coffee n. beverage

I drink my coffee black.

collar 97

coffeepot n.

This coffeepot makes good coffee.
coffeepot   coffeepots

cold adj.

It is cold outside today.
colder   coldest

coffin n.

He is burying the coffin.
He's burying the casket.

cold n. virus

He has a cold.
cold   colds

coin n. money

Nickles, dimes, pennies,
and quarters are coins.

collapse v.

The house may collapse.
It may cave in.

coke n.

He had a hamburger and a coke.
coke   cokes

collar n.

Her dress has a wide collar.
collar   collars

98 collect

collect v.

I collect stamps.
collects   collected   collecting

color n.

Red and blue are her favorite colors.
color   colors

collect v.

or

She will <u>collect</u> the papers.
She'll <u>gather</u> them.

colt n. *animal*

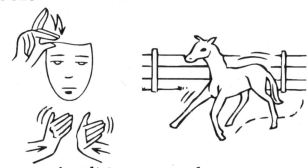

A colt is a young horse.
colt   colts

college n.

He graduated from college.
college   colleges

Columbus n.

Columbus was a famous explorer.

collision n. *accident*

The woman saw the collision.
collision   collisions

comb n.

or

This is a black comb.
comb   combs

company 99

comb v.
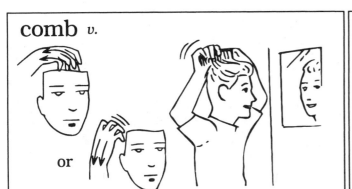
I must comb my hair.
combs   combed   combing

comfortable adj.

His collar is not comfortable.

come v.

When did she come home from her trip?
comes   came   coming   come

comma n. punctuation mark

He forgot to put in the comma.
comma   commas

come across v.

Did he come across his ball?
Did he find it?

communicate v.
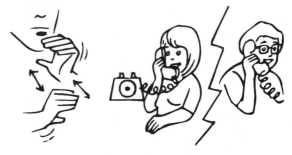
I communicate with my mother by telephone.

comfortable adj.

His bed is very comfortable.
more comfortable   most comfortable

company n. business group

He works for a large company.
company   companies

100 company

company n.

We are having company for dinner.
We're having guests for dinner.

complain v.

I always complain about the dog.
I always find fault with it.

compare v.

I must compare the purses.
compares   compared   comparing

complete v.

Did he complete the job?
Did he finish it?

compass n.
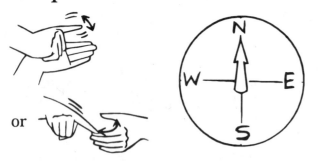
The compass points to north.
compass   compasses

computer n.

He likes to work on the computer.
computer   computers

compass n.
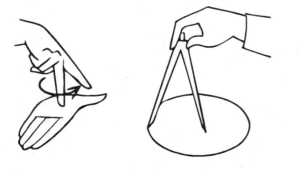
He uses a compass to draw a circle.

concrete n.

The sidewalk is made of concrete.

connect 101

condition n.

His car is in poor condition.

confused adj.

The boy is confused.
He doesn't know how to get home.

condition n.
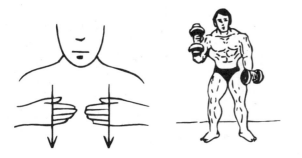
He is in good condition.
He's in good health.

congratulate v.

I must congratulate my son.

cone n.

He is eating an ice cream cone.
cone   cones

Congress n.
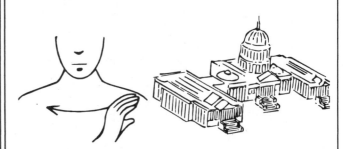
Congress meets in this building
in Washington, D.C.

confess v.
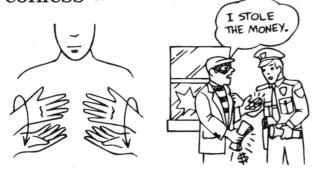
I confess. I admit that
I broke into the house.

connect v. fasten

He must <u>connect</u> the hose.
He must <u>attach</u> it.

102 consider

consider *v.*

I have to consider the problem.
I have to think about it.

contact lens *n.*

She wears contact lenses.
contact lens   contact lenses

consonant *n.*

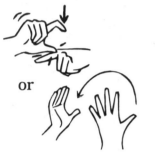

She pointed to the consonants.
consonant   consonants

contagious *adj.*

Small pox is a contagious disease.
It easily spreads to other people.

Constitution *n.*

The Constitution was signed in 1787.

contest *n.*

He won the contest.
contest   contests

contact *v.*

I will contact you this evening.
I'll call or see you then.

continue *v.*

It may continue to snow all day.
continues   continued   continuing

copper 103

control n.

The driver lost control of the car.

cookie n. cooky

The boy wants a cookie.
cookie   cookies

control v.
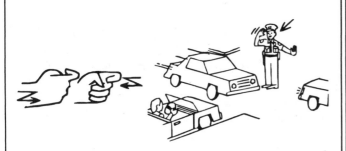
I must control the traffic.
controls   controlled   controlling

cool adj.

I need something cool to drink.
cooler   coolest

cook n. worker

The cook tasted the soup.
cook   cooks

copied pt. of copy

The woman copied the letter.

cook v.

I often cook my own breakfast.
cooks   cooked   cooking

copper n. metal
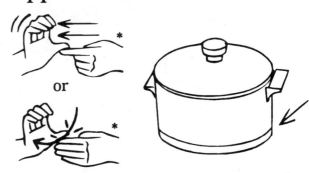
The bottom of the pot is copper.

104 copy

copy n.
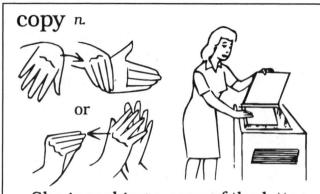
She is making a copy of the letter.
copy   copies

cork n.
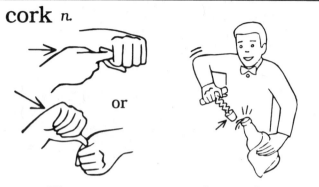
You must remove the cork.
You must remove the stopper.

copy v.
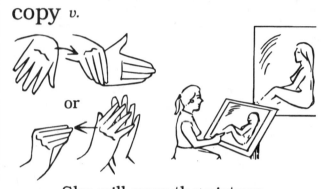
She will copy the picture.
copies   copied   copying

corkscrew n. tool

I need a corkscrew
to remove the cork.

copy v.
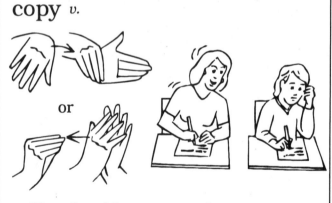
She should not copy the answers.

corn n. vegetable
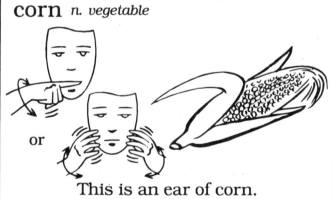
This is an ear of corn.
one ear of corn   two ears of corn

cord n.

The cord is too short.
cord   cords

corner n.

The accident happened at the corner.
corner   corners

cot 105

corral n.

The horse is in the corral.
corral   corrals

cosmetics n.

She bought some cosmetics.
She bought some make-up.

correct adj. right

The answer is correct.

cost v.

How much does asparagus cost?

correct v. check

The teacher will correct the paper.
corrects   corrected   correcting

costume n.

The children are wearing costumes.
costume   costumes

correspond v.

They correspond with each other.
They write to each other.

cot n. furniture

He sleeps on a cot.
He sleeps on a narrow bed.

106 cottage

cottage n.

The man lives in a small cottage.
cottage   cottages

cough v.

Why did the boy cough?
coughs   coughed   coughing

cotton n.
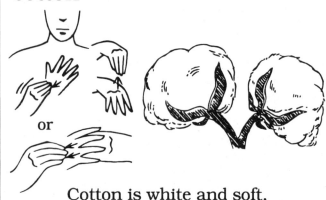
Cotton is white and soft.

could pt. of can

Mary could make her own lunch.
She was able to make her own lunch.

cotton candy n.

Cotton candy is made
of melted sugar.

couldn't contr. of could not

The boy couldn't reach the cookies.
He could not reach them.

couch n. furniture

We bought a new couch.
couch   couches

counselor n.

He talked to his counselor.
counselor   counselors

court 107

count v.

I must count count my money.
counts   counted   counting

couple n.

They make a nice <u>couple</u>.
They make a nice <u>pair</u>.

counter n.

or
She is sitting at the counter.
counter   counters

couple n.

He took a <u>couple of</u> cookies.
He took <u>several</u> cookies.

country n. nation

Spain is a country in Europe.
country   countries

courage n.

or
He has a lot of courage.
He is very brave.

country n. rural area

We took a drive in the country.

court n.

The man had to appear in court.

108 court

court n.

They walked to the tennis court.
court   courts

cover n.
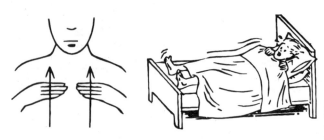
He pulled up the covers.
He pulled up the blankets.

courteous adj.

He is always very courteous.
He's always very polite.

cover v.

I must cover the baby.
covers covered covering

cousin n.

My aunt's children are my cousins.
cousin   cousins

cow n. animal
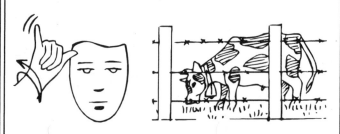
The cow has a bell around its neck.
cow   cows

cover n.

She put the cover on the pot.
She put the lid on the pot.

coward n.

He is a coward.
He is not brave.

crawl 109

cowboy n.

The cowboy is riding a horse.
cowboy   cowboys

Crackerjacks n. food

She loves Crackerjacks.

crab n.

or

She bought a crab for dinner.
crab   crabs

cradle n.

The baby sleeps in the cradle.
cradle   cradles

crack n.

The cup has a crack in it.
crack   cracks

cranberry n.

She served cranberries with the turkey.
cranberry   cranberries

cracker n. food

I ate some crackers with my soup.
cracker   crackers

crawl v. creep

The baby can crawl.
crawls   crawled   crawling

110 crayon

crayon n.

or

She has a box of crayons.
crayon   crayons

crib n. *furniture*

or

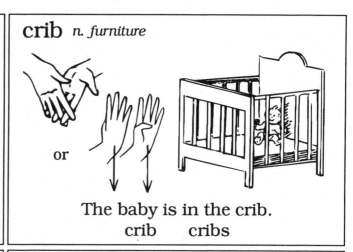

The baby is in the crib.
crib   cribs

crazy adj.

or

He did some crazy things.
crazier   craziest

cricket n. *insect*

I saw a cricket in the garden.
cricket   crickets

cream n.

Do you use cream in your coffee?

cried v. pt. *of* **cry**

The boy cried.

cream pitcher n. *creamer*

The cream pitcher is next
to the sugar bowl.

crime n.

or

The man is committing a crime.
He is doing something unlawful.

crowd 111

crocodile n. reptile

Crocodiles have long narrow heads.
crocodile   crocodiles

cross v.

Did the woman cross the street?
crosses   crossed   crossing

crooked adj.

One board is crooked.
more crooked   most crooked

crosswalk n.
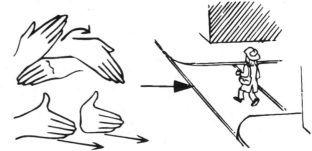
She is walking in the crosswalk.
crosswalk   crosswalks

cross adj. angry

Father becomes cross when he
sees the dog in the house.

crow n. bird

The crow has black feathers.
crow   crows

cross n.
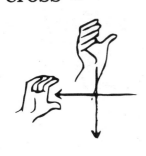 
She wore a cross around her neck.
cross   crosses

crowd n. many people

There was a crowd at the dance.
crowd   crowds

112 crown

crown n.
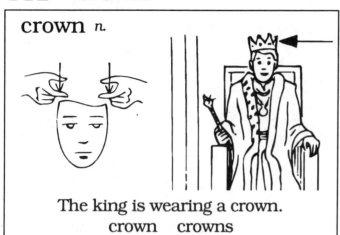
The king is wearing a crown.
crown   crowns

crust n.
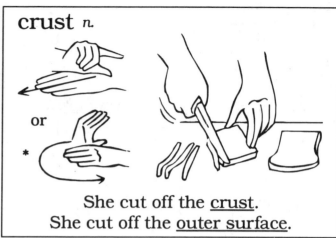
She cut off the crust.
She cut off the outer surface.

crumb n.
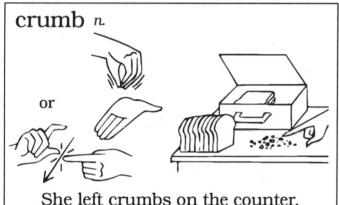
or
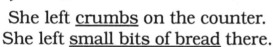
She left crumbs on the counter.
She left small bits of bread there.

crutch n.
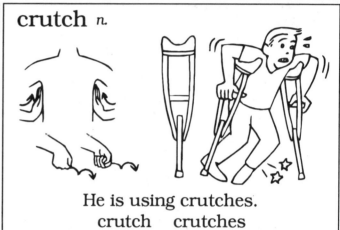
He is using crutches.
crutch   crutches

crush v. squeeze together
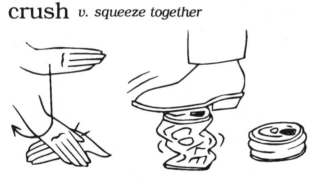
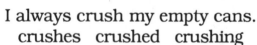
I always crush my empty cans.
crushes   crushed   crushing

cry v. shed tears
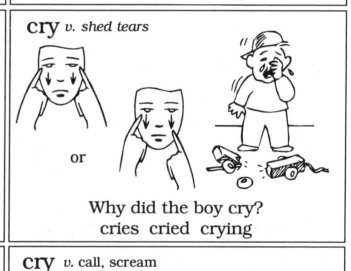
Why did the boy cry?
cries   cried   crying

crust n.
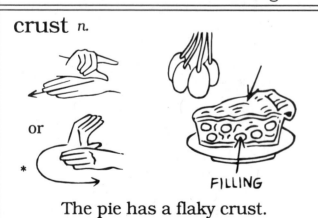
The pie has a flaky crust.
crust   crusts

cry v. call, scream

I must cry for help.
I must yell for help.

curl 113

cucumber n. vegetable

The woman is slicing the cucumber.
cucumber   cucumbers

cupcake n. food

I made some cupcakes.
cupcake   cupcakes

cuff n.

The shirt and pants have cuffs.
cuff   cuffs

curb n.

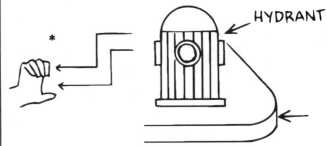

The hydrant is near the curb.
curb   curbs

cup n.

The cup is empty.
cup   cups

curious adj.

He is curious about the gift.
He's eager to learn what it is.

cupboard n. cabinet

The dishes are in the cupboard.
cupboard   cupboards

curl n.

She has long curls.
curl   curls

114 curtain

curtain n.
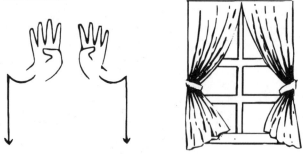
The curtains are white.
curtain   curtains

customer n.
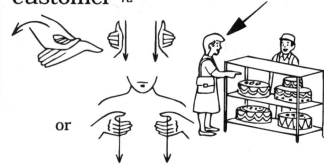
or
She is a good customer. She often buys things at this bakery.

cushion n.

She sat on a cushion.
cushion   cushions

cut v.

Why did she cut the paper?
cuts   cut   cutting

custard n. food

I made some custard.

cut v.

I will cut the candy bars in half.

custodian n. worker
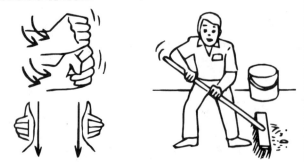
He is the school custodian.
He's the school caretaker.

cute adj.

The kitten is cute.
cuter   cutest

D d

Dad n. father

She asked her dad for some money.

dairy n.
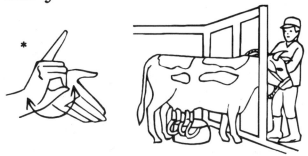
The dairy produces milk, cream and butter.

daffodil n. flower
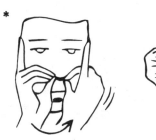
Daffodils are pretty.
daffodil   daffodils

daisy n. flower

The girl picked a daisy.
daisy   daisies

dagger n. weapon
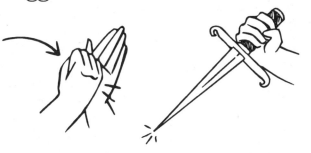
The dagger has a sharp point.
dagger   daggers

dam n.

or
The dam holds back the water.
dam   dams

daily adv.

I brush my teeth <u>daily</u>.
I brush them <u>every day</u>.

damage v.

or
Did the accident damage the cars?
damages   damaged   damaging

115

116 damp

damp adj.

The ground was damp after the rain.
It was a little wet.

dandelion n.

Dandelions are weeds.
dandelion   dandelions

dance n.

We had fun at the dance.
dance   dances

danger n.

or
The woman is in danger.

dance v.

They like to dance.
dances   danced   dancing

dangerous adj.

or
It is <u>dangerous</u> to skate on thin ice. It's <u>not safe</u>.

dancer n.
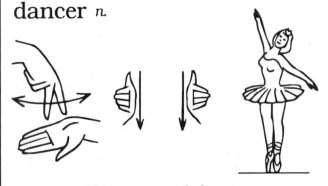
She is a good dancer.
dancer   dancers

dark adj.

It is dark outside.
darker   darkest

December 117

date n. month/day/year

The date is November 14.
date   dates

deaf adj.

The boy is deaf.
He can not hear.

daughter n. female child

They have one daughter.
daughter   daughters

dear adj.

His sweetheart is dear to him.
He loves her very much.

day n.

It will be a nice day today.
day   days

debt n.

He is in debt.
He owes a lot of money.

dead adj.

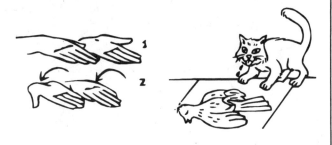

The bird is dead.
It is not alive.

December n. month

Christmas comes in December.

118 decide

decide v.

He must decide which way to go.
decides   decided   deciding

deduct v.

They deduct taxes from his wages.
deducts   deducted   deducting

decimal point n.
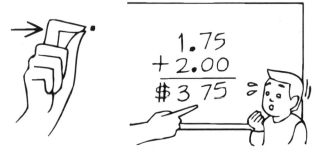
He forgot the decimal point.
decimal point   decimal points

deep adj.

The well is very deep.
deeper   deepest

decorate v.

We will decorate the Christmas tree.
We'll trim the Christmas tree.

deer n. animal

The deer lives in the woods.

decrease v. reduce
or

Why did they decrease the price?
Why did they lower it?

delicious adj.
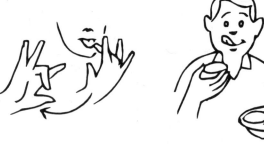
He thinks the cookies are delicious.
He thinks they taste good.

deny 119

deliver *v.*

The postman will deliver the package.
delivers   delivered   delivering

denominator *n.*

The denominator goes below the line.
denominator   denominators

demand *v.*
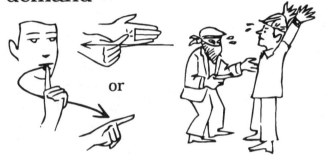
The robber will demand my money.
He'll order me to give him my money.

dental floss *n.*
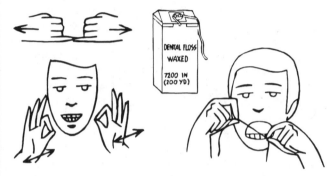
He uses dental floss every day.

demonstrate *v.*

I will demonstrate the vacuum.
I'll show you how to use it.

dentist *n.*

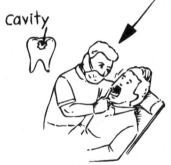
The dentist is filling a cavity.
dentist   dentists

Denmark *n. country*

Denmark is a country in Europe.

deny *v.*

Did he deny he took the candy?
Did he say he did not take it?

120 deodorant

deodorant n.
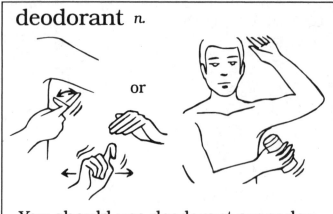
You should use deodorant every day.

describe v.
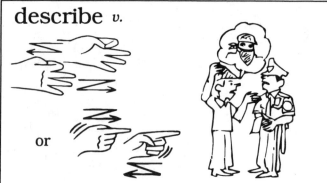
I can describe the robber.
describes   described   describing

dependent n.
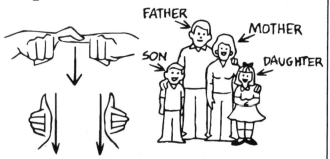
The man has three dependents.
dependent   dependents

desert n.

The desert is hot and dry.
desert   deserts

deposit v.

She must deposit some money.
She must put money into her account.

desk n.
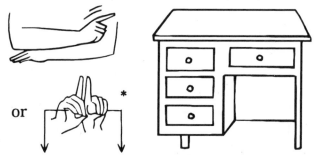
The desk has four drawers.
desk   desks

depth n.

Do you know the depth of the well?
Do you know how deep it is?

dessert n. food

What do you want for dessert?
dessert   desserts

diarrhea 121

destroy v.
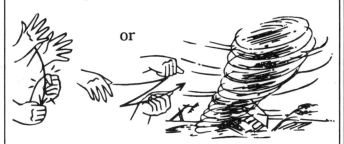
The storm will <u>destroy</u> the house.
It will <u>ruin</u> the house.

dial v.

I will dial the number.
dials   dialed   dialing

detach v.

He has to <u>detach</u> the hose.
He has to <u>unfasten</u> it.

diamond n. jewel

Diamonds cost a lot of money.
diamond   diamonds

devil n.

The devil has horns.
devil   devils

diaper n.
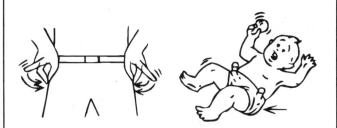
The baby is wearing a diaper.
diaper   diapers

dial n.
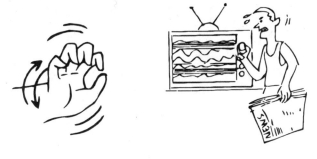
He is turning the dial.
dial   dials

diarrhea n.

The boy has diarrhea.

122 dice

dice *n.*
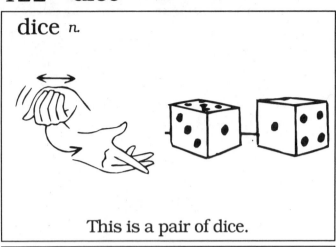
This is a pair of dice.

die *v.*
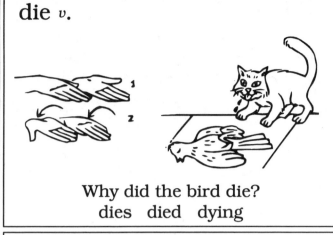
Why did the bird die?
dies   died   dying

dictionary *n.*
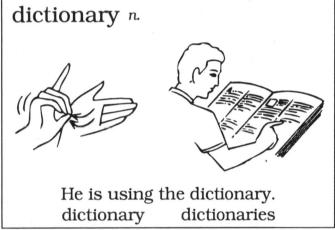
He is using the dictionary.
dictionary   dictionaries

die *v.*
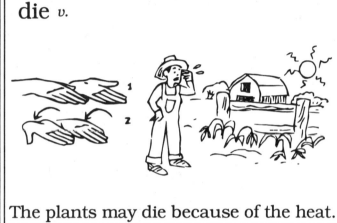
The plants may die because of the heat.

did *pt. of* do

I did the laundry.

diet *n.*

The woman is on a diet.
She wants to lose weight.

didn't *contr. of* did not

The boy didn't have enough money.
He did not have enough money.

difference *n.*

The difference between 6 and 8 is 2.

dinosaur 123

different *adj.*

Two are the same.
One is different.

dimple *n.*

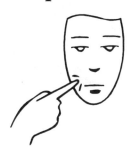 

She has dimples in her cheeks.
dimple   dimples

difficult *adj.*

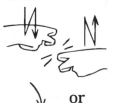 

or

The problem is difficult.
It is hard.

dining room *n.*

We always eat dinner
in the dining room.

dig *v.*

I must dig a hole.
digs   dug   digging

dinner *n. evening meal*

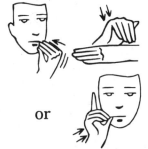

or

We had roast beef for dinner.
dinner   dinners

dime *n. coin: 10 cents*

He needs a dime to buy the candy.
dime   dimes

dinosaur *n. reptile*

or

Dinosaurs lived long ago.
dinosaur   dinosaurs

124 dip

dip n. food

She served potato chips and dip.
dip   dips

dirt n. soil

The boy is playing in the dirt.

diploma n.

or
He received his diploma when he graduated.

dirty adj.

The shoe is dirty.
It is not clean.

direction n.
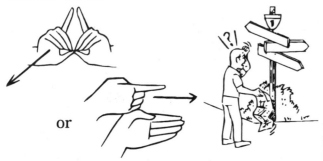
or
Which direction should I take?
Which way should I go?

disagree v.

They always disagree about where the dog should be kept.

direction n.

or
He is reading the directions.
He's reading the instructions.

disappear v.

or
Watch! The vase will disappear.
disappears   disappeared   disappearing

dishtowel 125

disappointed *adj.*

I am <u>disappointed</u> with your behavior.
I'm <u>not pleased</u> with your behavior.

disease *n. illness*

or

Chicken pox is a contagious disease.
disease   diseases

disconnect *v.*

I <u>disconnect</u> the phone at night.
I <u>unplug</u> it at night..

dish *n. plate*

or

The boy dropped his dish.
dish   dishes

discover *v. find*

What did Columbus discover in 1492?
discovers   discovered   discovering

dishonest *adj.*

The man is <u>dishonest</u>.
He is <u>not truthful and sincere</u>.

discuss *v.*

or

They will <u>discuss</u> the new building.
They'll <u>talk about</u> the new building.

dishtowel *n.*

She is holding a dishtowel.
dishtowel   dishtowels

126 dishwasher

dishwasher n. worker

The man is a dishwasher.
dishwasher   dishwashers

disobey v.

You always <u>disobey</u> me.
You <u>don't obey</u> me.

dishwasher n. household appliance
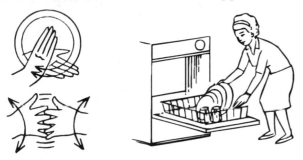
She is using the dishwasher.
dishwasher   dishwashers

distance n.

The rocket will go a great distance.
It will travel thousands of miles.

disk n.

He inserted the disk.
disk   disks

dive v.
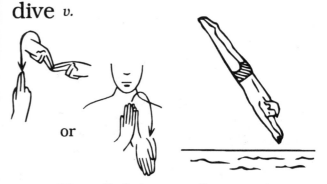
He will dive into the water.
dives   dived/dove   diving

Disneyland n.

We had fun at Disneyland.

divide v.

Did the boys <u>divide</u> the marbles?
divides   divided   dividing

doctor 127

divide v.

She will divide the pie into six pieces.

do v.

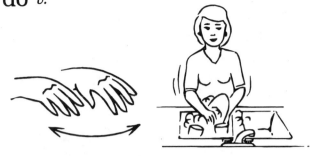

I always <u>do</u> the dishes.
I always <u>wash</u> the dishes.

divorce v.

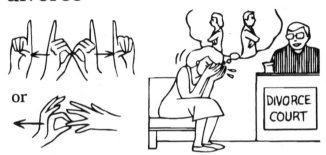

or

She will divorce her husband.
She'll end the marriage.

do v.

She must <u>do</u> her nails.
She must <u>polish</u> them.

dizzy adj.

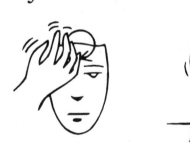

The woman feels dizzy.
dizzier   dizziest

dock n. pier

or

He tied the boat to the dock.
dock   docks

do v.

I always do well in school.
does did doing done

doctor n.

or

I went to the doctor because I was sick.
doctor   doctors

128 does

does *s-form of* **do**

He does want another cookie.

doll *n. toy*

She got a doll on her birthday.
doll   dolls

doesn't *contr. of* **does not**

He <u>doesn't</u> have enough money.
He <u>does not</u> have enough money.

dollar *n. money*

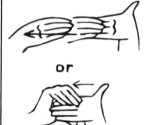 

Do you have a dollar?
dollar   dollars

dog *n. animal*

The dog is black and white.
dog   dogs

dolphin *n.*

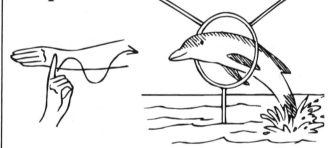

We saw a dolphin.
dolphin   dolphins

doghouse *n.*

The dog sleeps in the doghouse.
doghouse   doghouses

done *adj.*

The job is <u>done</u>.
It is <u>finished</u>.

door 129

done pp. of do
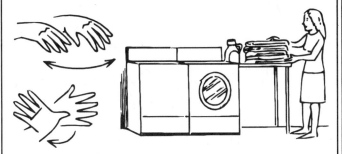
I have done the laundry.
I've finished the laundry.

don't know
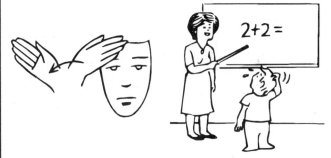
I don't know the answer.

donkey n. animal

The donkey has long ears.
donkey   donkeys

don't want

I don't want any peas and carrots.

don't contr. of do not

I <u>don't</u> have enough money.
I <u>do not</u> have enough money.

donut n. doughnut
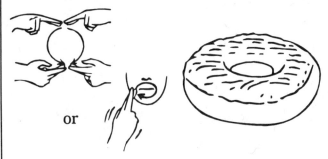
There is a hole in the donut.
donut   donuts

don't care
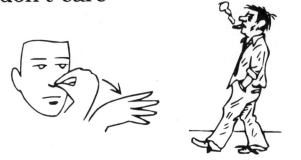
I don't care how I look.
That's not important to me.

door n.
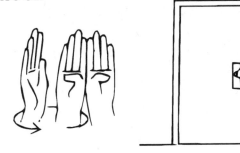
The door is closed.
door   doors

130 doorbell

doorbell n.

The mailman rings the doorbell.
doorbell   doorbells

double adj.

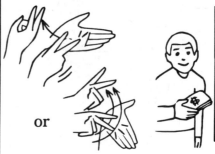

or

He received double pay.
He received twice as much as usual.

doorknob n.

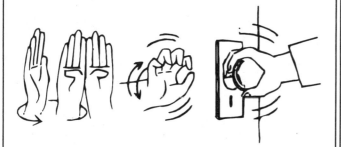

Turn the doorknob to open the door.
doorknob   doorknobs

doubt v.

I doubt that brick is real gold.
I don't believe it is real gold.

dope n. slang: pot, weed, grass

or

The man is on dope.
He uses marijuana.

dough n.

The baker is kneading the dough.

dot n.

Put a dot over the i. Put a
small round mark over the i.

doughnut n. donut

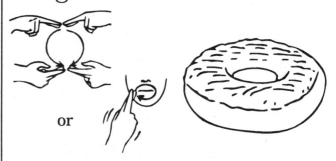

or

There is a hole in the doughnut.
doughnut   doughnuts

drag 131

dove n. bird
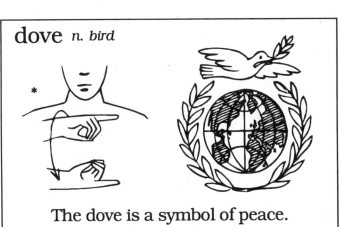
The dove is a symbol of peace.
dove   doves

downstairs adv.

The boy is downstairs.
The girl is upstairs.

dove pt. of dive
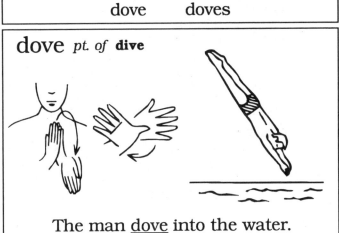
The man <u>dove</u> into the water.
He <u>dived</u> into the water.

dozen n. twelve
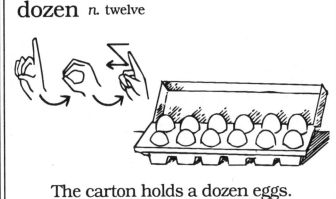
The carton holds a dozen eggs.
dozen   dozens

down adj.
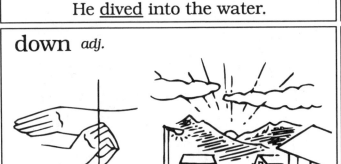
The sun is down.
It has set.

Dracula n.
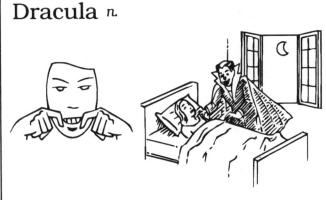
Dracula was a vampire.

down prep.
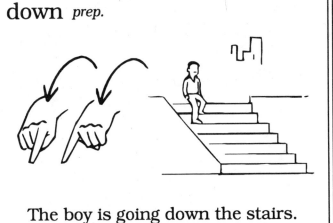
The boy is going down the stairs.

drag v.
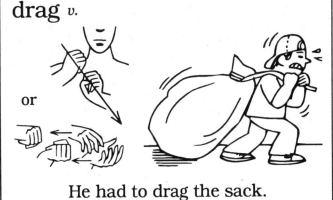
He had to drag the sack.
He had to pull it slowly.

132 dragon

dragon *n.*

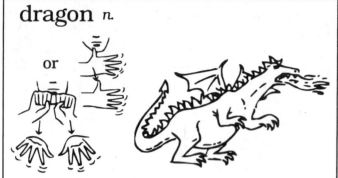

The dragon has wings and claws.
dragon   dragons

draw *v.*

I can draw a picture.
draws drew drawing drawn

drain *n.*

She poured the water down the drain.
drain   drains

draw *v.*

I will <u>draw</u> money out of the bank.
I'll <u>take</u> money out of my account.

drank *pt. of* **drink**

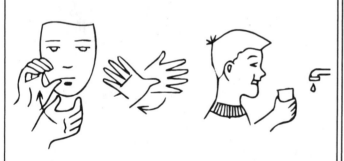

The boy drank some water.

drawer *n.*

The drawer is empty.
drawer   drawers

drape *n.*

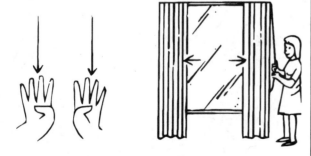

She is opening the drapes.
drape   drapes

drawn *pp. of* **draw**

She has drawn a picture.

dream v.

Did he dream about the dance?
dreams   dreamed/dreamt   dreaming

drew pt. of draw

The girl drew a picture.

dress n. clothing

She has a new dress.
dress   dresses

dried pt. of dry

Father dried the dishes.

dress v.

I must dress.
I must put on my clothes.

drift v.

Why did the boat drift away?
drifts   drifted   drifting

dresser n. furniture
or

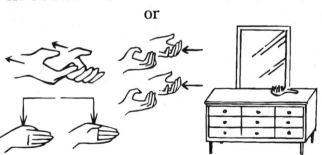

The brush is on the dresser.
dresser   dressers

drill n. tool

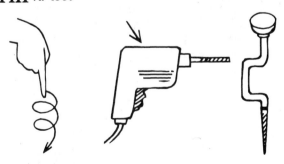

This is an electric drill.
drill   drills

134 drill

drill v.

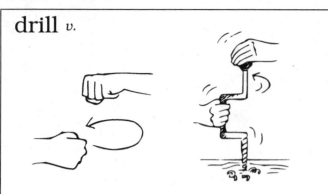

He will drill a hole.
drills   drilled   drilling

drinking fountain n.

She is using the drinking fountain.

drink n.

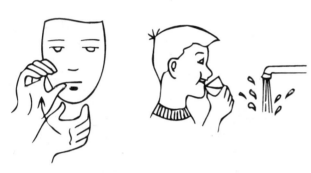

He took a drink of water.

drip v. leak

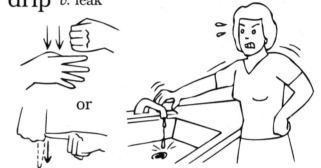

The faucet began to drip.
drips   dripped   dripping

drink n. beverage

He had a drink with his hamburger.
He had a beverage with his hamburger.

drive v.

I usually drive to work.
drives   drove   driving   driven

drink v.

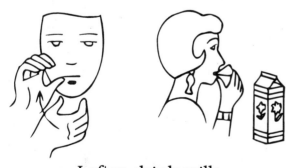

I often drink milk.
drinks   drank   drinking   drunk

driven pp. of **drive**

He has driven many miles.

drown 135

driveway n.

He parked the car in the driveway.
driveway   driveways

drop v.
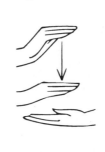

The price dropped $20.00.
The store lowered the price.

drool v.
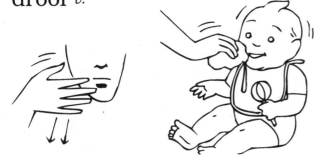
Babies drool. Saliva may run from a baby's mouth.

drove pt. of drive

The man drove all day.

drop n.

There is only a drop left.
There is only a small amount left.

drove pt. of drive
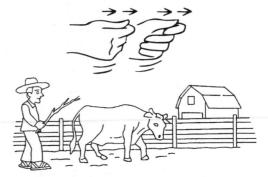
He drove the cow into the barn.

drop v.

I drop things because I am careless.
drops   dropped   dropping

drown v.

Did the boy almost drown in the pool?
drowns   drowned   drowning

136 drug

drug n.

I bought some drugs.
drug   drugs

drunk pp. of **drink**

We have drunk all of the coffee.

druggist n. worker

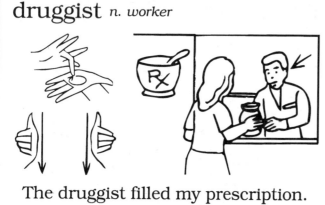

The druggist filled my prescription.
druggist   druggists

dry adj.

The clothes are dry.
They are not wet.

drugstore n.

She is in the drugstore.
drugstore   drugstores

dry adj.

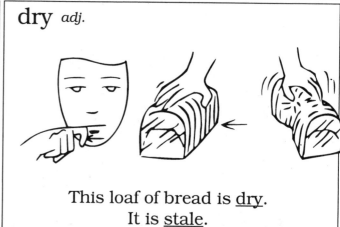

This loaf of bread is dry.
It is stale.

drum n.

The boy is beating the drum.
drum   drums

dry adj.

The dry weather harmed the crops.
The lack of rain harmed the crops.

dull 137

dry v.

I will dry the dishes.
I'll wipe the dishes.

due adj.

The rent is due on the first of the month. The rent must be paid then.

dryer n. household appliance

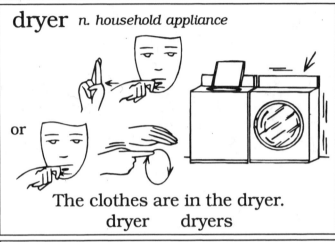

or

The clothes are in the dryer.
dryer   dryers

dug pt. of **dig**

The man dug a hole.

duck n. bird

The duck has white feathers.
duck   ducks

dull adj.

or

The knife is dull.
It's not sharp.

duckling n. young duck

The ducklings are cute.
duckling   ducklings

dull adj.

or

She has a dull job.
She has a boring job.

138 dumb

dumb *adj.*

My parents will think I am <u>dumb</u>.
They will think I'm <u>stupid</u>.

dustpan *n.*

Sweep the dust into the dustpan.
dustpan   dustpans

dump *v.*

Did he dump the wood in the yard?
dumps   dumped   dumping

dusty *adj.*

The table is dusty.
dustier   dustiest

during *prep.*

During the morning Father played
golf and Mother had her hair done.

duty *n.*

It's your <u>duty</u> to wash the dishes.
It's your <u>responsibility</u>.

dust *v.*

I must dust the table.
dusts   dusted   dusting

dye *v.*

She will dye the dress.
dyes   dyed   dyeing

E e

each *adj.*

He plays golf <u>each</u> Saturday.
He plays golf <u>every</u> Saturday.

eagle *n. bird*

Eagles have sharp beaks.
eagle   eagles

each *adv.*

The cookies are 25 cents each.

ear *n. body part*

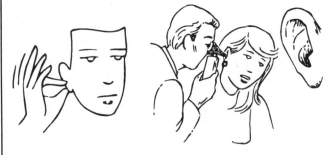

The doctor is examining her ear.
ear   ears

each other *pron.*

They love each other.
He loves her and she loves him.

ear *n. plant part*

Mary has one ear of corn.
Bob has two ears of corn.

eager *adj.*

They are <u>eager</u> to get to the bank.
They're <u>anxious</u> to get there.

earache *n.*

The boy has an earache.
The boy's ear hurts.

139

140 early

early *adj.*

He arrived at school too early.
He arrived before the usual time.

earphones *n.*

He's wearing earphones.

earmold *n.*

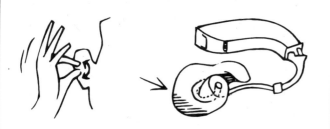

He got a new earmold.
earmold   earmolds

earring *n. jewelry*

She lost one earring.
earring   earrings

earmuffs *n.*

The boy is wearing earmuffs.

earrings *n.*

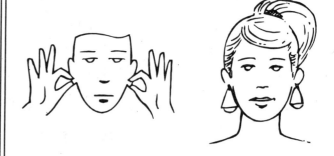

She is wearing a pair of earrings.

earn *v.*

I <u>earn</u> a lot of money.
I <u>am paid</u> a lot of money.

earth *n.*

The <u>earth</u> is a planet.
The <u>world</u> is a planet.

echo 141

earth n.

The earth was damp after the rain.
The soil was damp after the rain.

easy adj. simple
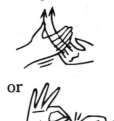
The problem is easy.
easier   easiest

earthquake n.

The earthquake did a lot of damage.
earthquake   earthquakes

eat v.

I eat an apple every day.
eats   ate   eating   eaten

east adj.

New York is on the east coast.

eaten pp. of eat

The boy has eaten too much.

Easter n. holiday

Easter is in April this year.

echo v.
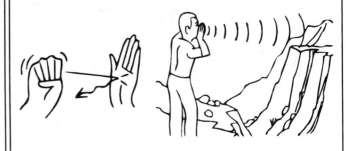
My will voice echo through the canyon.
echoes   echoed   echoing

142 edge

edge n.

The glass is near the edge of the table.
It's near the side of the table.

effect n.

The policy goes into effect 1/1/97.
The policy starts on 1/1/97.

edge n.
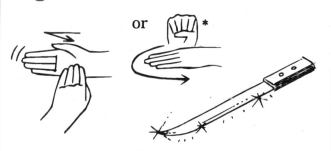
The knife has a sharp edge.
edge   edges

effort n.

He made an effort to get a cookie.
He tried to get one.

education n.
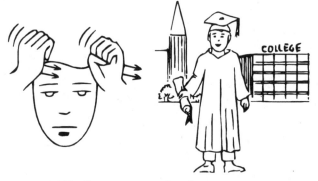
He has a good education.

effort n.
He puts a lot of effort into his job.
He puts a lot of energy into it.

effect n.

Smoking had a bad effect on his health.
Smoking harmed his health.

egg n. food

The man is frying some eggs.
egg   eggs

either 143

eggbeater n.

She is using an eggbeater.
eggbeater   eggbeaters

eighth fraction: 1/8

He cut off an eighth of an inch.
eighth   eighths

Egypt n. country

The pyramids are in Egypt.

eighth n. 8th

Today is the eighth of June.

eight number: 8

It is twenty-two minutes after eight.

eighty number: 80

Grandfather is eighty years old.

eighteen number: 18

or
She is eighteen years old.

either adj.

or
*
He doesn't like either cream or sugar in his coffee.

144 either

either adv.
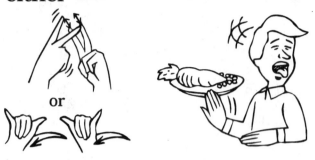
He doesn't like carrots.
He doesn't like peas, either.

electric adj.
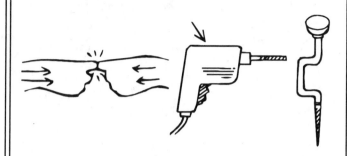
This is an electric drill.

elastic n.

Elastic stretches easily.

electric fan

The electric fan will cool the room.
electric fan   electric fans

elbow n. body part

He hurt his elbow.
elbow   elbows

electric shock n.
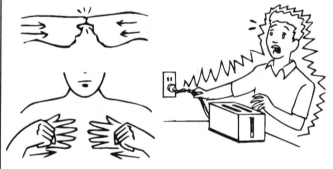
He received an electric shock.

elect v.

Did the voters elect Kennedy?
Did he receive the most votes?

electricity n.

The meter measures the electricity.

elves 145

elementary adj.

He is in elementary school.

elf n.

The elf lives in the woods.
elf   elves

elephant n. animal

The elephant has a long trunk.
elephant   elephants

elk n. animal
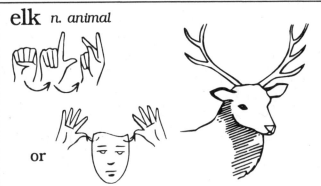
An elk is smaller than a moose.
elk   elks/elk

elevator n.
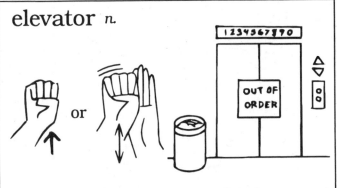
The elevator is out of order.
elevator   elevators

else adj.

Do you want anything <u>else</u>?
Do you want anything <u>in addition</u>?

eleven number: 11

Veterans Day is November 11.

elves plural of elf

The elves live in the woods.

146 embarrass

embarrass v.

Did his behavior embarrass the women? Did it make them feel uncomfortable?

employment n.

He is looking for employment. He's looking for a job.

emergency n.

The boy saw the emergency. He saw the need for immediate action.

empty adj.
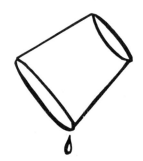
The glass is empty. There is nothing in it.

employ v.

or

We employ many workers here. We give jobs to many workers.

empty v.
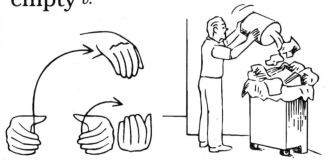
I will empty the wastebasket.
empties   emptied   emptying

employee n. worker
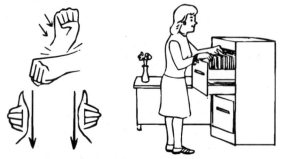
The woman is an employee. She gets paid for her work.

enchilada n. food
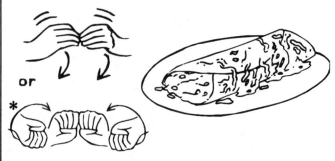
or
*
We had enchiladas for dinner.
enchilada   enchiladas

energy 147

encyclopedia n.

She is using the encyclopedia.
encyclopedia   encyclopedias

endorse v.

She must endorse the check.
She must sign the back of the check.

end n.

The short man is at
the end of the line.

endorse v.

I endorse more rights for women.
I support more rights for them.

end v.

or
When does school end?
When does it let out?

enemy n.

The soldiers attacked the enemy.
enemy   enemies

end table n. furniture

The lamp in on the end table.
end table   end tables

energy n.

or
The children are full of energy.
They are very lively.

148 engaged

engaged *adj.*

They are engaged.
They plan to get married.

English *n.*

They are studying English.

engine *n.*

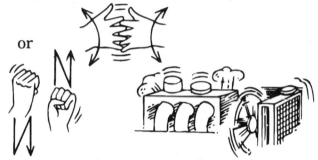

His car has a powerful engine.
It has a powerful motor.

enjoy *v.*

They enjoy themselves at the beach. They have a good time.

England *n.*

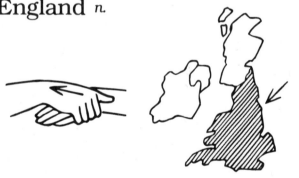

England is the southern part of Great Britain.

enough *adj.*

The woman has enough money.
She has plenty of money.

English *adj.*

The boy is English.
He was born in England.

enough *adj.*

The boy doesn't have enough money to buy the candy.

escalator 149

enter v.

The guests will <u>enter</u> the house.
They will <u>come into</u> the house.

erase v.
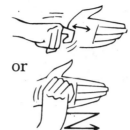 or
He will erase the blackboard.
erases   erased   erasing

envelope n.

He is addressing the envelope.
envelope   envelopes

eraser n.

He is using an eraser.
eraser   erasers

equal v.

Does five plus two equal seven?
Is five plus two the same as seven?

error n.

She made an <u>error</u>.
She made a <u>mistake</u>.

equipment n.

Playground equipment is expensive.

escalator n.
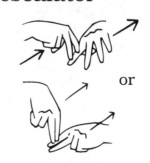 or
She took the escalator
to the second floor.

150 escape

escape v.
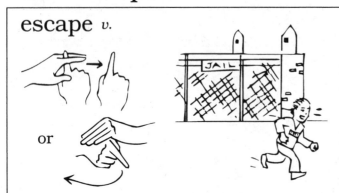
Prisoners seldom escape from the jail.
escapes   escaped   escaping

even adj.

The scores are even.
Each team has the same score.

Eskimo n.

Eskimos live in the Arctic.
Eskimo   Eskimos

even adj.
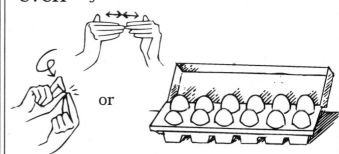
Twelve eggs make an even dozen.
Twelve eggs make exactly a dozen.

Europe n. continent

France and Germany are in Europe.

evening n.

I will see you this evening.
I'll see you after dark.

eve n.

Christmas eve is the night before Christmas day.

ever adv.

Don't ever write on the wall again.
Don't write on the wall at any time.

exaggerate 151

every *adj.*
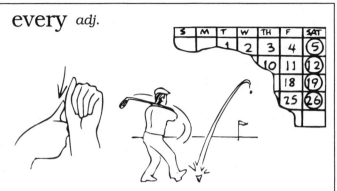
He plays golf every Saturday.
He plays golf each Saturday.

evidence *n.*
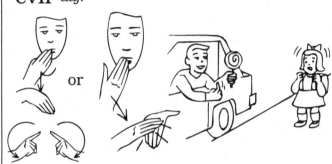
The policeman found some evidence.
He found some proof.

every day

I brush my teeth every day.
I brush them daily.

evil *adj.*

The stranger is an evil man.
He is a bad man.

everything *pron.*
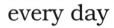

Eat everything on your plate.
Eat all the things on your plate.

exactly *adv.*
It is exactly 8 o'clock.
It's precisely 8 o'clock.

evict *v.*

I told you I would evict you
if you didn't pay your rent.

exaggerate *v.*

I think you exaggerate. I don't
think the fish was that big.

examination n.

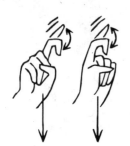

He passed the examination.
He passed the test.

except prep.

He works every day except Sunday.
He works every day but Sunday.

examination n.

The doctor gave him a physical examination.

excited adj.

The children are excited.
more excited   most excited

examine v.

I must examine the scene of the crime.
I must look at the scene carefully.

excuse v.

Excuse me. Pardon me. Forgive me.

example n.

He showed me examples of his work.
He showed me samples of his work.

exercise n.

Exercise is good for your health.

explain 153

exercise *v.*

I exercise every day.
exercises   exercised   exercising

expect *v.*

I expect the ballon to pop.
I think it will pop.

exhausted *adj.*
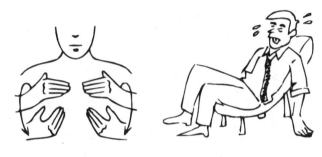
The man is exhausted.
He is very tired.

expensive *adj.*

or

The dress is expensive.
The price is high.

exit *n.*

The theater has an emergency exit.
It has an emergency way out.

expert *adj.*
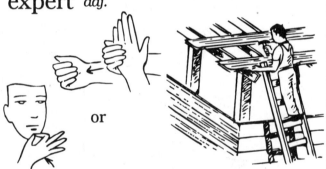
or

He is an expert builder.
He's a skillful builder.

expect *v. anticipate*

They expect to have a good time.
They hope to have a good time.

explain *v. make clear*

I will explain the lesson.
explains   explained   explaining

154 explode

explode v.

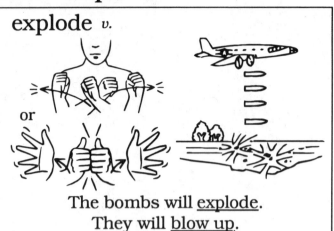

The bombs will explode.
They will blow up.

eye n. body part

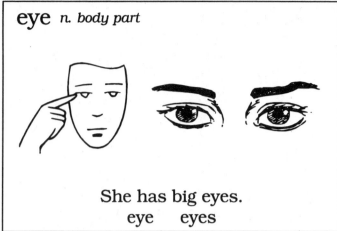

She has big eyes.
eye   eyes

explorer n.

Columbus was a famous explorer.
explorer   explorers

eyebrow n. body part

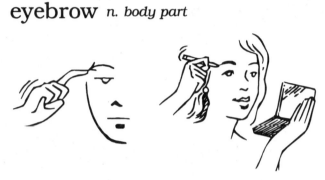

She darkens her eyebrows.
eyebrow   eyebrows

extinguisher n.

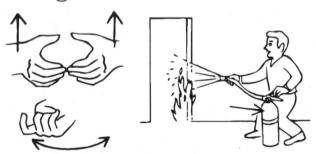

He is using the fire extinguisher.
extinguisher   extinguishers

eyelash n. body part

She has long eyelashes.
eyelash   eyelashes

extra adj.

The boy wants an extra cookie.
He wants an additional cookie.

eyelid n. body part

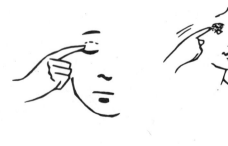

She puts make-up on her eyelids.
eyelid   eyelids

F f

fabric *n.*

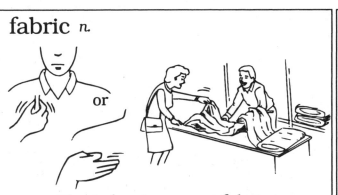

She is buying some <u>fabric</u>.
She's buying some <u>cloth</u>.

fail *v.*

I always fail some classes.
fails   failed   failing

face *n. body part*

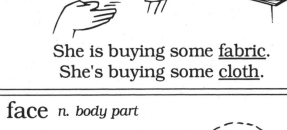

This is a man's face.
face   faces

faint *v.*

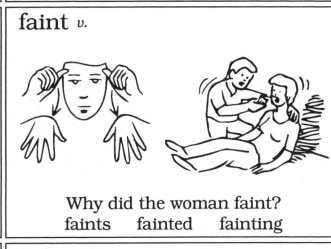

Why did the woman faint?
faints   fainted   fainting

fact *n.*

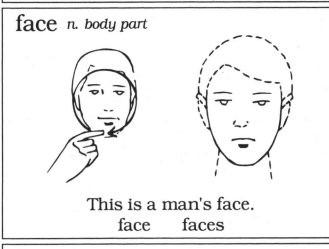

I didn't do it. That's a fact.
I didn't do it. That's the truth.

fair *adj.*

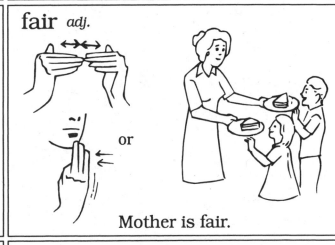

Mother is fair.

factory *n.*

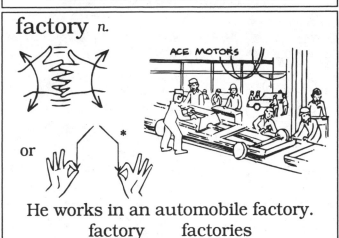

He works in an automobile factory.
factory   factories

not **fair** *adj.* unfair

Mother is not fair.

155

156 fair

fair n.

We went to the fair.
fair   fairs

fall n. season

<u>Fall</u> comes after summer.
<u>Autumn</u> comes after summer.

fairy n.

The fairy is carrying a wand.
fairy   fairies

fall v.

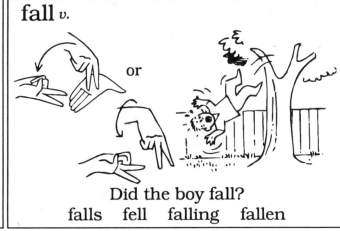

Did the boy fall?
falls   fell   falling   fallen

faith n.

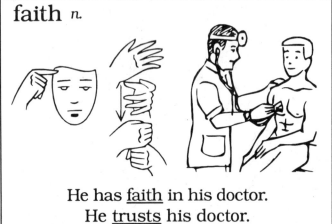

He has <u>faith</u> in his doctor.
He <u>trusts</u> his doctor.

fallen pp. of **fall**

The boy has fallen.

fake n.

The gold brick is a <u>fake</u>.
The gold brick is a <u>fraud</u>.

false adj.

He made a <u>false</u> statement.
He made an <u>untrue</u> statement.

farm 157

family n. parents & children

There are four people in our family.
family   families

fang n. animal body part

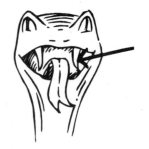

Rattlesnakes have fangs.
fang   fangs

famous adj.

Edison was a <u>famous</u> inventor.
He was a <u>well-known</u> inventor.

far adv.

Spacecraft travel far from Earth.
farther   farthest

fan n.

or

You need a fan in the summer.
fan   fans

fare n.

The bus fare is $1.25.
It costs $1.25 to ride the bus.

fancy adj.

or

She wore a very fancy dress.
fancier   fanciest

farm n.

The farm is close to the hills.
farm   farms

158 farmer

farmer n. worker

The farmer is stacking hay.
farmer   farmers

fat n
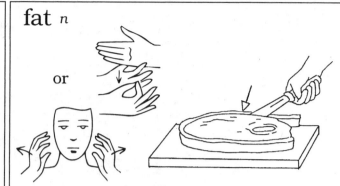
The steak has too much fat on it.
I will cut off some of the fat.

fast adj.

An airplane is fast.
A turtle is slow.

fatal adj.
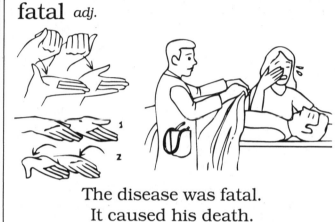
The disease was fatal.
It caused his death.

fast adj.

He is driving too fast.
faster   fastest

father n. male parent

The boy and his father are walking.
father   fathers

fasten v. connect
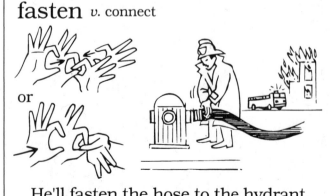
He'll fasten the hose to the hydrant.
He'll attach it to the hydrant.

faucet n.

He turned on the faucet.
faucet   faucets

fed 159

fault n.
or

It is his fault.
He is to blame.

fear v.
or

I fear the lion.
I am afraid of the lion.

favor n. kind act
or

Do me a favor and
mail this letter.

feather n.
or

All birds have feathers.
feather   feathers

favorite adj.
or

Cherry pie is my favorite dessert.
I like cherry pie best of all.

February n. month
*
or

Lincoln's Birthday is in February.

fear n.
or

The girl has a great fear of mice.
fear   fears

fed pt. of feed

Father fed the dog.

160 fed up

fed up adj.

She is <u>fed up</u> with her job.
She's <u>bored</u> with it.

feet n. body part
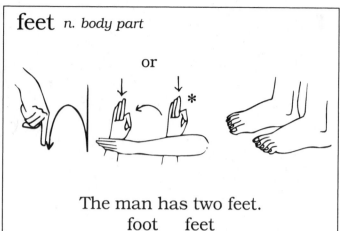
The man has two feet.
foot   feet

federal adj.

He pays federal and state taxes.

feet n. measurement
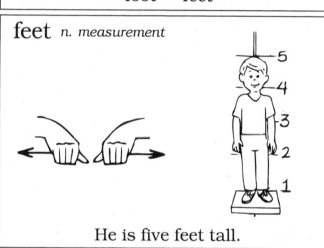
He is five feet tall.

feed v.

I always feed the chickens myself.
feeds   fed   feeding

fell pt. of fall

The boy fell.

feel v.
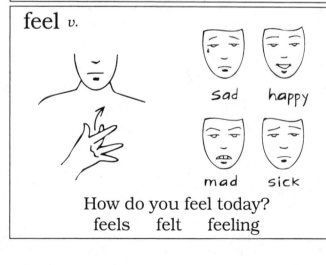
How do you feel today?
feels   felt   feeling

felt pt. of feel
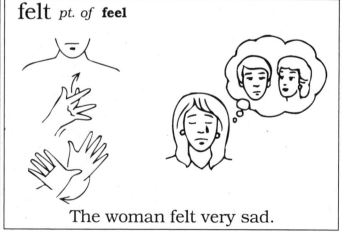
The woman felt very sad.

fib 161

female *n. woman or girl*

Girls and women are females.
female   females

ferry *n. boat*

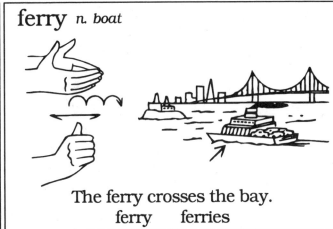

The ferry crosses the bay.
ferry   ferries

fence *n.*

A man is building a fence.
fence   fences

fever *n.*

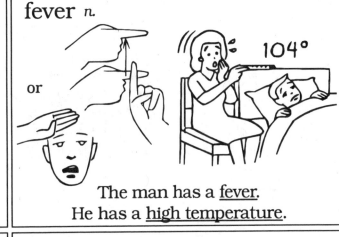

The man has a <u>fever</u>.
He has a <u>high temperature</u>.

fence *v.*

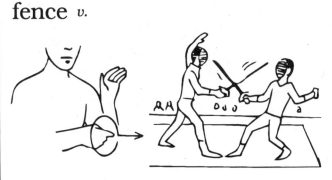

They often fence with each other.
fences   fenced   fencing

few *n. not many*

He only had a few pennies.
fewer   fewest

Ferris wheel *n.*

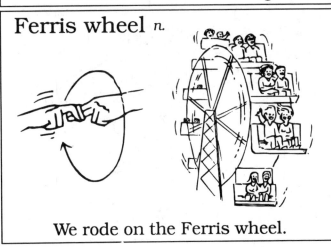

We rode on the Ferris wheel.

fib *n.*

He told a <u>fib</u>.
He told a <u>lie</u>.

162 fiction

fiction *n.*

This story is fiction.
It's not a true story.

fifty *number: 50*
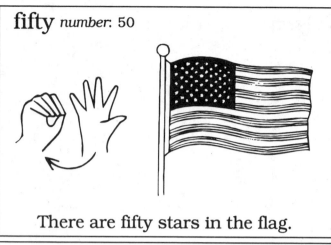
There are fifty stars in the flag.

field *n.*
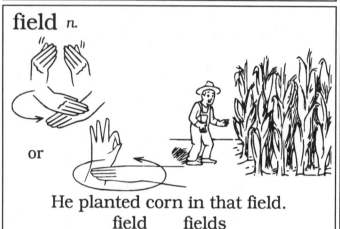
He planted corn in that field.
field   fields

fight *n.*
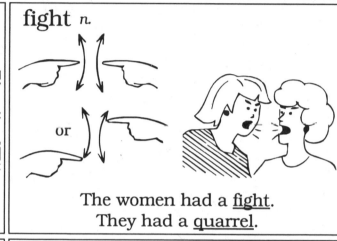
The women had a <u>fight</u>.
They had a <u>quarrel</u>.

fifteen *number: 15*

Eight plus seven equals fifteen.

fight *v.*

Why did the men fight?
fights   fought   fighting

fifth *adj. 5th*

The short man is fifth in line.

figure *n.*

The <u>figure</u> shocked him.
The <u>total</u> shocked him.

fin 163

figure n.

She has a nice <u>figure</u>.
She has a nice <u>shape</u>.

fill v.
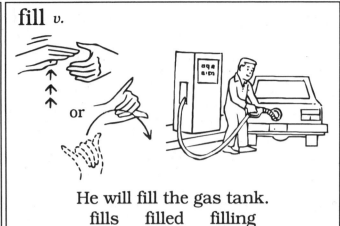
He will fill the gas tank.
fills   filled   filling

file n. tool

He is using the file to smooth the rough edges.

film n.

They enjoyed the <u>film</u>.
They enjoyed the <u>movie</u>.

file n.
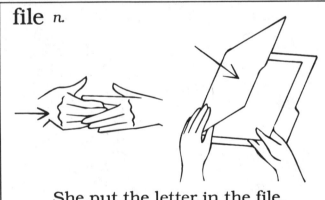
She put the letter in the file.
file   files

filthy adj.

The kitchen was <u>filthy</u>.
It was <u>very dirty</u>.

file cabinet n.

The file cabinet has three drawers.
file cabinet   file cabinets

fin n.

The fish has fins.
fin   fins

164 final

final *adj.*

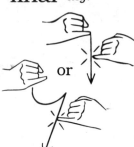

He couldn't do the <u>final</u> problem.
He couldn't do the <u>last</u> one.

finger *n. body part*

The boy cut his finger.
finger   fingers

finally *adv.*

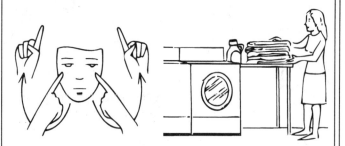

She <u>finally</u> finished the laundry.
<u>At last</u> she finished the laundry.

fingernails *n.*

She is polishing her fingernails.

find *v.*

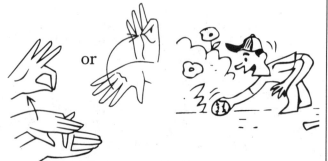

I knew I would find my ball.
finds found finding

finish *v.*

Did he <u>finish</u> his work?
Did he <u>complete</u> it?

fine *adj.*

The man feels <u>fine</u> today.
He feels <u>well</u> today.

Finland *n. country*

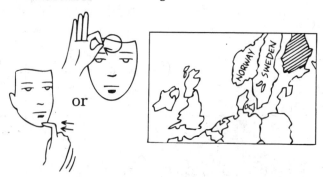

Finland is a country in Europe.

fireplace 165

fire n.
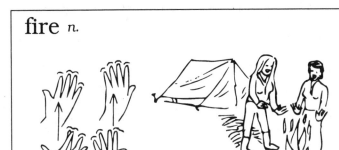
Someone built a fire.
fire   fires

fire escape n.
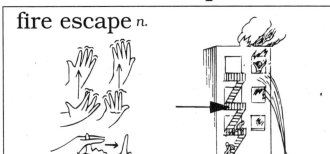
We ran down the fire escape.
fire escape   fire escapes

fire v.

He will fire her. She will lose her job.
fires   fired   firing

fire extinguisher n.

He is using a fire extinguisher.

fire alarm n.

The boy ran to the fire alarm.

fireman n. firefighter

The fireman attached the hose.
fireman   firemen

fire engine n. fire truck

The fire engine is red.
fire engine   fire engines

fireplace n.
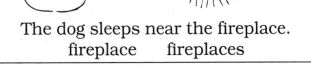
The dog sleeps near the fireplace.
fireplace   fireplaces

166 fire station

fire station n.

The boy visited the fire station.
He visited the firehouse.

first name
Her first name is Mary

fireworks n.

or
We watched the fireworks.

fish n.
Fish live in water.
fish   fish/fishes

first adj.
January is the first
month of the year.

fish v.
I often fish here.
fishes   fished   fishing

first adj.

or
The tall man is first in line.

fishing pole n.
He has a new fishing pole.
fishing pole   fishing poles

flashlight 167

fit v.

That dress doesn't fit her.
fits   fitted   fitting

flake n.

I like corn flakes.
flake   flakes

five number. 5

He goes to school five days a week.

flame n.

The house is in flames.
It is on fire.

fix v.

He will fix the broken chair.
fixes   fixed   fixing

flash v.

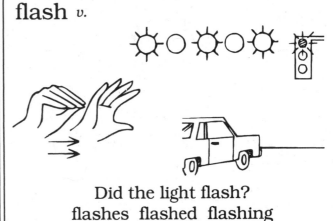

Did the light flash?
flashes   flashed   flashing

flag n.

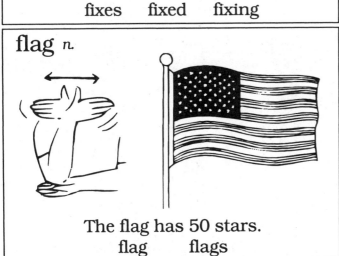

The flag has 50 stars.
flag   flags

flashlight n.

The officer is holding a flashlight.
flashlight   flashlights

168 flat

flat *adj.*

The tire is flat.
There is no air in the tire.

flea *n.*

The dog has fleas.
flea   fleas

flat *adj.*

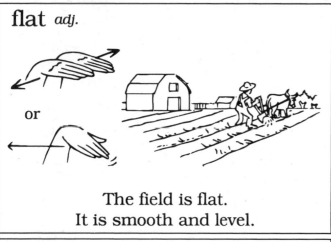

The field is flat.
It is smooth and level.

flew *pt. of* **fly**

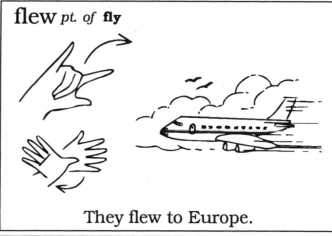

They flew to Europe.

flatter *v.*

You always flatter me.
You say things to please me.

flies *n. plural of* **fly**

He wants to get rid of the flies.

flavor *n.*

What flavor do you want?
flavor   flavors

flies *s-form of* **fly**

He flies an airplane.

floor 169

flirt v.

I always flirt with him.
flirts   flirted   flirting

flock n.

I look after the flock of sheep.
flock   flocks

float n.

The float was beautiful.
float   floats

flock v.

Children flock to the truck.
They run in a group to the truck.

float v.

Can the ball float?
floats   floated   floating

flood n.

The flood damaged the house.
flood   floods

float v.

The balloon will float away.

floor n.
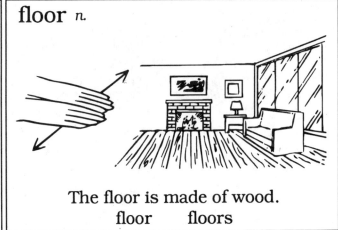
The floor is made of wood.
floor   floors

170 floor

floor n.
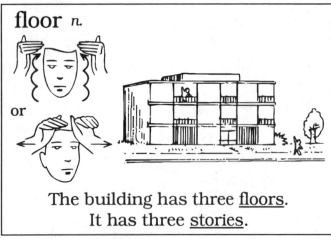
The building has three <u>floors</u>.
It has three <u>stories</u>.

flown pp. of **fly**
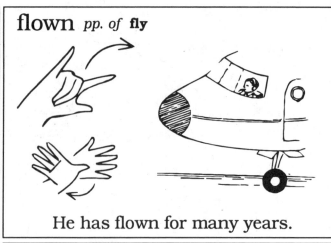
He has flown for many years.

flour n. *ground grain*
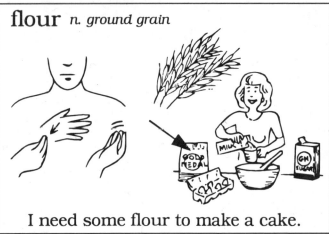
I need some flour to make a cake.

flu n. *sickness*
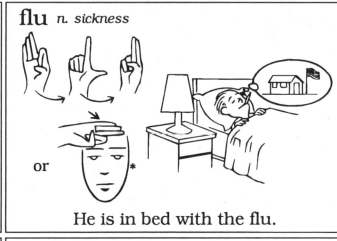
He is in bed with the flu.

flow v.

Does the water <u>flow</u> over the cliff?
Does it <u>move</u> over the cliff?

fluid n.
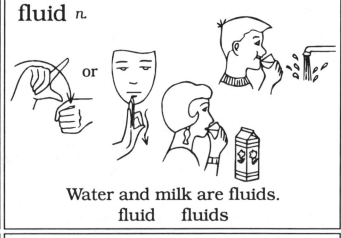
Water and milk are fluids.
fluid   fluids

flower n.

The flowers are pretty.
flower   flowers

flush v.
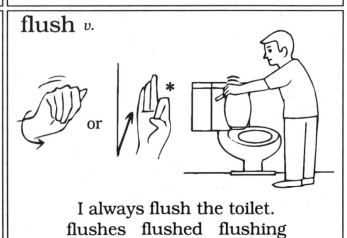
I always flush the toilet.
flushes   flushed   flushing

fold 171

flute n. musical instrument

She plays the flute.
flute   flutes

foam v.

Root beer foams if you pour it too fast.

fly n. insect

The man tried to kill the fly.
fly   flies

fog n.

The fog was terrible.
He couldn't see the street.

fly v.

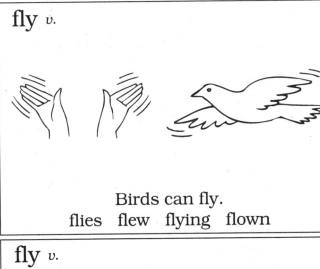

Birds can fly.
flies   flew   flying   flown

foil n.

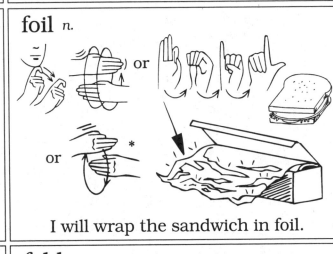

I will wrap the sandwich in foil.

fly v.

They will fly to New York.

fold v.

I always fold the towels.
folds   folded   folding

172 follow

follow v.

I will follow that boy.
I'll walk behind him.

fool around
Please don't fool around.
Please don't waste time.

food n.

or

You must eat all the food on your plate.

foolish adj.

or

She was foolish to buy that brick.
She was silly to buy that brick.

fool v. deceive

or

He's trying to fool that woman.
fools   fooled   fooling

foot n. 12 inches
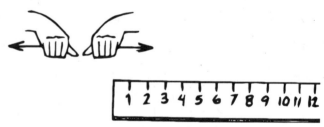
There are 12 inches in a foot.
one foot   two feet

fool v.

or

I like to fool her..
I like to tease her.

foot n. body part
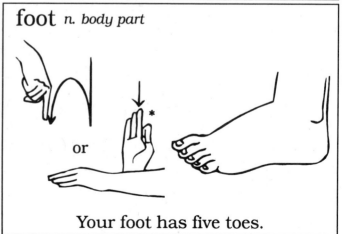
or

Your foot has five toes.

force 173

football n. game

They are playing football.

forbidden pp. of **forbid**

The doctor has forbidden me to smoke. He ordered me to stop.

football n.

He has a new football.
football   footballs

force v.

I force him to mow the lawn.
I make him do it against his will.

for prep.

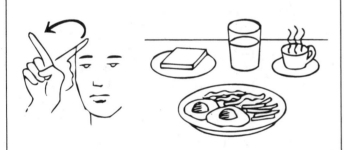

I had bacon and eggs for breakfast.

force v.

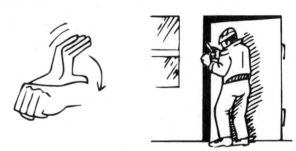

He will force the door open.
He'll break open the door.

forbid v.

or

Laws forbid drunk driving.
Drunk driving is illegal.

force v.

I must <u>force</u> this dress into the suitcase. I must <u>jam</u> it in.

174 forehead

forehead n. body part
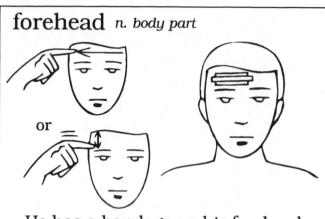
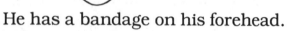
He has a bandage on his forehead.

forgive v. excuse, pardon

Please forgive me.
forgives forgave forgiving forgiven

foreign adj.

She wants to visit a foreign country.

forgot pt. of forget

She forgot to watch the meat.

forest n.

They walked through the <u>forest</u>.
They walked through the <u>woods</u>.

forgotten pp. of forget

She has forgotten her purse.

forget v. can't remember

I forget where I put my money.
forgets forgot forgetting forgotten

fork n.

The boy bent the fork.
fork forks

found 175

form n.

He filled out the form.
He filled out the application.

forty number. 40

She is forty years old.

form n.
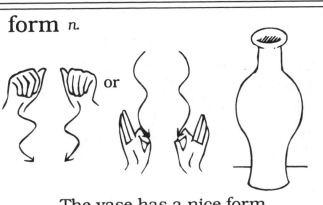
The vase has a nice form.
It has a nice shape.

forward adv.

The boy wheeled himself forward.
He wheeled himself ahead.

formula n.

The formula for water is two parts of hydrogen and one part oxygen.

fought pt. of **fight**

The men fought.

fort n.

The Indians attacked the fort.
fort   forts

found pt. of **find**

The boy found his ball.

176 fountain

fountain n.

There is a fountain in the park.
fountain   fountains

fourth adj. 4th

The short man is fourth in line.

fountain n.

The girl is using the fountain.

fourth n. fraction: 1/4

He ate a fourth of the pie.
He ate a quarter of the pie.

four number: 4

There are four people in line.

fox n. animal

The fox has a bushy tail.
fox   foxes

fourteen number: 14

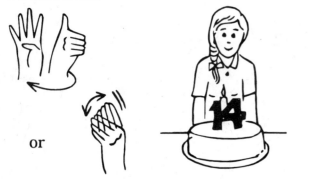

She is fourteen years old.

fraction n.

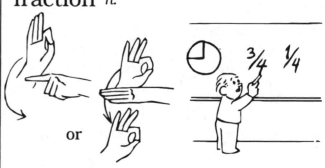

He is studying fractions.
fraction   fractions

freezer 177

frame n.

The picture has a wooden frame.
frame   frames

free adj.

The woman took a free sample.

France n. country
 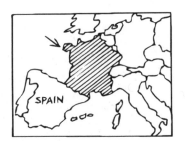
France is a country in Europe.

freeway n.

We drove on the freeway.
freeway   freeways

Frankenstein n.

Frankenstein was a monster.

freeze v.

Does the lake freeze in the winter?
freezes   froze   freezing   frozen

freckles n.
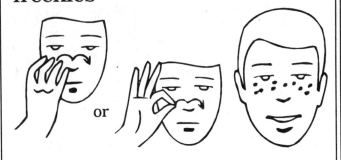
The boy has freckles.
freckle   freckles

freezer n.

The ice cream is in the freezer.
freezer   freezers

178 french fries

french fries n. food

He ordered some french fries.
french fry   french fries

Friday n. day of week
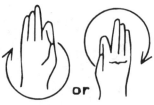
Friday comes after Thursday.

frequently adv.

They frequently dine out.
They often dine out.

fried pt. of fry

He fried the eggs.

fresh adj.
or
*

This is a fresh tomato.
fresher   freshest

friend n.

The boys are friends.
friend   friends

fresh adj.
or
*

This loaf of bread is fresh.
The other one is stale.

friendly adj.
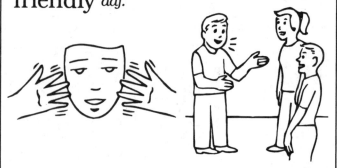
Bob is always friendly.
He is kind and courteous.

from time to time 179

frighten *v.*

Mice <u>frighten</u> the girl.
Mice <u>scare</u> her.

from *prep.*

They came to the United
States from Mexico.

frightened *adj.*

The girl is <u>frightened</u>.
She is <u>afraid</u>.

from *prep.*

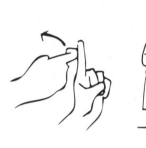

The boy brought his report
card home from school.

Frisbee *n. toy*

He tossed the Frisbee to his friend.
    Frisbee   Frisbees

from now on

<u>From now on</u>, keep that dog outside.
<u>Hereafter</u>, keep it outside.

frog *n. animal*

The frog is green.
   frog   frogs

from time to time

He calls me from time to time.
He calls me once in a while.

180 front

front *adj.*

He knocked on the front door.

frown *v.*
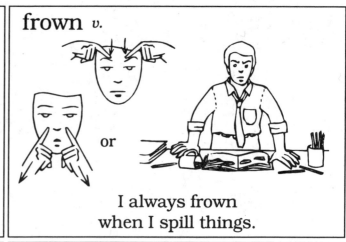
I always frown when I spill things.

front *n.*

They are standing in front of their house.

froze *pt. of* **freeze**

The lake froze.

frost *n.*

The windshield is covered with frost.

frozen *adj.*

She bought some frozen vegetables.

frosting *n.*
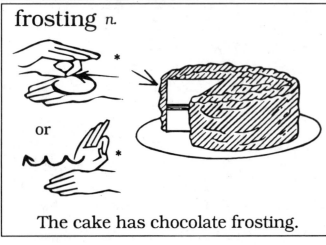
The cake has chocolate frosting.

fruit *n. food*

I like to eat fresh fruit.

fun 181

frustrated *adj.*
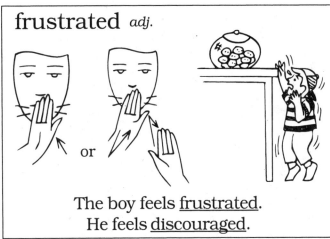
The boy feels <u>frustrated</u>.
He feels <u>discouraged</u>.

fuel *n.*
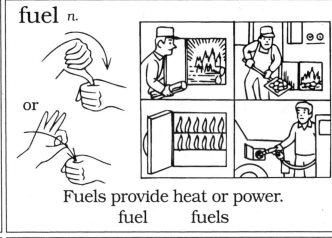
Fuels provide heat or power.
fuel   fuels

fry *v.*

I usually fry my eggs.
fries   fried   frying

full *adj.*

The glass is full.
It can't hold any more.

frying pan *n.*

The eggs are in the frying pan.
frying pan   frying pans

full *adj.*

The boy is full.
He can't eat any more.

fudge *n. candy*

I made some fudge.

fun *n.*

They had fun at the beach.
They enjoyed themselves.

182 function

function v.

The elevator will not function.
The elevator will not work.

fur n. animal hair
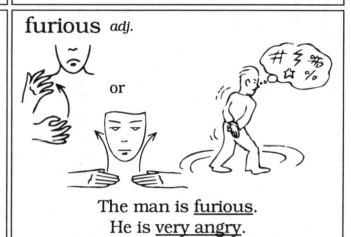
The fox has soft fur.

funeral n.

We went to the funeral.
funeral   funerals

furious adj.
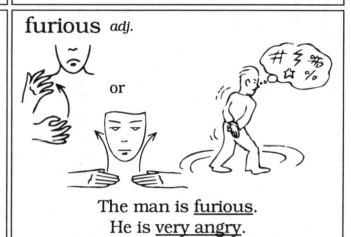
The man is furious.
He is very angry.

funnel n.
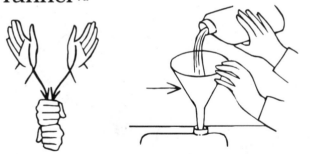
I used a funnel to fill the bottle.
funnel   funnels

furniture n.

We bought some new furniture.

funny adj.

The clown was very funny.
The clown caused us to laugh.

future n.

The boy is thinking of his future.

G g

gag *v.*

The judge gagged the jury. He ordered them not to talk about the case.

gallon *n.*

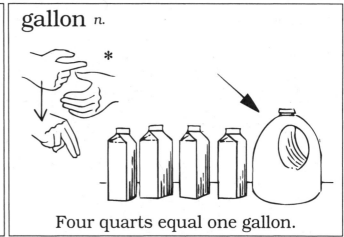

Four quarts equal one gallon.

gag *v.*

I gag when I taste that medicine.
I choke and want to vomit.

gamble *v.*

I gamble and lose my money.
gambles   gambled   gambling

gain *v.*

I always <u>gain</u> weight.
I always <u>put on</u> weight.

game *n.*

They are playing a game.
game   games

Gallaudet *n.*

Gallaudet is a college for the deaf.

gang *n.*

He belongs to a gang.
gang   gangs

183

184 garage

garage n.

Her car is in the garage.
garage   garages

gardener n. worker
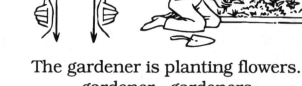
The gardener is planting flowers.
gardener   gardeners

garbage n.

She threw the fish in the garbage.

gargle v.

I gargle every morning.
gargles   gargled   gargling

garbage can n. container
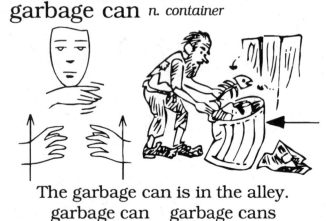
The garbage can is in the alley.
garbage can   garbage cans

gas n. gasoline

The car needs gas.

garden n.

or
They have a nice garden.
garden   gardens

gas n.

She turned on the gas.

gave 185

gasoline *n.* gas

He bought some gasoline.

gather *v.*

I often gather flowers.
gathers   gathered   gathering

gas pedal
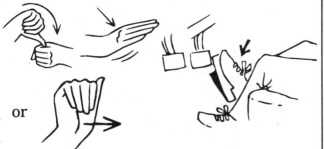
He stepped on the gas pedal.
He stepped on the accelerator.

gather *v.*
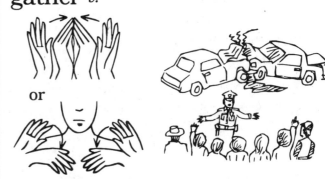
Crowds gather near most accidents.

gas station *n.* filling station

He drove to the gas station.
gas station   gas stations

gauge *n.*
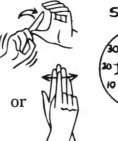  
The temperature gauge
is on the dashboard.

gate *n.*

The dog is near the gate.
gate   gates

gave *pt. of* give

The boy gave the girl a gift.

186 geese

geese n. plural of **goose**

The geese are near the pond.

germ n.

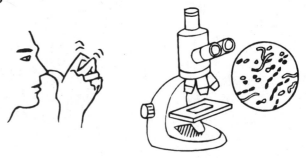

Germs cause disease.
germ germs

gentleman n.

He always acts like a gentleman.
He is courteous to others.

Germany n. country

Germany is a country in Europe.

genuine adj.

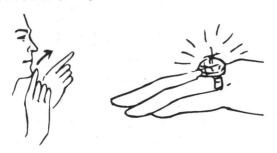

This is a <u>genuine</u> diamond.
This is a <u>real</u> diamond.

gesture v. use hand movements

They don't speak the same language,
so they gesture to each other.

geometry n.

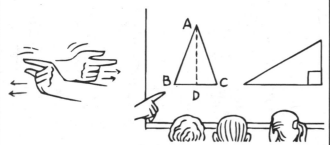

They are studying geometry.

get v. receive

I often get letters from friends.
gets got getting gotten

get

When did she <u>get</u> home?
When did she <u>arrive</u> home?

get on v.

They will <u>get on</u> the plane.
They'll <u>board</u> the plane.

get v. grow

I <u>get</u> angry when I see the dog.
I <u>become</u> angry when I see it.

get out v.

I want you to <u>get out</u> now.
I want you to <u>leave</u> now.

get away v.

You must <u>get away</u> from the stove.
You must <u>move away</u> from it.

get rid of v.

He should <u>get rid of</u> that junk!
He should <u>dispose of</u> it!

get off v.

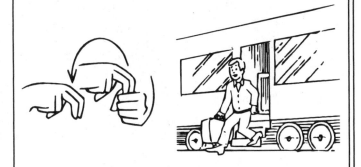

I have to get off the train here.

get to

He will <u>get to</u> L.A. at 7 o'clock.
He'll <u>arrive in</u> L.A. then.

188 get up

get up v. arise

I usually <u>get up</u> at 6:30.
I usually <u>get out of bed</u> then.

giggle v.

We always giggle when we see that boy.
giggles   giggled   giggling

ghost n.

The woman thought she saw a ghost.
ghost   ghosts

gingerbread n. food

Mother made some gingerbread.

giant n.

The man is a <u>giant</u>.
He is a <u>huge</u> <u>man</u>.

giraffe n. animal

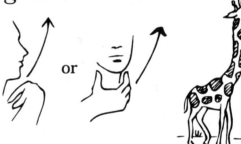

The giraffe has a long neck.
giraffe   giraffes

gift n.

The <u>gift</u> has a pretty ribbon.
The <u>present</u> has a pretty ribbon.

girl n. female child

The girl has long curls.
girl   girls

glass 189

girlfriend n.
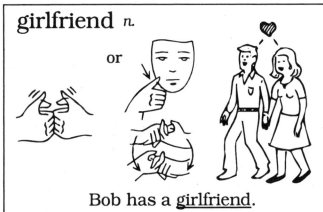
Bob has a girlfriend.
He has a sweetheart.

given pp. of give
The boy has given the girl a gift.

give v.
The boy will give the girl a gift.
gives   gave   giving   given

glad adj.
The woman was glad to see him.
She was happy to see him.

give up v.
You must give up smoking.
You must stop smoking.

glass n.
I would like a glass of water.
glass   glasses

give up v.
We give up.
We surrender.

glass n.
The window is made of glass.

glasses n.

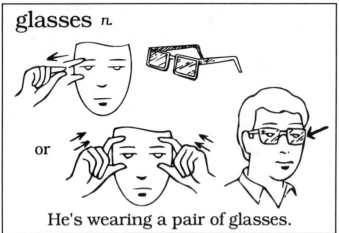

He's wearing a pair of glasses.

glue n.

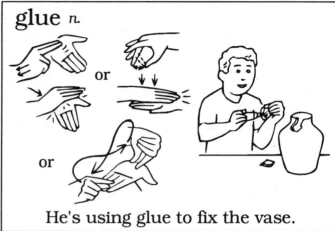

He's using glue to fix the vase.

globe n.

The lamp needs a new globe.
It needs a new bulb.

glutton n.

He was a glutton.
He ate too much.

globe n.

The plane circled the globe.
It circled the earth.

go v.

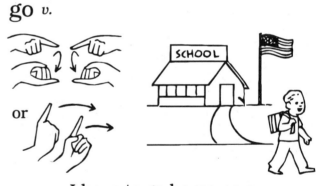

I have to go home now.
goes   went   going   gone

glove n.

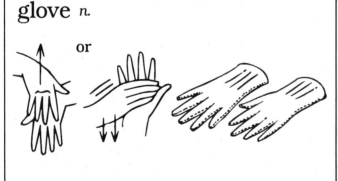

This is a pair of gloves.
glove   gloves

go v.

You must go.
You must leave.

gold 191

goal *n. objective*

His goal is to become an adventurer.
goal   goals

goes *s-form of* **go**

or

He goes to school in the morning.

goat *n. animal*

The goat has horns and a beard.
goat   goats

goggles *n.*

I wear goggles to protect my eyes.

gobble *v.*

Don't gobble your food.
Don't eat so rapidly.

going on *v.*

or

What is <u>going on</u>?
What is <u>happening</u>?

God *n.*

or

People go to church or
temple to worship God.

gold *n. precious metal*

or

The miner discovered gold.

192 golf

golf *n. game*

The man is playing golf.

gone *pp. of* **go**

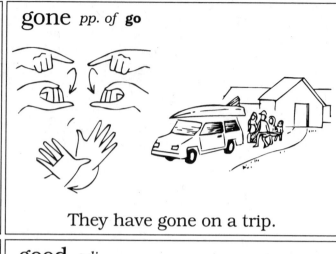

They have gone on a trip.

gone *adj.*

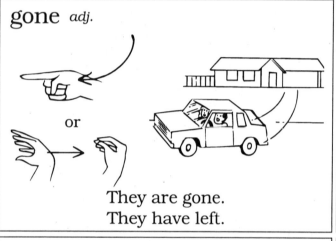

They are gone.
They have left.

good *adj.*

His grades are good.
good better best

gone *adj.*

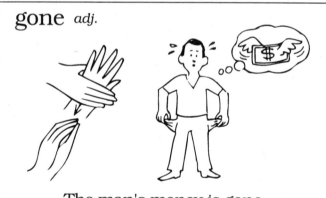

The man's money is gone.
He has lost his money.

good *adj.*

He is in good health.
He is healthy.

gone *adj.*

The milk is gone.
The milk has been used up.

not good *adj.*

The girl's behavior is not good.

government 193

good *adj.*

We had a good time.
We enjoyed ourselves.

gossip *v*

She likes to gossip.
She likes to talk about other people.

goodbye *n.* goodby, good-by, good-bye

She waved goodbye to her friends.

got *pt. of* get
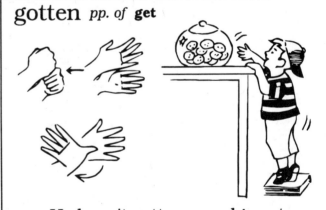
The woman got some letters.
She received some letters.

goose *n. bird*

The goose is near the pond.
goose   geese

gotten *pp. of* get

He hasn't gotten a cookie yet.

gorilla *n. animal*
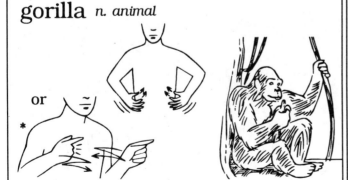
The gorilla is very strong.
gorilla   gorillas

government *n.*
The president is the head
of the federal government.

194 gown

gown n. dress

She wore a beautiful gown.
She wore a beautiful evening dress.

grain n.
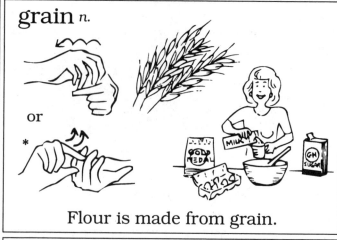
Flour is made from grain.

grab v. seize

I will grab a cookie and run outside.
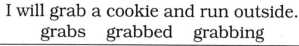
grabs   grabbed   grabbing

grammar n.

The class is studying grammar.

grade n.

He received poor grades.
grade   grades

grand adj.

They dined at a grand restaurant.
They dined at an elegant restaurant.

graduate v.

He will graduate in June.
He'll finish college in June.

grand adj. informal

We had a grand time at the circus.
We had a wonderful time.

grave 195

grandfather *n.* grandpa

He is my grandfather.
grandfather   grandfathers

grandmother *n.* grandma

She is my grandmother.
grandmother   grandmothers

grape *n. fruit*

This is a bunch of grapes.
grape   grapes

grapefruit *n. fruit*

The grapefruit is sour.

grass *n.*
Cows like to eat grass.

grasshopper *n. insect*
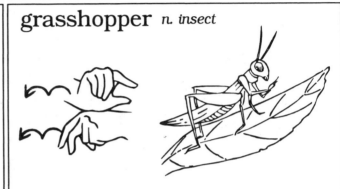
The grasshopper has wings.
grasshopper   grasshoppers

grate *v.*
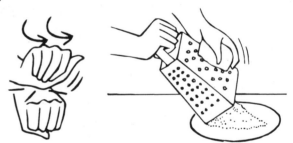
I have to grate some cheese.
grates   grated   grating

grave *n.*
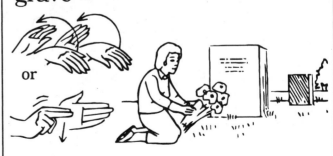
She put flowers on the grave.
grave   graves

196 gravel

gravel n. small pieces of rock

Some gravel flew into the air.

grease n.

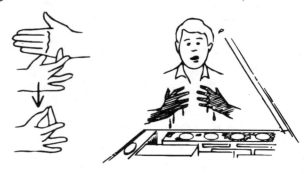

He has grease on his hands.

gravity n.

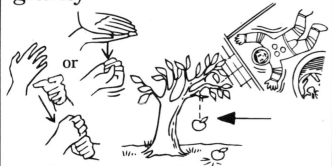

Gravity causes objects to move toward the center of the earth.

great adj.

We had a great time at the circus.
We had a wonderful time.

gravy n. food

He likes gravy on his potatoes.

Greece n. country

Greece is a country in Europe.

gray adj. color: grey

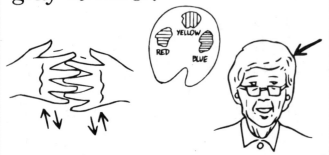

Grandmother has gray hair.
She has grey hair.

greedy adj. selfish

The man is very greedy.
greedier   greediest

groceries 197

green *adj. color*

The grass is green.

grey *adj. color: gray*

Grandmother has grey hair.
She has gray hair.

green *adj.*

The peach is green.
It is not ripe.

grin *v.*

Why did the boy grin?
grins   grinned   grinning

grenade *n. weapon*

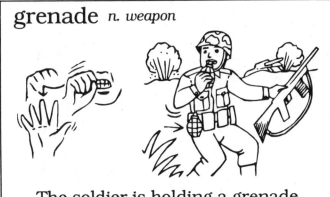

The soldier is holding a grenade.
grenade   grenades

grind *v.*

The woman must grind her corn.
grinds   ground   grinding

grew *pt. of* **grow**

The farmer grew corn.

groceries *n.*

The basket is full of groceries.

198   grocery cart

grocery cart n.

She is pushing the grocery cart.
grocery cart   grocery carts

group n.

A group of people stood near the policeman.

grocery store n.

The woman is in the grocery store.
grocery store   grocery stores

grow v.

Some trees grow to be very tall.
grows   grew   growing   grown

ground n.

The ground is ready for planting.
The soil is ready for planting.

grow v. become, get

I always grow angry when
I see the dog in the house.

ground pt. of grind

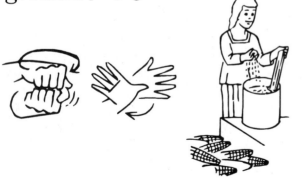

The woman ground the corn.

growl v.

Dogs growl.
They make an angry sound.

guide 199

grown *pp. of* grow

The boy has grown tall.

guard *v.*

or

The soldier must guard the prisoners.
guards   guarded   guarding

grown-up *n.*

or

He is a grown-up.
He's an adult.

guess *n.*

The boy made a guess.
guesses   guessed   guessing

guarantee *n.*

or

The pills come with
a money-back guarantee.

guest *n.*

or

We had guests for dinner.
We had visitors for dinner.

guard *n. worker*

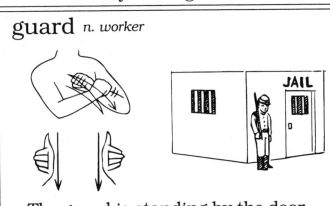

The guard is standing by the door.
guard   guards

guide *v. lead*

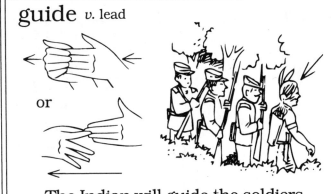

or

The Indian will guide the soldiers
through the woods.

200 guilty

guilty adj.

The man is guilty.
The man is not innocent.

gum n. body part

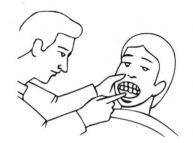

The dentist examined his gums.

guinea pig n. animal

or

The guinea pig has a short tail.
guinea pig   guinea pigs

gun n. weapon

The sheriff has two guns.
gun   guns

guitar n. musical instrument

He plays the guitar.
guitar   guitars

gym n. gymnasium

The boys are in the gym.

gum n.

or

Would you like a stick of gum?

gypsy n.

The gypsy will tell your fortune.
gypsy   gypsies

H h

habit n.

Smoking is a bad habit.
habit   habits

hail v.

I must hail the ship.
I must try to attract attention.

had pt. of have

The boy had a ball, but he lost it.

hail v.

Did the crowd hail the hero?
Did the crowd cheer him?

had pt. of have

He had broken the window.

hair n. boby part
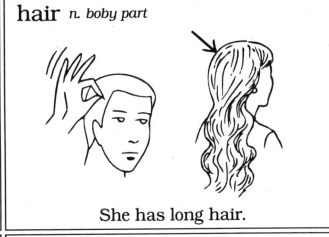
She has long hair.

hail n.
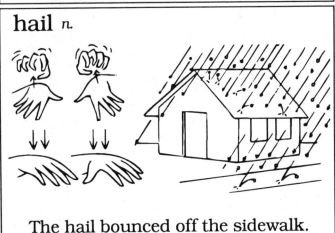
The hail bounced off the sidewalk.

hairbrush n.
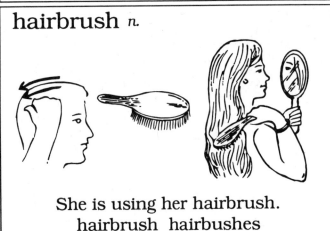
She is using her hairbrush.
hairbrush   hairbushes

202 haircut

haircut n.

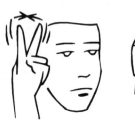

The boy is getting a haircut.
haircut   haircuts

half n.

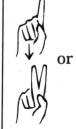 or

He ate half of the pie.
one half   two halves

hairdresser n. worker

The hairdresser enjoys her work.
hairdresser   hairdressers

half a dozen

She bought half a dozen eggs.
She bought six eggs.

hair dryer n.

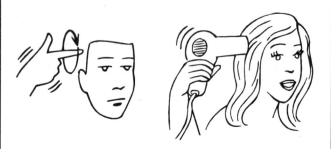

She is using a hairdryer.
hairdryer   hairdryers

half hour n.

He's been waiting for a half hour.
He's been waiting for 30 minutes.

hair ribbon

She's wearing a hair ribbon.
hair ribbon   hair ribbons

halitosis n.

She has halitosis. She has bad breath.

hammock 203

hall *n. corridor*

They walked down the hall.
hall   halls

ham *n. meat*

I baked a ham for dinner.
ham   hams

Halloween *n. holiday*

Halloween is October 31st.

hamburger *n. food*

He ate a hamburger for lunch.
hamburger   hamburgers

halt *n.*

He came to a halt.
He stopped.

hammer *n. tool*

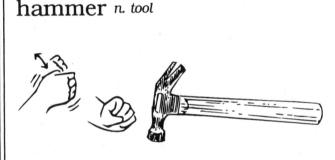

The hammer has a wooden handle.
hammer   hammers

halves *n. pural of* **half**

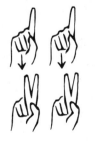

She cut the candy bars into halves.
She cut them in half.

hammock *n.*

The man is asleep in the hammock.
hammock   hammocks

204 hamper

hamper n.

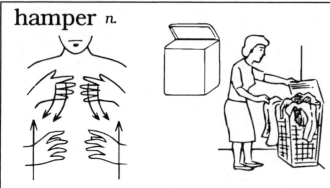

I put the dirty clothes in the hamper.
hamper   hampers

hand n.

The clock has two hands,
a minute hand and an hour hand.

hamper v.

Snow will <u>hamper</u> our progress.
It will <u>hinder</u> our progress.

hand n.

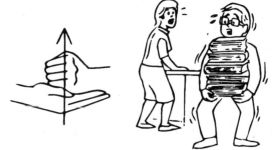

Please <u>give me a hand</u>.
Please <u>help me</u>.

hamster n. animal

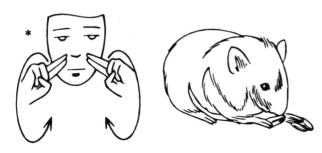

The hamster has a short tail.
hamster   hamsters

hand v. give

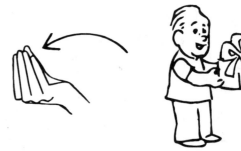

He will <u>hand</u> the gift to the girl.
He'll <u>give</u> it to her.

hand n. body part

There are five fingers on each hand.
hand   hands

hand in v.

Please hand in your papers.
Please give me your papers.

hang 205

handbag n. purse

The handbag is made of leather.
The purse is made of leather.

handle v. touch

Don't handle the merchandise.
handles   handled   handling

handcuffs n.
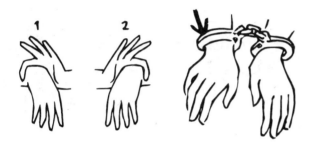
This is a pair of handcuffs.

handle v.

Father can't handle the children.
He can't control them.

handkerchief n.

She is using a handkerchief.
handkerchief   handkerchiefs

handsome adj.

The man is handsome.
He is good-looking.

handle n.
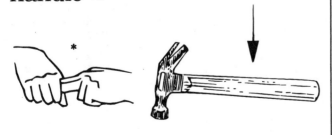
The hammer has a long handle.
handle   handles

hang v.

Please hang the picture on that wall.
hangs   hung/hanged   hanging

206 hang

hang v.

I hang my clothes in the closet.

hanger n.
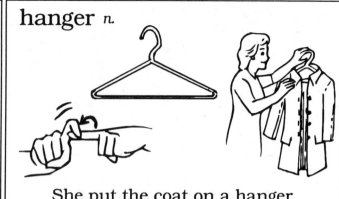
She put the coat on a hanger.
hanger   hangers

hang v.
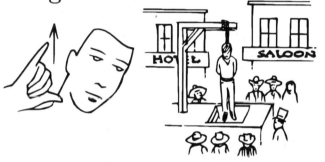
Why did they hang the man?
Why was he put to death?

Hanukkah n. Chanukah

They are celebrating Hanukkah.

hang up v.

Why did she hang up the phone?

happen v. occur

How did the accident happen?
happens   happened   happening

hangar n.
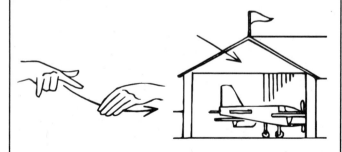
The airplane is in the hangar.
hangar   hangars

happy adj. glad
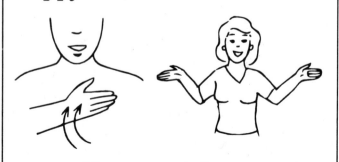
The woman is happy.
happier   happiest

harvest 207

harbor n.

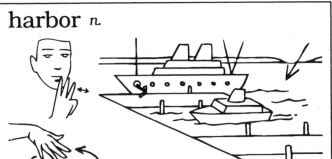

The ship is in the harbor.
harbor   harbors

harm v.

Dry weather can <u>harm</u> the plants.
Dry weather can <u>damage</u> them.

hard adj.

My homework is <u>hard</u>.
It is <u>difficult</u>.

harmonica n.

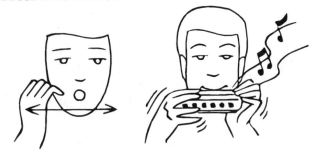

He plays the harmonica.
harmonica   harmonicas

hard adj.

The stale bread is <u>hard</u>.
It is <u>not soft</u>.

harp n. musical instrument

She is playing a harp.
harp   harps

hardware n.

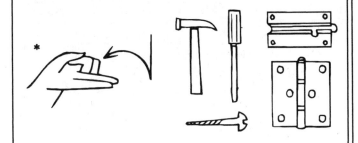

The store carries hardware.

harvest v.

We <u>harvest</u> the crops in the fall.
We <u>gather</u> the crops then.

208 has

has *s-form of* **have**

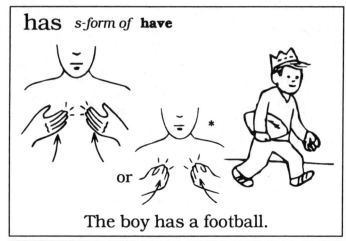

The boy has a football.

hatchet *n.* small ax

The man is using a hatchet.
hatchet hatchets

has *s-form of* **have**

He has broken the window.

hate *v.* dislike

I hate peas and carrots.
hates hated hating

hat *n.*

Do you like my new hat?
hat hats

haul *v.*

He must <u>haul</u> water from the lake.
He must <u>carry</u> it from the lake.

hatch *v.*

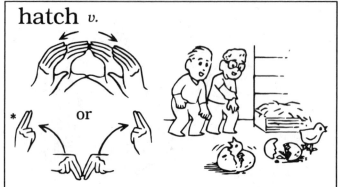

They watched the chickens hatch.
hatches hatched hatching

haunted *adj.*

That house is haunted.
There is a ghost in the house.

hay 209

have v.

I have only three pennies.
has   had   having

have to v.

You have to keep that dog outside.
You must keep it outside.

have v.
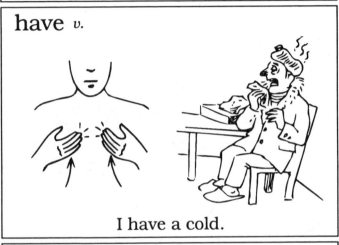
I have a cold.

Hawaii n. state: HI

Hawaii became a state in 1959.

have v.

I have eaten too much.

hawk n. bird

The hawk has long claws.
hawk   hawks

have on v.

I have on a coat.
I am wearing a coat.

hay n.

Hay is dried grass.
Cows and horses eat hay.

210　hayloft

hayloft *n.*

We store hay in the hayloft.
hayloft　haylofts

head *v.*

We will <u>head</u> up the mountain.
We'll <u>go</u> up the mountain.

haystack *n.*

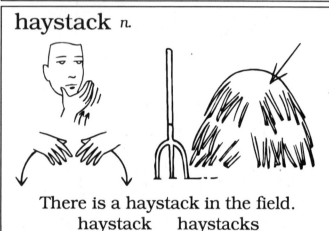

There is a haystack in the field.
haystack　haystacks

head *v.*

The guide will <u>head</u> the party.
He will <u>lead</u> the party.

he *pron. boy or man*

<u>He</u> wants a cookie.
<u>The boy</u> wants a cookie.

headache *n.*

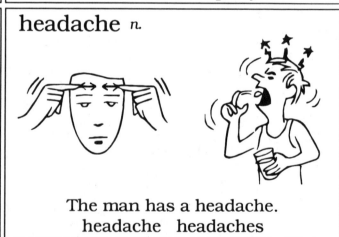

The man has a headache.
headache　headaches

head *n. body part*

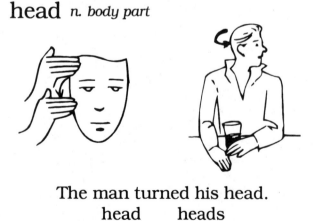

The man turned his head.
head　heads

headlight *n.*

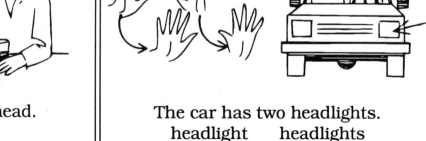

The car has two headlights.
headlight　headlights

heart 211

headphone n.

He's wearing a pair of headphones.
He's wearing a pair of earphones.

heard pt. of hear
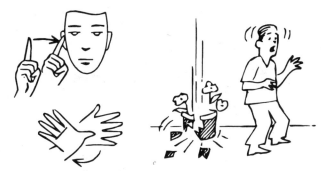
The man heard a loud noise.

health n.
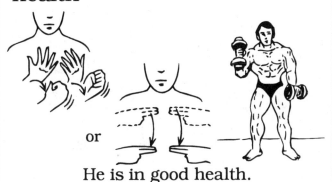
or
He is in good health.
He is not sick.

hearing adj.

She is a hearing person.
She is not deaf.

healthy adj.
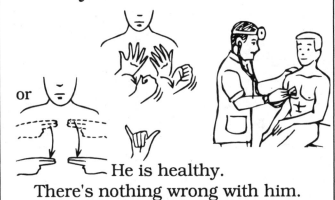
or
He is healthy.
There's nothing wrong with him.

hearing aid n.

or
He wears a hearing aid.
hearing aid   hearing aids

hear v.

We didn't hear my father come in!
hears   heard   hearing

heart n. body part
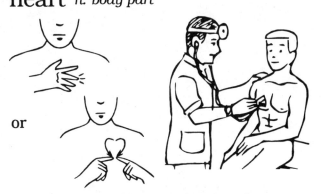
or
The doctor listened to my heart.

212 heart

by heart
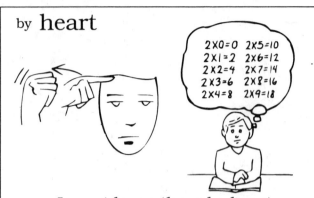
I must learn these by heart.
I must memorize them.

heavy adj.

The box is very heavy.
It is difficult to lift.

heat n.

The heat is terrible today.
It is very hot today.

heel n. body part
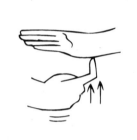
He has a blister on his heel.
heel   heels

heat v.

I must heat the soup.
heats   heated   heating

heel n. shoe part
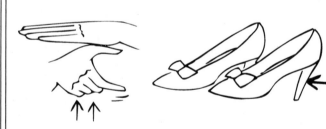
The shoes have high heels.

heaven n.

Some people believe they will
go to heaven when they die.

height n.
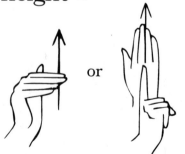 
What is your height?
How tall are you?

here 213

held *pt. of* **hold**

The hunter held a rifle.

help *v. aid*

I always help my mother.
helps helped helping

helicopter *n.*

The helicopter has no wings.
helicopter helicopters

hen *n.*

A hen is a female bird.
hen hens

hello *greeting*

Bob waved and said, "Hello."

her *adj., pron. girl or woman*

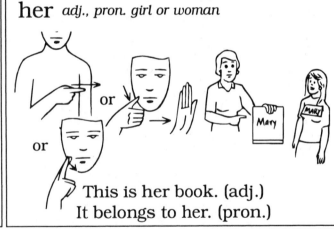

This is her book. (adj.)
It belongs to her. (pron.)

helmet *n.*

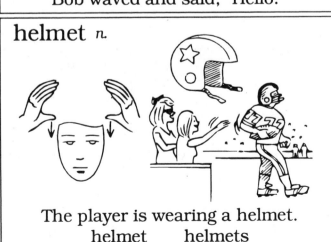

The player is wearing a helmet.
helmet helmets

here *adv.*

We live here.
We live in this house.

214 hero

hero n.
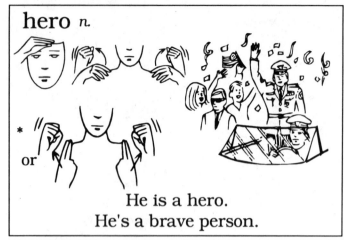
He is a hero.
He's a brave person.

hiccups n.
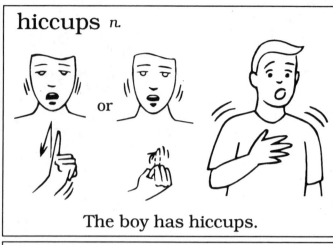
The boy has hiccups.

hers pron. girl or woman

That is <u>Mary's</u> book.
That book is <u>hers</u>.

hid pt. of hide

The girl hid behind the tree.

herself pron. girl or woman

She drew the picture herself.
No one helped her.

hidden pp. of hide

Mother has hidden the gifts.

hi interjection

Bob waved and said, "Hi."

hide v.

Where did the girl hide?
hides hid hiding hidden

highway 215

hide *v.*

I will hide the gifts.
I'll put them out of sight.

high *adv.*

He kicked the ball high.

high *adj. tall*

He likes to climb high mountains.
higher   highest

highchair *n. furniture*
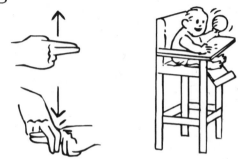
The baby sits in a highchair.
highchair   highchairs

high *adj.*

Asparagus is very high.
Asparagus is expensive.

high school *n.*

He goes to high school.
high school   high schools

high *adj.*

He drove at high speed.
He drove very fast.

highway *n.*
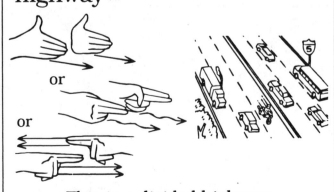
This is a divided highway.

216 hike

hike n.

They went on a hike.
They took a long walk.

hinge n.
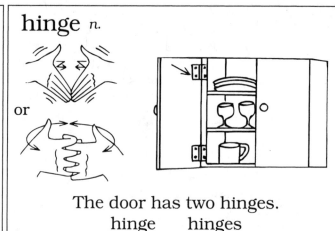
The door has two hinges.
hinge   hinges

hill n.
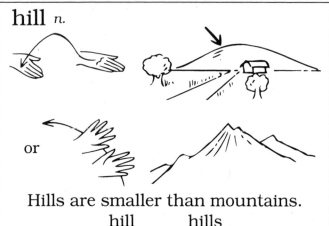
Hills are smaller than mountains.
hill   hills

hip n. body part
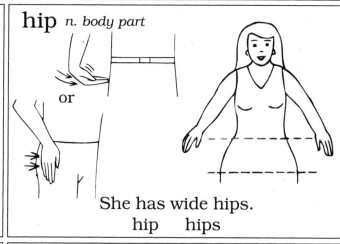
She has wide hips.
hip   hips

him pron. boy or man
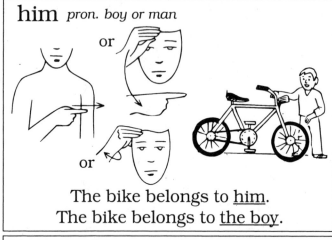
The bike belongs to him.
The bike belongs to the boy.

hippopotamus n. animal

The hippopotamus has short legs.
hippopotamuses or hippoptami

himself pron. boy or man
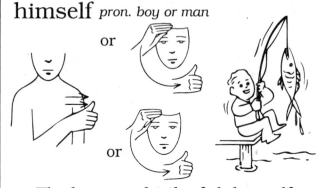
The boy caught the fish himself.
No one helped him.

hire v.

I must hire a janitor.
hires   hired   hiring

his *adj., pron.* boy or man

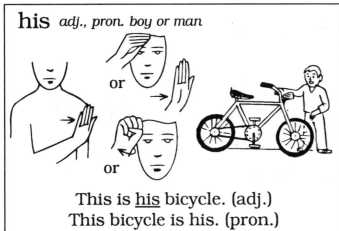

This is his bicycle. (adj.)
This bicycle is his. (pron.)

hit *v.*

I always hit the target.

history *n.*

The class is studying history.

hitchhike *v.*

He will hitchhike.
He'll try to get a free ride.

hit *v.* bat, strike

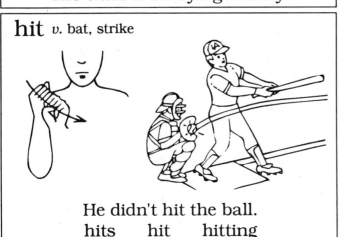

He didn't hit the ball.
hits   hit   hitting

hobby *n.*

His hobby is collecting stamps.
hobby   hobbies

hit *v.*

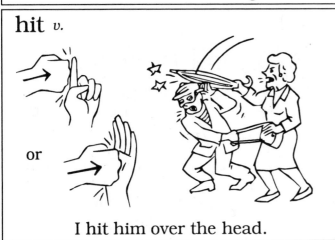

I hit him over the head.

hockey *n. game*

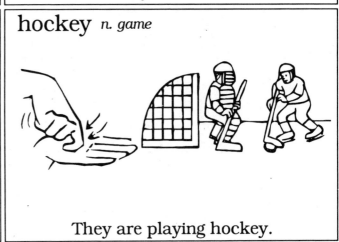

They are playing hockey.

218 hoe

hoe n. tool

She is using a hoe.
hoe   hoes

hole n.

There is a hole in his sock.

hold v.

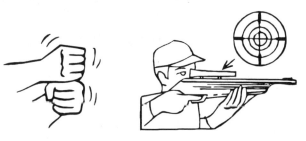

You must hold a rifle with both hands.
holds   held   holding

holiday n.

School is closed on holidays.
holiday   holidays

hold still

Please hold still.
Please don't move.

Holland n. country

Holland is another name
for the Netherlands.

hole n.

The man is digging a hole.
hole   holes

holler v. yell

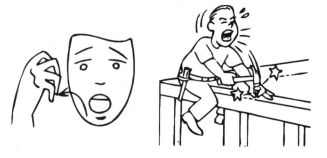

Why did the man holler?
hollers   hollered   hollering

homework 219

hollow adj.
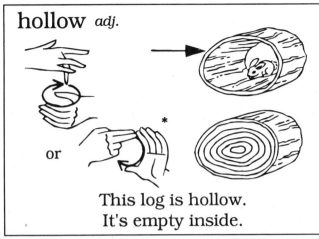
This log is hollow.
It's empty inside.

home adv.

The boy is going home.

holly n.
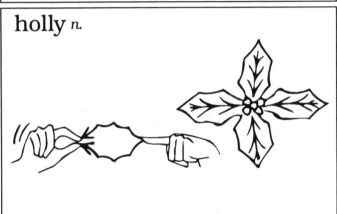
She decorated the table with holly.

home n.

This is our home.
We live here.

holster n.
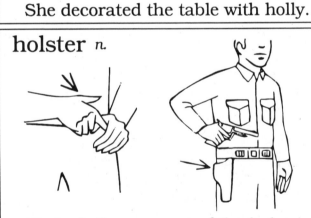
He took the gun out of the holster.
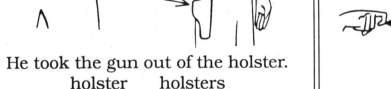
holster   holsters

homely adj.

The witch is <u>homely</u>.
The witch is <u>ugly</u>.

holy adj. sacred

He is a holy man.
He has devoted his life to God.

homework n.

The teacher assigned some homework
- some work for us to do at home.

220 honest

honest *adj. truthful*

The boy is honest.
more honest   most honest

hood *n. auto part*

The man is lifting the hood.

honey *n. food*

Bees make honey.

hood *n. clothing*

The raincoat has a hood.
hood   hoods

honk *v.*

Why did he honk his horn?
honks   honked   honking

hoof *n. animal body part*

He nailed the horseshoe to the hoof.
hoof   hoofs/hooves

honor *v.*

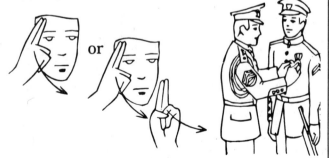

We honor heroes.
We treat them with respect.

hook *n.*

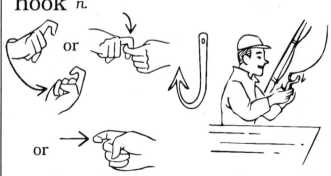

He put a worm on the hook.
hook   hooks

horn 221

hooked on v.

He is <u>hooked on</u> drugs.
He's <u>addicted to</u> drugs.

hope v.
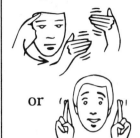
I hope I find my ball soon.
hopes   hoped   hoping

hook up v.

He will <u>hook up</u> the washer.
He'll <u>connect</u> the washer.

horn n. toy

The children are blowing horns.
horn   horns

hop v.

The girl can hop.
hops   hopped   hopping

horn n. auto part

The man honked his horn.

hop v.

I can <u>hop</u> over the fence.
I can <u>jump</u> over it.

horn n. animal body part
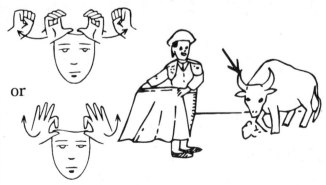
The bull has sharp horns.

222 horrible

horrible *adj.*

The girl has a horrible temper.
She has a terrible temper.

hose *n.*

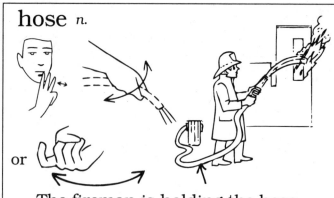

The fireman is holding the hose.
hose   hoses

horse *n. animal*

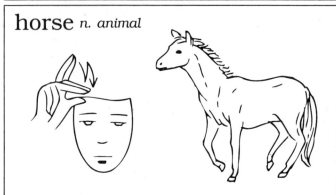

The horse has a long tail.
horse   horses

hosiery *n. clothing*

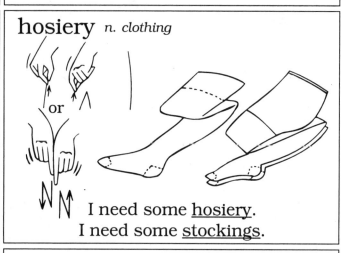

I need some hosiery.
I need some stockings.

horseshoe *n.*

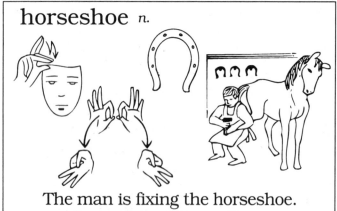

The man is fixing the horseshoe.
horseshoe   horseshoes

hospital *n.*

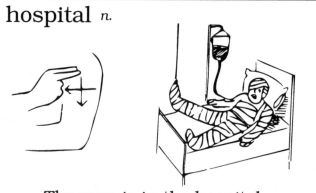

The man is in the hospital.
hospital   hospitals

hose *n. clothing*

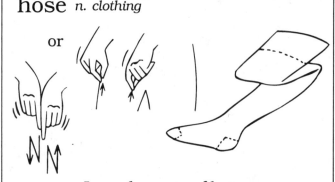

I need a pair of hose.
I need a pair of stockings.

hot *adj.*

It is hot today.
hotter   hottest

how come 223

hot cakes n. food
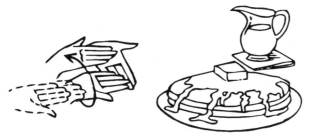
I had <u>hot cakes</u> for breakfast.
I had <u>pancakes</u> for breakfast.

house n.

We bought a large house.
house houses

hot dog n. food

He ate a hot dog for lunch.
hot dog hot dogs

how adv.
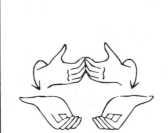
sad happy

mad sick
How do you feel today?

hotel n.
or

We stayed at a nice hotel.
hotel hotels

how conj.

I don't know how the window got broken.

hour n.

There are 60 minutes in an hour.
hour hours

how come informal

How come I have to mow the lawn?
Why do I have to mow the lawn?

224 how many

how many

How many do you want?

huge *adj.*

The man is carrying a huge box.
He's carrying a very large box.

howl *v.*

or

Wolves often howl at the moon.
howls   howled   howling

human *n.*

Men, women, and children are humans.
human   humans

howl *v.*

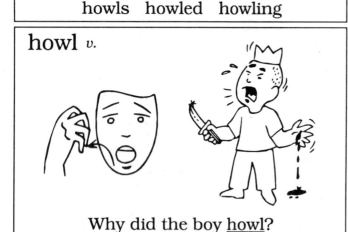

Why did the boy howl?
Why did he yell?

hundred *number:* 100

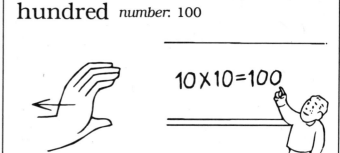

Ten times ten equals a hundred.

hug *v.*

They often hug each other.
hugs   hugged   hugging

hung *pt. of* **hang**

He hung the picture over the couch.

hurry 225

hungry *adj.*

The man is very hungry.
He needs to eat.

hurrah *interj.* hooray

They shouted, "Hurrah!"

hunt *v.*

I hunt deer every year.
hunts   hunted   hunting

hurricane *n. storm*

The hurricane did a lot of damage.
hurricane   hurricanes

hunt *v.*

I must <u>hunt for</u> my ball.
I must <u>look for</u> it.

hurried *pt. of* **hurry**

The man hurried to catch the bus.

hunter *n.*

The hunter saw a deer.
hunter   hunters

hurry *n.*

The man is in a <u>hurry</u>.
The man is in a <u>rush</u>.

226 hurry

hurry *v.* rush

I had to hurry to catch my plane.
hurries   hurried   hurrying

hush *v.*

Please hush.
Please be quiet.

hurt *v.*

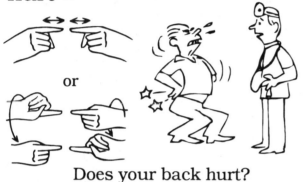

Does your back hurt?
hurts   hurt   hurting

hut *n.*

He lives in a <u>hut</u>.
He lives in a <u>small cabin</u>.

hurt *v.*

How did he <u>hurt</u> his ankle?
How did he <u>injure</u> it?

hydrant *n.*

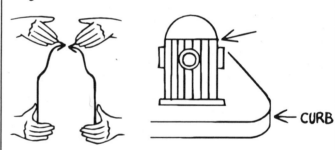

The hydrant is near the curb.
hydrant   hydrants

husband *n.*

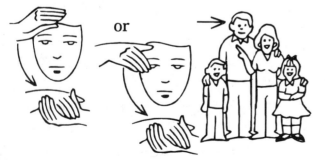

This is my husband.
I am married to this man.

hypnotize *v.*

The magician will hypnotize the man.
hypnotizes   hypnotized   hypnotizing

I i

I *pron.*

I didn't do it!

ice-cream soda *n. food*

She ordered an ice-cream soda.
ice-cream soda   ice-cream sodas

ice *n.*

The ice will soon melt.

ice skate *n.*

This is a pair of ice skates.
ice skate   ice skates

ice cream *n. food*

Do you like ice cream?

ice-skate *v.*

He can't ice-skate yet.
ice-skates ice-skated ice-skating

ice-cream cone *n. food*

The boy has an ice-cream cone.
ice-cream cone   ice-cream cones

ice tea *n. beverage*

This is a glass of ice tea.
This is a glass of iced tea.

228 icicle

icicle n.

Icicles hung from the roof.
icicle   icicles

identical adj.

They are identical twins.
They look exactly alike.

icing n.

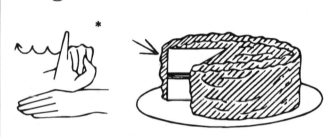

The cake has chocolate icing.
It has chocolate frosting.

identify v.

I can identify the robber.
I can recognize the robber.

ID n.

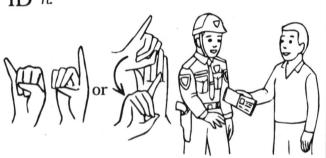

I showed him my ID.
I showed him my identification.

idol n.

The natives worshiped an idol.
idol   idols

idea n.

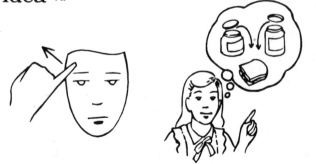

Mary has an idea for her lunch.
idea   ideas

if conj.

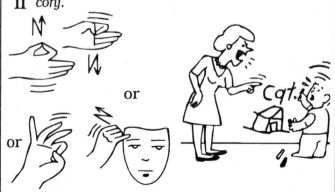

I will spank you if you are bad.

immediately 229

igloo n.
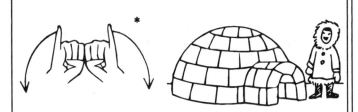
The Eskimo lives in an igloo.
igloo   igloos

illegal adj.

Stealing is illegal.
It's against the law.

ignorant adj.

My parents will think I'm ignorant.
They'll think I don't know anything.

I love you

The boy said, "I love you."

ignore v.

I always ignore that sign.
I always disregard it.

imagine v.

I like to imagine a life at sea.
I like to think about that.

ill adj.
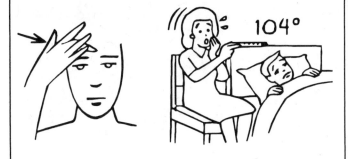
The man is very ill.
He's very sick.

immediately adv.

I want you to leave immediately.
I want you to leave right now.

230 important

important *adj.*

Doing your homework is important.
Doing your homework means a lot.

in *prep.*

The bird is in the cage.

impossible *adj.*

It's <u>impossible</u> for me to come now.
It's <u>not possible</u> for me to come.

in all *adv.*

He has three cents <u>in all</u>.
He has three cents <u>altogether</u>.

improve *v.*

His health did improve.
He feels a little better now.

in a while

I'll call you back <u>in a while</u>.
I'll call you back <u>later</u>.

in *adv.*

The doctor is in.
The doctor is here.

in back of

The lady is <u>in back of</u> the tall man.
She's <u>behind</u> the tall man.

Independence Day 231

in case
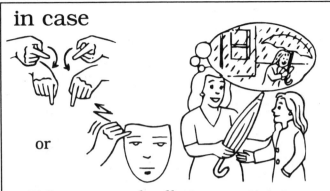
Take your umbrella in case it rains.
Take it in the event it rains.

inches *plural of* inch
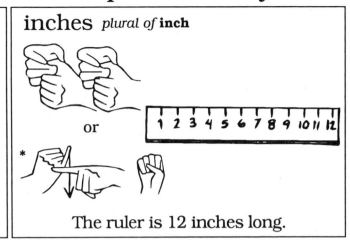
or
*
The ruler is 12 inches long.

in charge of

He is in charge of the business.
He manages the business.

include *v.*

I didn't include the tax.
I forgot to add in the tax.

in front of
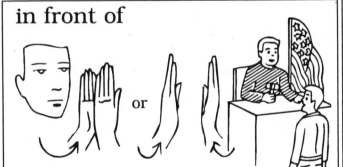
The man stood in front of the judge.
He stood before the judge.

increase *v.*

We will increase your salary.
We'll raise your salary.

inch *n. 1/12 of a foot*
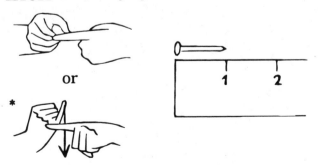
or
*
The nail is 1 inch long.
inch   inches

Independence Day *n. holiday*

Independence Day is July 4th.

232 India

India *n. country*
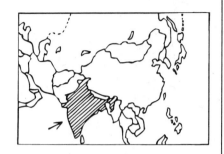
India is a country in Asia.

infection *n.*
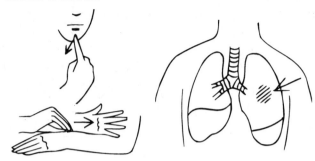
He has an infection in his lung.
infection   infections

Indian *n. native American.*

The Indians attacked the fort.
Indian   Indians

influence *v.*

His behavior can influence my decision.
It can affect my decision.

inexpensive *adj.*

The dress is inexpensive.
It's cheap.

inform *v.*

Did he inform her he was leaving?
Did he tell her he was leaving?

infant *n.*

The infant is sitting on the floor.
The baby is sitting on the floor.

ingredient *n.*

She has the ingredients for the cake. She has the things listed.

insert 233

initial n.
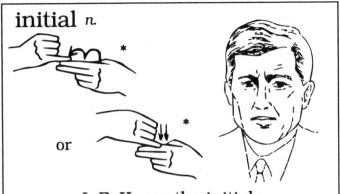
J. F. K. are the initials of John Fitzgerald Kennedy.

innocent adj.

I'm innocent.
I didn't do it.

injection n.

The doctor gave him an injection.
The doctor gave him a shot.

insane adj.

I must be insane.
I must be crazy.

injure v.

How did he injure his ankle?
How did he hurt his ankle?

insect n.
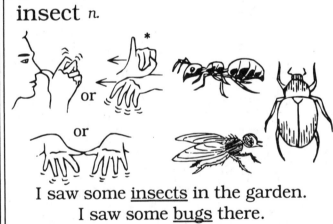
I saw some insects in the garden.
I saw some bugs there.

ink n.

He dipped the pen into the ink.

insert v.

You must insert the disk in the drive.
You must put it in the drive.

234 inside

inside *adv.*

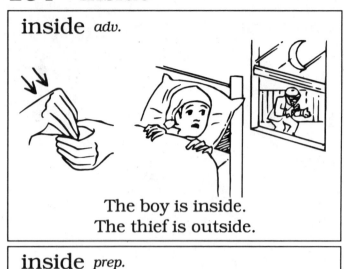

The boy is inside.
The thief is outside.

inspect *v.*

I must inspect the scene.
I must examine it.

inside *prep.*

The children are inside the house.

instead *adv.* in place of

He had to mow the lawn
instead of playing baseball.

inside out *adv.*

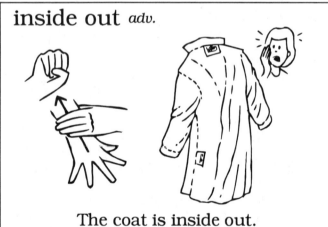

The coat is inside out.

instruction *n.*

You must follow the instructions.
You must follow the directions.

insist *v.*

I insist that you mow the lawn.
I demand that you mow the lawn.

insult *v.*

Did the man insult the woman?
Was he rude to her?

into 235

insurance n.

Drivers must have insurance.

intersection n.
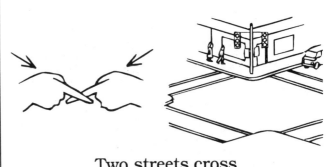
Two streets cross at an interesction.

interesting adj.

Fred's new job is very interesting.

interview v.

The employer will interview her.
He will talk to her and ask questions..

interpreter n. worker

The man needs an interpreter.
interpreter   interpreters

into prep.

The bird flew into the house.
It entered the house.

interrupt v.

I must <u>interrupt your</u> call.
I must <u>break in on</u> your call.

into prep.

8 into 40 is 5.
40 divided by 8 is 5.

236 into

run into v.

Did the car run into the fence?
Did it hit the fence?

invent v.

What did Edison invent?
invents   invented   inventing

turn into v.

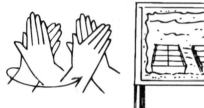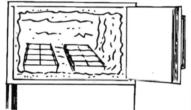

Water can turn into ice.
It can become ice.

investigate v.

The officer will investigate the scene.
He'll examine the scene.

intoxicated adj.

The man is intoxicated.
He is drunk.

invitation n.

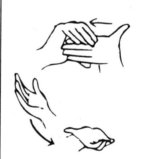

I received a wedding invitation.
invitation   invitations

introduce v.

I will introduce you to my parents.
introduces   introduced   introducing

Ireland n. country

Ireland is an island.

island 237

Irish *adj.*

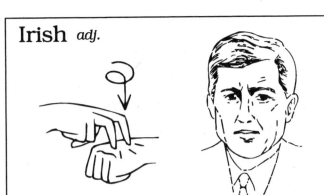

President Kennedy was Irish.
His ancestors came from Ireland.

ironing board *n.*

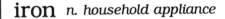

This is an ironing board.
ironing board   ironing boards

iron *n. household appliance*

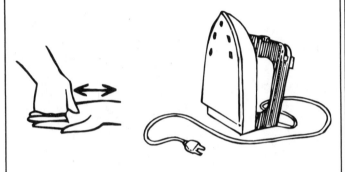

The iron has a long cord.

irresponsible *adj.* unreliable

or

She is irresponsible.
She doesn't attend to her duties.

iron *n. metal*

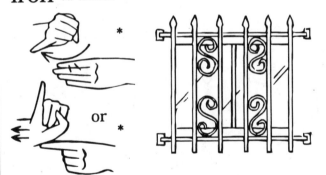

or

The bars are made of iron.

is *v. pres. 3rd sing. of* **be**

or

It is raining.

iron *v.*

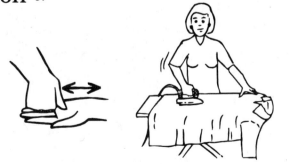

I must <u>iron</u> this dress.
I must <u>press</u> it.

island *n.*

or

The man is on an island.
island   islands

238 Israel

Israel *n. country*

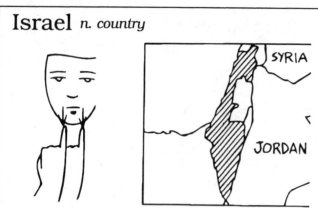

Israel is a country in Asia.

item *n.*

She bought several <u>items</u>.
She bought several <u>things</u>.

it *pron.*

The boy broke <u>it.</u>
The boy broke <u>the window</u>.

its *adj.*

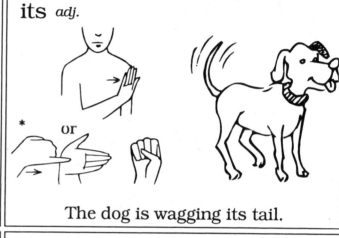

The dog is wagging its tail.

Italy *n. country*

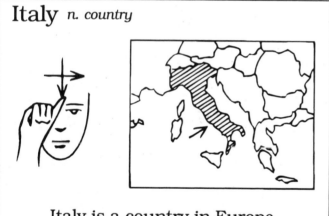

Italy is a country in Europe.

itself *pron.*

The dog is ashamed of itself.

itch *v.*

The sweater made him itch.
It made him want to scratch.

ivy *n.*

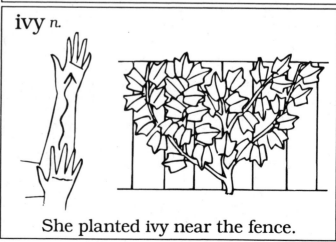

She planted ivy near the fence.

J j

jab *v. poke*

Why did she jab him in the ribs?
jabs   jabbed   jabbing

jacket *n. clothing*

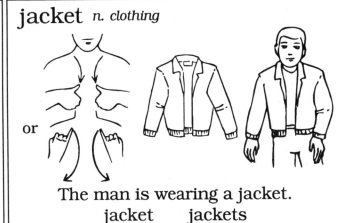

The man is wearing a jacket.
jacket   jackets

jabber *v.*

She can jabber for hours.
She can talk and talk and talk.

jackhammer *n. tool*

The jackhammer makes a lot of noise.
jackhammer   jackhammers

jack *n. tool*

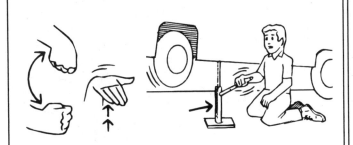

The man is using a jack.
jack   jacks

jack-in-the-box *n. toy*

The baby opened the jack-in-the-box.

jack *n. toy*

She is playing with her jacks.

jack-o'-lantern *n.*

We made a jack-o'-lantern.

239

240 jagged

jagged *adj.*

The edge is jagged.
The edge has sharp points.

jam *n.*

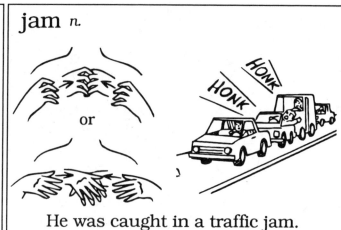

He was caught in a traffic jam.

jail *n.*

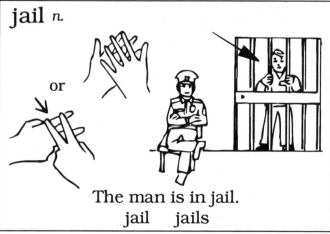

The man is in jail.
jail   jails

jam *n. informal*

He got himself in a jam.
He got himself into trouble.

jail *v.*

Did they jail the man?
Did they put him in jail?

jam *v.*

I must jam this dress into the suitcase. I must force it in.

jam *n. food*

She likes strawberry jam.
jam   jams

janitor *n. worker*

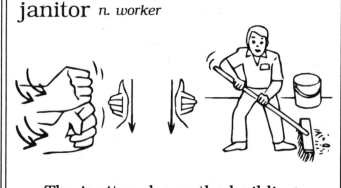

The janitor cleans the building.
janitor   janitors

jeans 241

January n. month

January is the first month of the year.

jar v.

The noise will jar his nerves. It will make him nervous.

Japan n. country

Japan is a country in Asia.

jaw n. body part

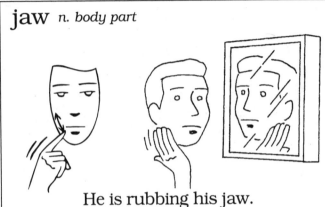

He is rubbing his jaw.
jaw   jaws

jar n. container

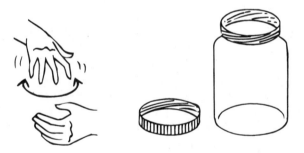

The jar is made of glass.
jar   jars

jealous adj.

She is jealous of her friend.
She's envious of her friend.

jar v. shake

Don't jar the table.
jars   jarred   jarring

jeans n. clothing

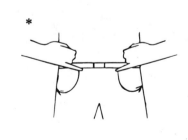 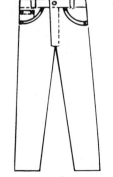

This is a pair of jeans.

242 jeep

jeep n. vehicle

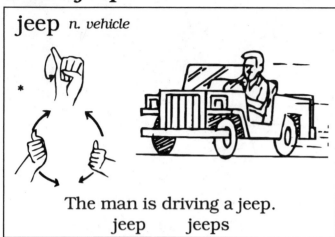

The man is driving a jeep.
jeep   jeeps

jerk v.

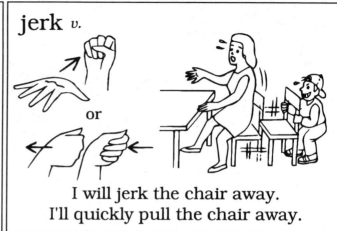

I will jerk the chair away.
I'll quickly pull the chair away.

Jello n. food

I made Jello for dessert.

Jesus n.

Jesus was born in Bethlehem.

jelly n. food

He likes apple jelly.
jelly   jellies

jet n. plane

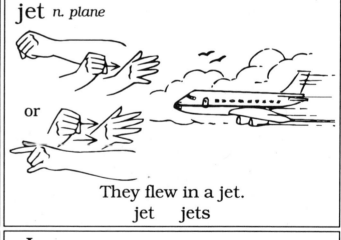

They flew in a jet.
jet   jets

jerk v.

Why did the train jerk to a stop?
jerks   jerked   jerking

Jew n.

Jews worship in the temple.
Jew   Jews

joy 243

jewelry n.

She has a lot of jewelry.

join v.

I must join the pieces of rope.
I must fasten them together.

job n.
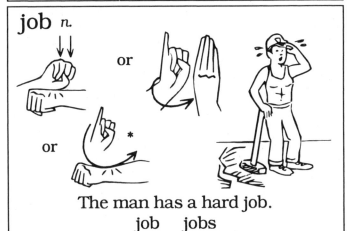
The man has a hard job.
job   jobs

joke n.

His jokes made us laugh.
His funny stories made us laugh.

jog v.

I jog every morning.
jogs   jogged   jogging

jolly adj.
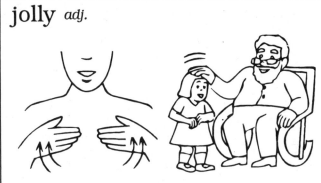
He is a jolly person.
He's a cheerful person.

join v.

He will join the army.
joins   joined   joining

joy n.

The woman is full of joy.
She's full of happiness.

244 judge

judge *n.* worker

The judge sent him to jail.
judge judges

juggle *v.*

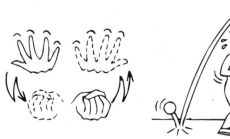

The boy tried to juggle the balls.
juggles juggled juggling

judge *v.*

I must judge the distance.
I must estimate the distance.

juice *n.*

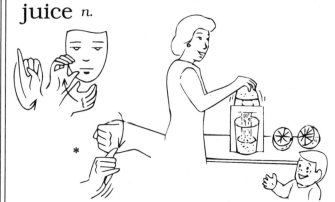

I want a glass of orange juice.

judge *v.*

They will judge the building plan.
They'll form an opinion about it.

juicy *adj.*

The grapefruit is juicy.
juicier juiciest

jug *n.* container

I bought a jug of apple cider.
jug jugs

July *n.* month

or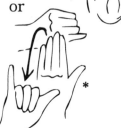

The 4th of July is Independence Day.

jump rope   245

jump *v.*

I always jump into the pool.
jumps   jumped   jumping

jump over *v.*

I usually jump over this fence.

jump *v.*
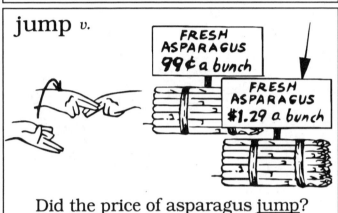
Did the price of asparagus jump?
Did it increase?

jump over *v.*

Why did she jump over my name?
Why did she skip it?

jump *v.*

Did she jump to the wrong conclusion?

jumper *n. clothing*

The girl is wearing a jumper.
jumper   jumpers

jump at

I always jump at the chance to ride in a plane. I'm always eager to do that.

jump rope *n. toy*

She got a jump rope for her birthday.

246 June

June *n. month*

They got married in June.

just *adj.*

The judge made a just decision.
He gave a fair decision.

jungle *n.*

Many animals live in the jungle.
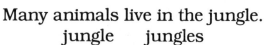
jungle   jungles

just *adv.*

He has just three cents.
He has only three cents.

junk *n.*

The lot is covered with junk.
It is covered with trash.

just *adv.*

They just moved away.
They recently moved away.

jury *n.*

The jury found him not guilty.
jury   juries

juvenile *n. child*

They are juveniles.
They're young people.

K k

kangaroo *n. animal*

The kangaroo has a long tail.
kangaroo   kangaroos

keep on

I must <u>keep on</u> looking for my ball.
I must <u>continue</u> to look for it.

karate *n.*

He is an expert at karate.

keep quiet

Please keep quiet.
Please be quiet.

keep *v.*

I keep my money in the bank.
keeps   kept   keeping

kept *pt. of* **keep**

He kept my ball. He took it and
he wouldn't give it back to me.

keep *v.*

I will keep your ball. I'll take it
and I won't give it back to you.

ketchup *n.*

He likes <u>ketchup</u> on his hot dog.
He likes <u>catsup</u> on his hot dog.

247

248 kettle

kettle n.
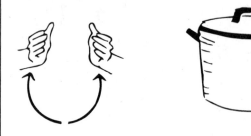
The kettle is made of metal.
kettle   kettles

keyboard n.

Pianos and computers have keyboards.
keyboard   keyboards

key n.

She used the key to open the door.
key   keys

keyhole n.
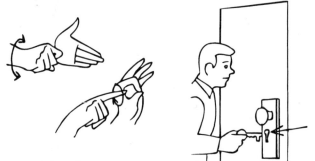
The key goes into the keyhole.
keyhole   keyholes

key n.
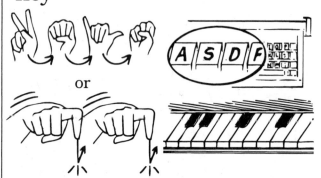
Pianos and computers have keys.

kick v.

He can kick the ball far.
kicks   kicked   kicking

key n.

Hard work was the key to his success.
That was important to his success.

kid n. *informal:* child

The kids made a lot of noise.
The children made a lot of noise.

kind 249

kid *n. animal*

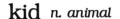

A kid is a young goat.

kill *v.*

Did the cat kill the bird?
kills   killed   killing

kid *v. tease*

I always kid him about his old car.
kids   kidded   kidding

kill *v.*

He took aspirin to <u>kill</u> the pain.
He took aspirin to <u>get rid of</u> the pain.

kidnap *v.*

Did the man <u>kidnap</u> the baby?
Did he <u>abduct</u> the baby?

kind *adj.*

The girl is <u>kind</u> to her pet.
She is <u>good</u> to her pet.

kidney *n. body part*

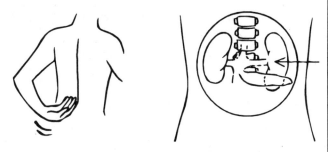

The doctor will treat his kidney.
kidney   kidneys

not **kind** *adj. unkind, cruel*

She is <u>not kind</u> to her pet.
She is <u>cruel</u> to her pet.

250 kind

kind *n.* type
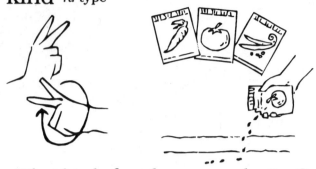
What <u>kind</u> of seeds are you planting?
What <u>sort</u> of seeds are you planting?

kiss *n.*
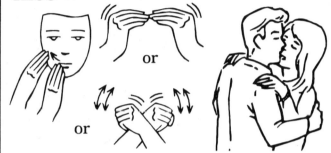
Mother gave the baby a kiss.
kiss   kisses

kindergarten *n.*

My son is in kindergarten.

kiss *v.*
Did the man kiss the woman?
kisses   kissed   kissing

king *n.* ruler

The king is wearing a crown.
king   kings

kitchen *n.*

Our home has a large kitchen.
kitchen   kitchens

King Kong
*
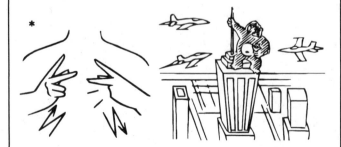
King Kong climbed to the
top of the building.

kite *n.* toy

The boy is flying a kite.
kite   kites

knight 251

kitten *n.* young cat

The kitten is cute.
kitten   kittens

knelt *pt. of* **kneel**

The priest knelt before the altar.

kleenex *n.*

He took a piece of kleenex.

knew *pt. of* **know**

The boy knew the answer.

knee *n.* body part

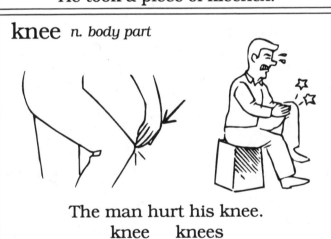

The man hurt his knee.
knee   knees

knife *n.*

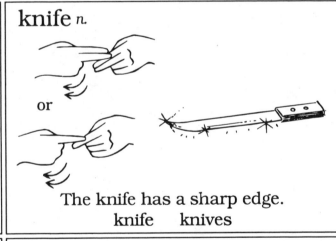

The knife has a sharp edge.
knife   knives

kneel *v.*

I must kneel to look at my toys.
kneels   knelt/kneeled   kneeling

knight *n.*

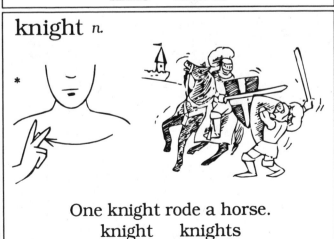

One knight rode a horse.
knight   knights

252 knit

knit v.

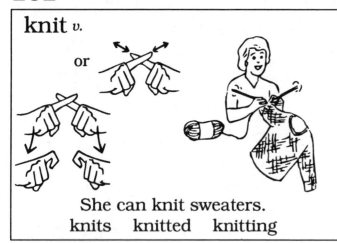

She can knit sweaters.
knits   knitted   knitting

knot n.

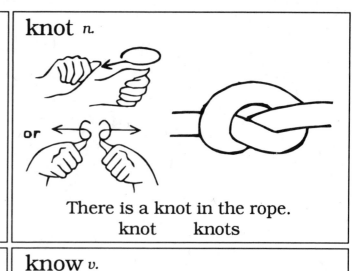

There is a knot in the rope.
knot   knots

knives n. pural of **knife**

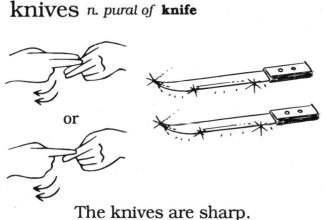

The knives are sharp.

know v.

Did the boy know the answer?
knows   knew   knowing   known

knob n.

He is turning the knob.
knob   knobs

known pp. of **know**

They have known each
other a long time.

knock v.

I will knock on the door.
knocks   knocked   knocking

Korea n. country

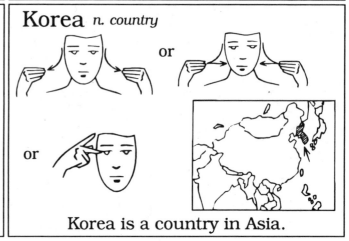

Korea is a country in Asia.

L l

label n.

He is reading the label.
label　labels

lack n.
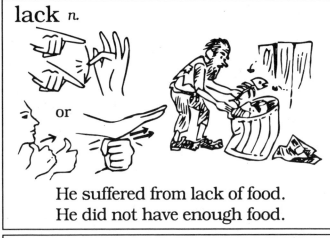
He suffered from lack of food.
He did not have enough food.

labor n.

He gets paid for his labor.
He gets paid for his work.

ladder n.

The painter will use the ladder.
ladder　ladders

Labor Day n. holiday

Labor Day is in September.

lady n. woman

The ladies are talking.
lady　ladies

lace n.
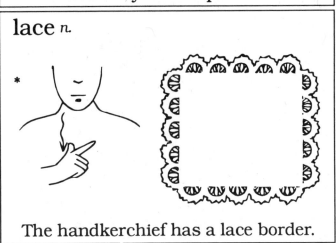
The handkerchief has a lace border.

laid pt. of **lay**
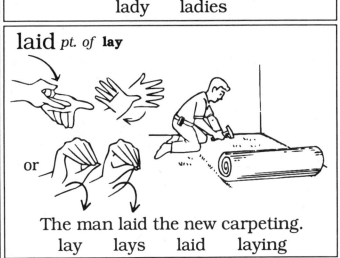
The man laid the new carpeting.
lay　lays　laid　laying

253

254 lain

lain *pp. of* **lie**

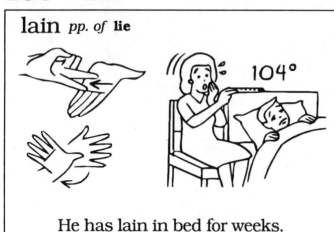

He has lain in bed for weeks.

land *n.*

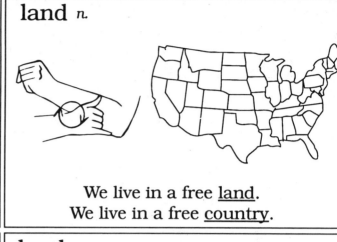

We live in a free land.
We live in a free country.

lake *n.*

or

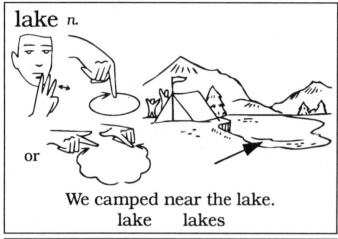

We camped near the lake.
lake   lakes

land *n.*

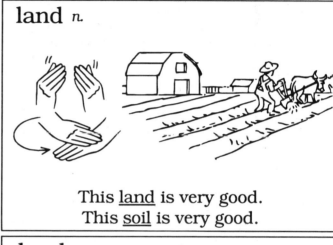

This land is very good.
This soil is very good.

lamb *n. animal*

or

A lamb is a young sheep.
lamb   lambs

land *v.*

or

When did the plane land?
lands   landed   landing

lamp *n.*

or

She bought a new lamp.
lamp   lamps

lane *n.*

or
*

They walked down the lane.
They walked down the narrow path.

last name 255

lane n.
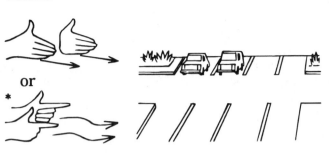
The street has four lanes.
lane lanes

large adj.

One bear is large.
One bear is big.

language n.

They don't speak the same language.
language languages

last adj.
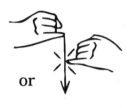
December is the last month of the year.

lantern n.

The man is holding a lantern.
lantern lanterns

last v.

The storm may last for a week.
It may continue for a week.

lap n.
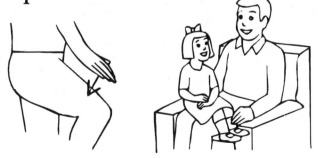
She sat on her father's lap.
lap laps

last name n.

Her last name is Smith.

256 late

late *adj.*

The boy is late.
He came in after the class started.

laundry *n.*

She is doing the laundry.
She's washing the dirty clothes.

late *adv.*

He got there too late.
He arrived after the plane took off.

law *n.*

You must obey the law.
law   laws

later *adv.*

I'll call you back later.
I'll call you back after a while.

lawn *n.*

The boy is mowing the lawn.
He's cutting the grass.

laugh *v.*

What made him laugh?
laughs   laughed   laughing

lawn mower *n. tool*

The woman pointed to the lawn mower.
lawn mower   lawn mowers

lawyer n.

The lawyer asked a question.
The attorney asked a question.

layer n.

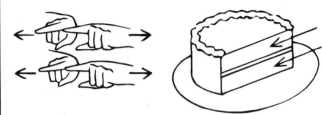

The cake has two layers.
layer layers

lay pt. of lie

The boy lay under the tree.
lie lay lying lain

lazy adj.

The boy is lazy.
He doesn't like to work.

lay v. put down

or

The man will lay the new carpet.
lay lays laid laying

lead n. metal

or
*

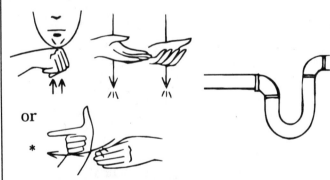

The pipe is made of lead.

lay v.

or

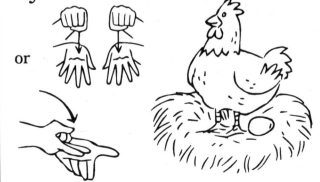

Hens can lay eggs.

lead v. guide

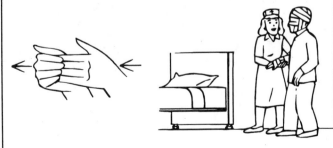

The nurse must lead the patient.
leads led leading

258 leader

leader n. worker

The boys followed their leader.
leader leaders

lean v.

I will lean against the wall and wait.
I'll rest against the wall and wait.

leaf n. plant part

A leaf fell from the tree.
leaf leaves

leapfrog n. game

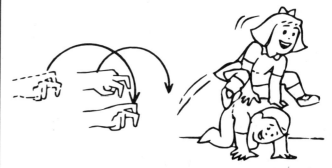

The children are playing leapfrog.

leak n.

There is a leak in the roof.
There's a hole in the roof.

learn v.

He must learn addition.
learns learned/learnt learning

leak v.

The bucket began to leak.
leaks leaked leaking

leather n.

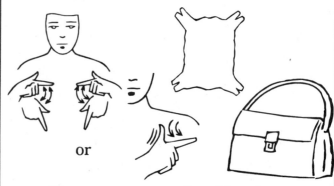

or

The purse is made of leather.

left 259

leave *v.*

They will leave on a trip.
leaves   left   leaving

lecture *n.*

The students listen to the lecture.
They listen to the speech.

leave *v.*

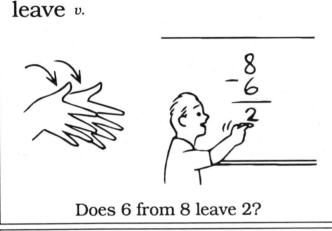

Does 6 from 8 leave 2?

led *pt. of* **lead**

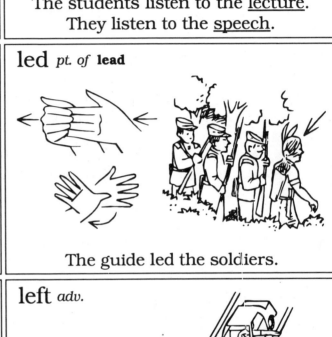

The guide led the soldiers.

leave *v.*

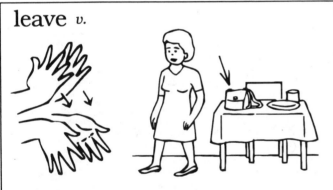

Did she leave her purse on the table?
Did she forget to take it?

left *adv.*

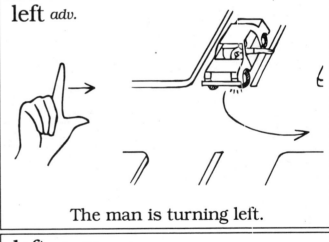

The man is turning left.

leaves *n. pural of* **leaf**

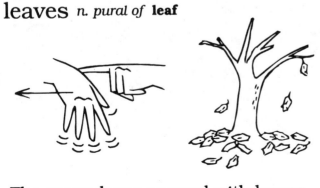

The ground was covered with leaves.
leaf   leaves

left *pt. of* **leave**

He left his ball in the park.

260 left

left pt. of leave

They left on their trip.

leisure adj.
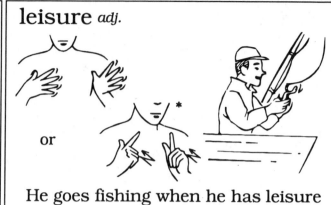
He goes fishing when he has leisure time - when he has free time.

leg n. body part
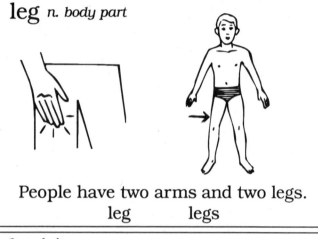
People have two arms and two legs.
leg   legs

lemon n. fruit

The lemon is sour.
lemon   lemons

leg(s) n. chair part
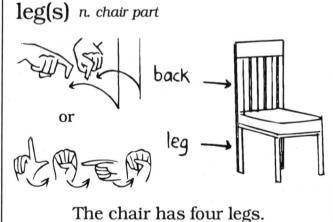
The chair has four legs.

lemonade n. beverage

She made some lemonade.

legislature n.

The state legislature makes laws to govern our state.

lend v. loan
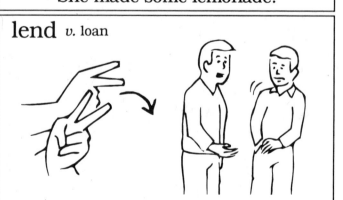
Please lend me some money.
lends   lent   lending

let go 261

length n.
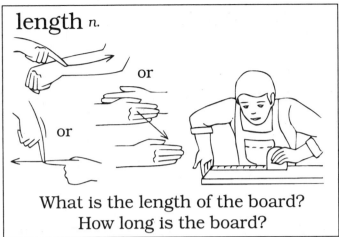
What is the length of the board?
How long is the board?

less than

Chicken costs less than steak.

leopard n. animal
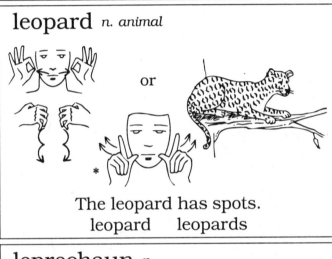
The leopard has spots.
leopard   leopards

lesson n.

The teacher explained the lesson.
lesson   lessons

leprechaun n.

The leprechaun lived in the forest.
leprechaun   leprechauns

let v.

She won't <u>let</u> him play.
She won't <u>allow</u> him to play.

less adj.

Bob has less marbles than Jim.

let go
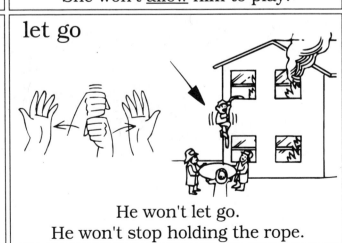
He won't let go.
He won't stop holding the rope.

262 let up

let up *v. informal*

The rain may <u>let up</u> soon.
It may <u>stop</u> soon.

lettuce *n. vegetable*

This is a head of lettuce.
one head   two heads

letter *n.*

abcdefghijklm
nopqrstuvwxyz

The alphabet has 26 letters.
letter   letters

level *adj.*

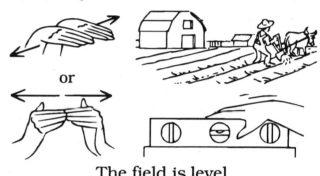

The field is <u>level</u>.
It is <u>flat</u>.

letter *n.*

He is writing a letter.

liar *n.*

The boy is a liar.
He did not tell the truth.

letter carrier *n.*

The <u>letter carrier</u> delivers mail.
The <u>mailman</u> delivers mail.

liberty *n.*

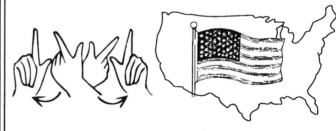

We enjoy <u>liberty</u> in America.
We enjoy <u>freedom</u> in America.

library *n.*

The students are in the library.
library   libraries

lid *n.*

He put the <u>lid</u> on the catsup.
He put the <u>cap</u> on the catsup.

license *n.*

He keeps his license in his wallet.
license   licenses

lie *n.*

The boy told a lie.
He did not tell the truth.

lick *v.*

Don't lick the plate.
licks   licked   licking

lie *n.*

I often lie in bed and read.
lies lay lying lain

lid *n. cover*

He removed the lid.
lid   lids

lie *v.*

Please don't lie to me.
lies   lied   lying

lie 263

264 life

life *n.*
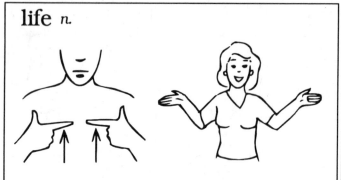
The woman has a happy life.
life   lives

light *adj.*
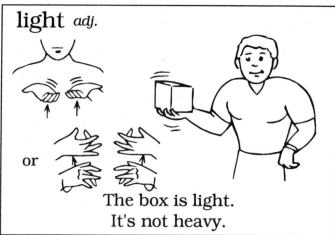
The box is light.
It's not heavy.

lifeguard *n. worker*

Some beaches have lifeguards.
lifeguard   lifeguards

light *n.*
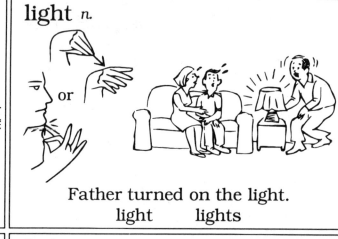
Father turned on the light.
light   lights

lift *v.*
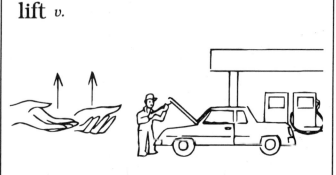
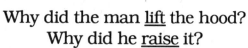
Why did the man lift the hood?
Why did he raise it?

light *n.*
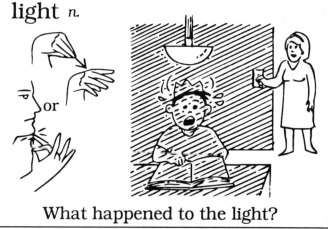
What happened to the light?

light *adj.*
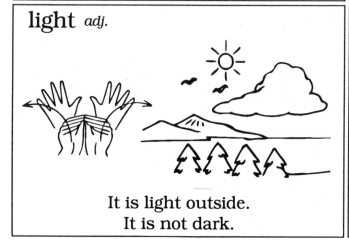
It is light outside.
It is not dark.

light *v.*
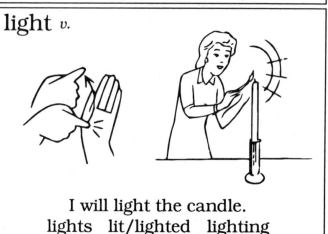
I will light the candle.
lights   lit/lighted   lighting

lime 265

light bulb *n.*

The lamp needs a new light bulb.
light bulb   light bulbs

like *v.*

I really <u>like</u> my job.
I really <u>enjoy</u> my job.

lightning *n.*

I saw a flash of lightning.

don't **like** *v.* dislike

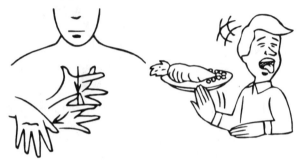

I <u>don't like</u> peas and carrots.
I <u>don't enjoy</u> peas and carrots.

like *prep.*

My bike is <u>like</u> yours.
My bike is <u>the same as</u> yours.

lily *n. flower*

The lily is beautiful.
lily   lilies

like *v.*

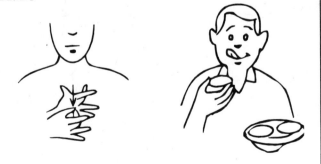

I like these cookies.
likes   liked   liking

lime *n. fruit*

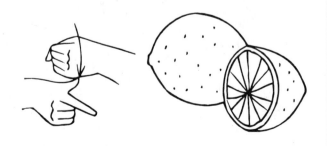

Limes are green and they
are smaller than lemons.

266 limit

limit n.

The speed limit is 25 miles an hour.
The maximum allowable speed is 25.

line up v.

They had to line up at the counter.
They had to form a line.

Lincoln n.

Lincoln's birthday is a holiday.

lion n. animal

The man is training the lion.
lion   lions

line n.

She hung the washing on the line.
line   lines

lip n. body part

She put Vaseline on her lips.
lip   lips

line n.
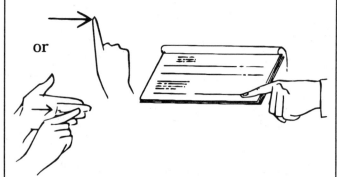
or

Sign your name on this line.

lipreading n.

or

He must practice lipreading.
He must practice speechreading.

little 267

lipstick n.

She wears lipstick.

listen v.

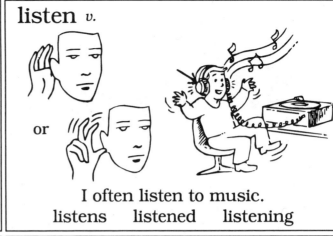

I often listen to music.
listens   listened   listening

liquid n.

Milk and water are liquids.
You can pour them.

lit pt. of **light**

She lit the candle.

liquor n.

Liquor caused his problems.
Alcohol caused his problems.

litter v.

I litter my room with things.
I scatter my things about.

list n.

She made a shopping list.
list   lists

little adj.

One bear is little.
One bear is small.

268 little

little *n.*

She added a <u>little</u> milk.
She added a <u>small amount of</u> milk.

living room *n.*

The couch is in the living room.

little bit

She ate a <u>little bit</u> of cake.
She ate a <u>small piece</u> of cake.

lizard *n.*

This is a lizard.
lizard   lizards

live *v. reside*

We live in this house.
lives   lived   living

load *v.*

He has to load the truck.
He has to put things in the truck.

liver *n. body part*

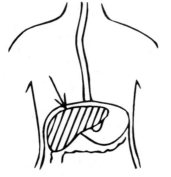
He had problems with his liver.

loaf *n.*

This is a loaf of bread.
loaf   loaves

locomotive 269

loaf v.

He will loaf all day.
He will not do his work.

location n.
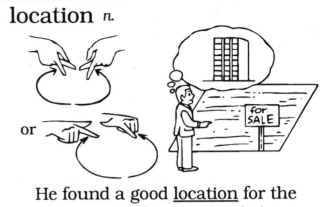
He found a good location for the building. He found a good place.

loaves plural of loaf
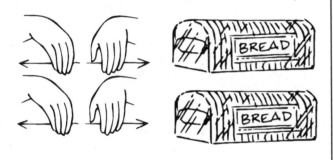
She bought two loaves of bread.

lock v.

I always lock my door.
locks   locked   locking

lobster n.

The lobster has large claws.
lobster   lobsters

locked adj.
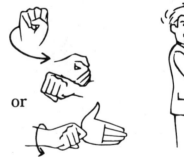 
The door is locked.
You need a key to open the door.

locate v.

I knew I would locate my ball.
I knew I would find it.

locomotive n.

The locomotive pulls the train.
locomotive   locomotives

270 log

log n.
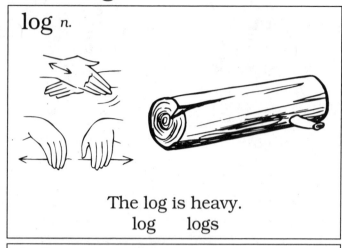
The log is heavy.
log   logs

long ago

Long ago, ships used sails.
In the past, they used sails.

lollipop n. candy
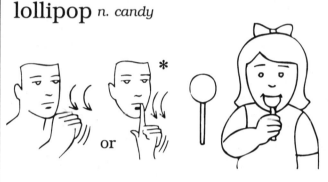
or
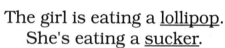
The girl is eating a lollipop.
She's eating a sucker.

long for v.

I long for my parents.
I miss them.

lonesome adj.

She is lonesome.
She's lonely.

look v.
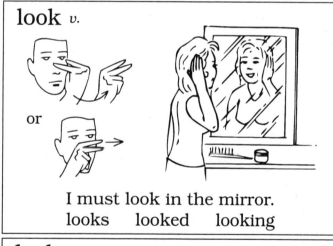
I must look in the mirror.
looks   looked   looking

long adj.
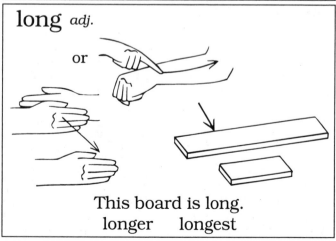
This board is long.
longer   longest

look v.

It does look like it may rain.
It does appear that it may rain.

Lord 271

look after *v.*

I <u>look after</u> the baby.
I <u>take care of</u> the baby.

looking glass *n.*

The <u>looking glass</u> is on the wall.
The <u>mirror</u> is on the wall.

look for *v.*

I must <u>look for</u> my ball.
I must <u>search for</u> it.

loose *adj.*

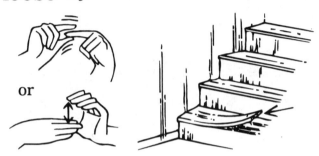

The board is <u>loose</u>.
It's not nailed down.

look out *v.*

<u>Look out</u>! The stove is hot.
<u>Be careful</u>! It is hot.

loose *adj.*

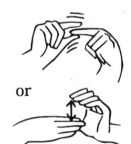 

The dress is <u>loose</u>.
It's <u>too big</u>.

look up *v.*

I have to <u>look up</u> the number.
I have to <u>search for</u> the number.

Lord *n.* God

People go to temple or church
to worship the Lord.

272 Los Angeles

Los Angeles *n. city*

Los Angeles is a large city.

lost *adj.*

The boy is lost.
He can't find his way home.

lose *v.*

Where did I lose my ball?
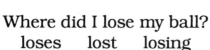
loses   lost   losing

lot *adv. informal*

He feels <u>a lot</u> better.
He feels <u>much</u> better.

loss *n.*

The loss of his money upset him.
loss   losses

lot *n.*

The lot is covered with junk.
lot   lots

lost *pt. of* **lose**

I lost my money.

lot *n. informal*

<u>A lot of</u> people ran to the bank.
<u>Many</u> people ran to the bank.

lower 273

lotion n.

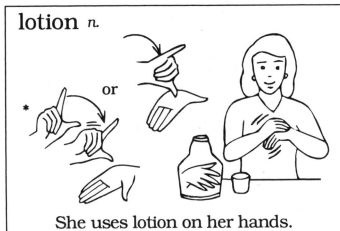

She uses lotion on her hands.

low adj.

One shelf is low.
One shelf is near the floor.

loud adj.

He heard a loud noise.
louder   loudest

low adj.

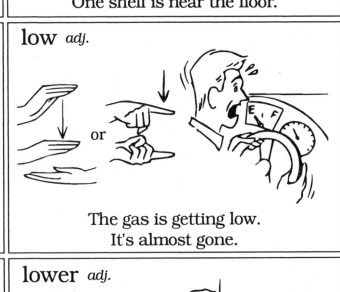

The gas is getting low.
It's almost gone.

love v.

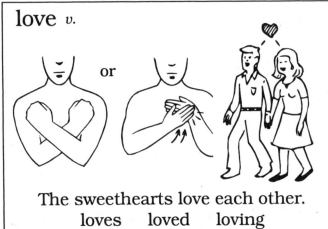

The sweethearts love each other.
loves   loved   loving

lower adj.

He put his hat on the lower shelf.

love v.

I love these cookies.
I like them very much.

lower v.

I will lower the blind.
I'll let down the blind.

274 luck

luck n.

She had good luck.

lump n.

or

The boy has a <u>lump</u> on his head.
He has a <u>bump</u> on his head.

lucky adj. fortunate

The man is very lucky.
luckier   luckiest

lunch n.

or

She makes her lunch herself.
lunch   lunches

luggage n.

My <u>luggage</u> is on the cart.
My <u>baggage</u> is on the cart..

lying v. -ing form of lie

The boy is lying under the tree.

lumber n.

or

He bought some lumber.
He bought some wooden boards.

lying v. -ing form of lie

or

The boy is lying.
He is not telling the truth.

M m

macaroni n. food

I will cook some macaroni.

mad adj.

The man must be mad.
He must be crazy.

machine n.
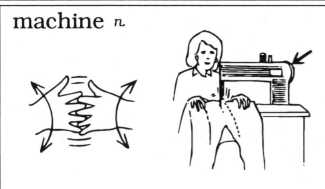
She is using a sewing machine.
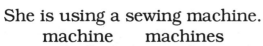
machine   machines

maddening adj. irritating

The noise was maddening.
It was very annoying.

machine gun n. weapon

The soldier has a machine gun.
machine gun   machine guns

made pt. of make

I made a cake.

mad adj. informal

The man is mad.
He is very angry.

magazine n.

The magazines are on the table.
magazine   magazines

275

276 magic

magic *adj.*

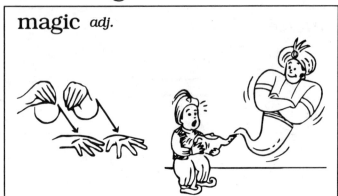

The boy has a magic lantern.

maid *n. worker*

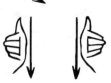

The <u>maid</u> opened the door.
The <u>servant</u> opened the door.

magnet *n.*

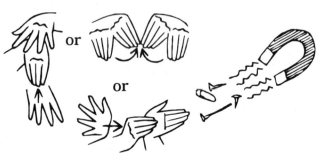

A magnet attracts iron and steel.
magnet   magnets

mail *n.*

She received some mail.

magnifying glass *n.*

He is using a magnifying glass.
magnifying glass   magnifying glasses

mail *v.*

I will mail this letter.
mails   mailed   mailing

maid *n. maiden*

She is a <u>maid</u>.
She's a <u>young girl</u>.

mailbox *n.*

The mailbox is empty.
mailbox   mailboxes

make fun of 277

mailman n. worker

The mailman delivers the mail.
mailman   mailmen

make v. equal
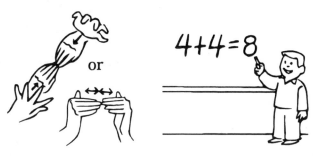
Does four plus four make eight?
Does four plus four add up to eight?

main adj. chief
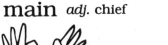
or

His main problem is money.
His most important problem is money.

make v.

I make him mow the lawn.
I force him to mow the lawn.

make v.

I will make a cake.
makes   made   making

make believe v.

We can make believe we are pirates.
We can pretend we're pirates.

make v.

I can make my bed.

make fun of v. ridicule

I always make fun of his car.
I always tease him about it.

278 make up

make up v.

They will make up.
They'll become friends again.

man n. male adult

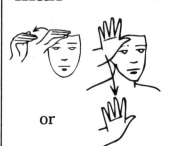 or

The man is happy.
man   men

make up v.

 or

I have to make up my face.
I must put on some make-up.

manage v.

I <u>manage</u> the business.
I <u>control</u> the business.

make up v.

I had to <u>make up</u> an excuse.
I had to <u>invent</u> an excuse.

manager n. worker

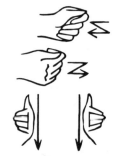 

The manager is explaining
the job to the young man.

male n. man or boy

Men and boys are males.
male   males

mane n. animal body part

He brushed the horse's mane.

march 279

manicure n.
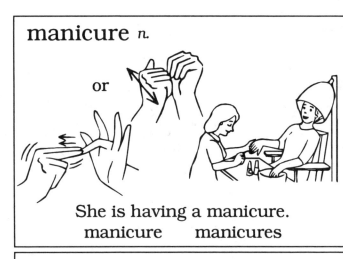
She is having a manicure.
manicure   manicures

map n.
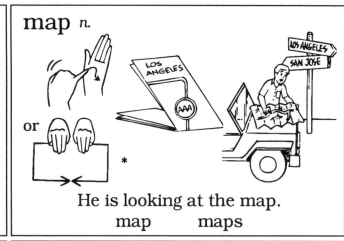
He is looking at the map.
map   maps

manners n. *polite behavior*

The boy has good manners.
He is polite.

marble n. *toy*

The boys divided the marbles.
marble   marbles

bad manners n.

He has bad manners.
He is not polite. He's rude.

March n. *month*

St. Patrick's Day is March 17.

many adj.

He ate many donuts.
more   most

march v.

The band will march in the parade.
marches   marched   marching

280 margarine

margarine n. food
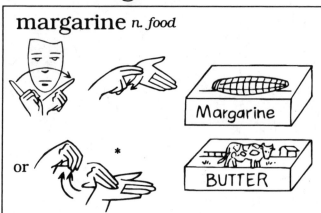
or
We use margarine instead of butter.

mark n.

He made some marks on the wall.
mark   marks

margin n.

The paper has a one inch margin.
margin   margins

mark v.
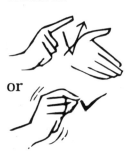 
or
The teacher must mark the papers.
She has to check the papers.

marijuana n. pot, weed, grass
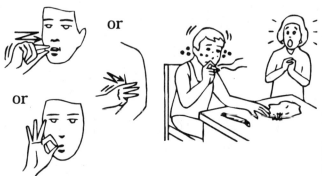
or
He smokes marijuana.

market n.

She went to the market to buy food.
She went to the store to buy food.

marine n.

He is a marine.
He joined the Marine Corps.

marriage n.

They have a happy marriage.
marriage   marriages

mat 281

marry v.
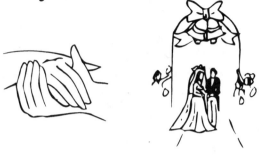
They will marry in June.
marries   married   marrying

massage v.

I will <u>massage</u> your back.
I will <u>rub</u> your back.

marshmallow n. food

Marshmallows are soft and white.
marshmallow   marshmallows

master n.

The worker must obey his <u>master</u>.
He must obey his <u>owner</u>.

mash v.

She will mash the potatoes.
mashes   mashed   mashing

master v.

He must master the times tables.
He has to memorize them.

mask n.

The thief wore a mask.
mask   masks

mat n.
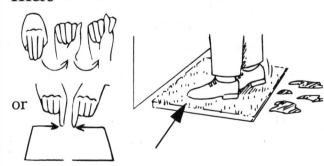
He wiped his feet on the mat.
mat   mats

282 match

match n.

He used a match to start the fire.
match   matches

material n. fabric
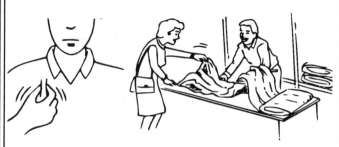
She bought some material.
She bought some cloth.

match v.

The shoes don't match.
They don't belong together.

material n.
or
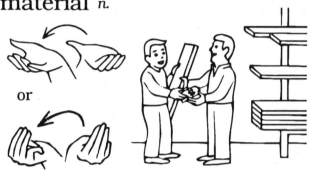
He bought some building materials.
He bought some building supplies.

matchbook n.
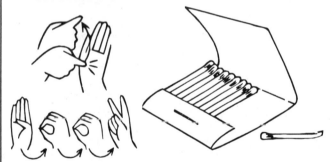
This is a matchbook.
This is a book of matches.

math n.

He is good at math.
He is good at mathematics.

mate n.
or

She can not find the mate.
She can't find the other shoe.

matter n.

What's the matter?
What's the problem?

matter v.

Good grades <u>matter</u> to him.
They <u>are important</u> to him.

mattress n.

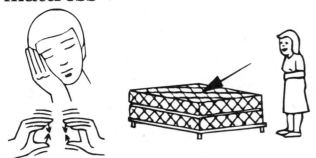

She bought a new mattress.
mattress   mattresses

mature adj.

One boy is very <u>mature</u>.
He acts like an adult.

maximum adj.

The <u>maximum</u> speed allowed is 25.
The <u>greatest</u> speed allowed is 25.

May n. month

or

Memorial Day is the last day of May.

may v.

It may rain.
It's possible that it will rain.

may v.

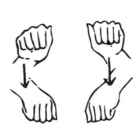 

You may go to the park.
I will allow you to go to the park.

maybe adv.

<u>Maybe</u> I left my ball in the park.
<u>Perhaps</u> I left it there.

284 mayonnaise

mayonnaise *n. food*
or
or

She put mayonnaise on the bread.

mean *adj.*
or

She did a mean thing.
She was not kind to her pet.

McDonald's *n.*
or

We went to Mc Donald's.

mean *v.*

What does the word *spatula* mean?
means   meant   meaning

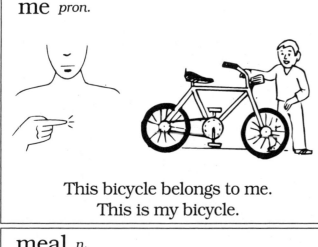

me *pron.*

This bicycle belongs to me.
This is my bicycle.

mean *v. intend*

I didn't mean to break the window.
It was an accident.

meal *n.*

I eat three meals a day.
meal   meals

meant *pt. of* **mean**

I meant to burn the wood.
I intended to burn the wood.

medium 285

measles n. disease

The girl has measles.

mechanic n. worker

The mechanic is fixing the car.
mechanic   mechanics

measure v.

I must measure this board.
measures   measured   measuring

medal n.

He received a medal for bravery.
medal   medals

measuring cup n.

Do you have a measuring cup?
measuring cup   measuring cups

medicine n.

The medicine was bitter.
medicine   medicines

meat n. animal flesh

What kind of meat would you like to have for dinner?

medium adj.
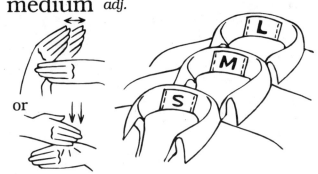
Which size do you want?
Small, medium, or large?

286 meet

meet v.
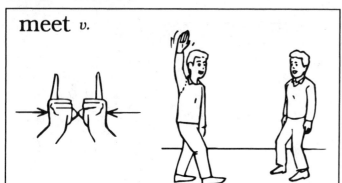
We often meet on the way to school.
meets   met   meeting

member n.
I am a member of the club.
I belong to the club.

meeting n.

The men are having a meeting.
meeting   meetings

Memorial Day n. holiday

Memorial Day is May 31.

melon n. fruit
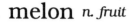

The melon is very sweet.
melon   melons

memorize v.
or
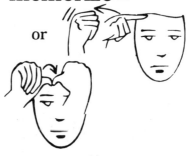
He will memorize the times tables.
He'll learn them by heart.

melt v.

The ice will soon melt.
It will soon turn into water.

memory n.
or

He has a good <u>memory</u>.
He has good <u>ability to remember</u>.

mess 287

men *plural of* **man**

The men are taking a coffee break.
man   men

merely *n.*

She thinks he is merely a child.
She thinks he is only a child.

mend *v.*
or

I must mend this shirt.
mends   mended   mending

merry *adj.*
or

We had a <u>merry</u> holiday.
We had a <u>happy</u> holiday.

menu *n.*
or
*
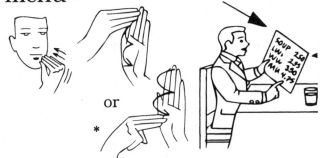
He looked at the menu.
menu   menus

merry-go-round *n.*

The children enjoy
the merry-go-round.

merchant *n.*

The merchant is making a sale.
merchant   merchants

mess *n.*
or

His room is a mess.
He does not put his things away.

288 message

message n.

She handed him a message.
message   messages

method n.
I don't like his methods. I don't like his way of doing things.

met pt. of **meet**

He met a friend.

Mexico n. country
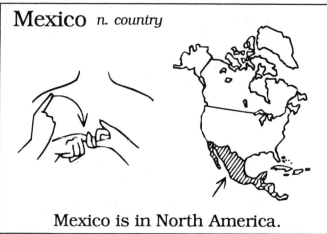
Mexico is in North America.

metal n.
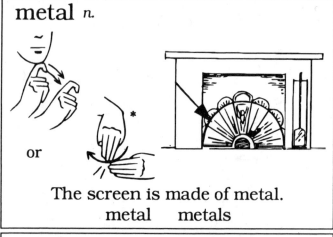
The screen is made of metal.
metal   metals

mice plural of **mouse**

Mice like cheese.

meter n.

He put coins in the parking meter.
meter   meters

Micky Mouse n.

The children enjoy Micky Mouse.

midnight 289

microphone n. mike

He spoke into the microphone.
microphone   microphones

microscope n.

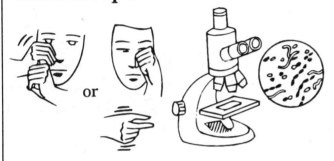

A microscope magnifies things.
microscope   microscopes

microwave oven

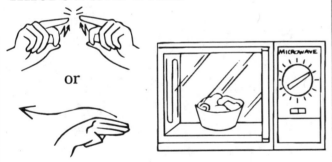

We have a microwave oven.

middle adj.

The middle bear is large.
The bear in the center is large.

middle n. center

The candles are in the
middle of the table.

middle n.

The apple is in the middle.
The apple is between two pears.

middle name n.

Her middle name is Jane.

midnight n. 12 o'clock at night

Cinderella danced with the
prince until midnight.

290 might

might n.

He pushed with all his <u>might</u>.
He used all his <u>strength</u>.

milk n. beverage

The woman is drinking milk.

might pt. of may

He might have fallen, but he didn't.

milk v.

I milk the cow every day.
milks   milked   milking

mile n. 5,280 ft.

The speed limit is 25 miles an hour.
mile   miles

milkman n. worker
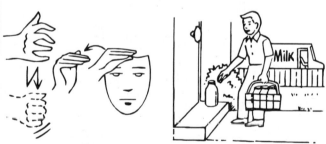
The milkman delivers the milk.
milkman   milkmen

military adj.

They are wearing military uniforms.

milk shake n.

He is making a milk shake.
milk shake   milk shakes

mine 291

million *1,000,000*

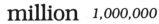

She won a million dollars.

mind *v.*

You didn't <u>mind</u> me.
You didn't <u>obey</u> me.

mince *v.*

She will mince the onion.
She'll chop it into small pieces.

mind *v.*

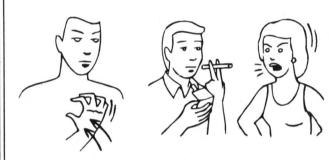

Do you <u>mind</u> if I smoke?
Do you <u>care</u> if I smoke?

mind *n.*

or

He has a good mind.
He is very smart.

mine *n.*

We visited a diamond mine.
mine   mines

make up one's **mind**

He can't <u>make up his mind</u>.
He can't <u>decide</u> what to do.

mine *pron.*

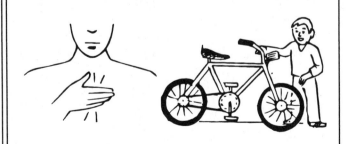

This bicycle is mine.
This is my bicycle.

292 miner

miner n. worker

The miner is using a pick.
miner   miners

minus prep.

Eight minus six is two.
Eight take away six is two.

minimum adj.

He is paid the minimum wage.
He's paid the lowest possible wage.

minute n.

There are 60 seconds in a minute.
minute   minutes

minister n. pastor

The minister asked us to rise.
minister   ministers

mirror n.

She looked in the mirror.
mirror   mirrors

minor n.

He is a minor.
He's not an adult.

mischief n.

You always get into mischief.
You always do harmful or bad things.

misunderstand 293

miser *n.*

The man is a miser.
He will not share his money.

miss *v.*

He will miss school for a week.
He'll be absent for a week.

Miss *n. Ms.*

This is Miss Jones.
She is not married.

miss *v.*

I miss my family.
I feel lonely.

miss *v.*

I always miss the ball.
misses   missed   missing

mistake *n.*

The boy made a mistake.
The boy made an error.

miss *v.*

Why did he miss the plane?

misunderstand *v.*

I sometimes misunderstand orders.
I don't understand them correctly.

294 mitt

mitt n.

The mitts protect my hands.
mitt   mitts

mob n.

The mob threw stones.
The angry people threw stones.

mitten n. clothing

The girl is wearing mittens.
mitten   mittens

moccasin n. clothing

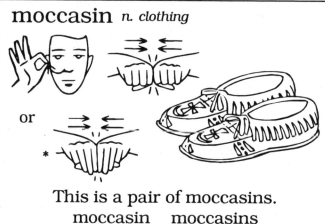

This is a pair of moccasins.
moccasin   moccasins

mix v.

You must mix the sugar and eggs.
mixes   mixed   mixing

model adj.

He made a model plane.
He made a small copy of a plane.

mixer n. household appliance

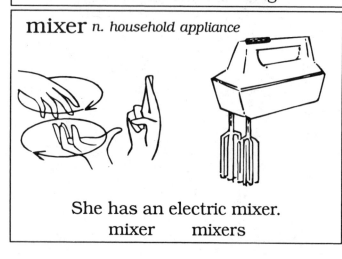

She has an electric mixer.
mixer   mixers

model v.

She will model many dresses.

Monday 295

modern *adj.*

Their house is modern.
more modern   most modern

mold *v.*

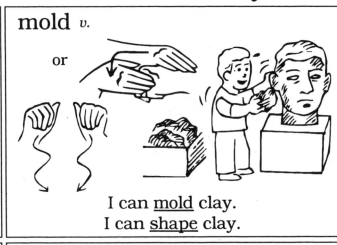

I can mold clay.
I can shape clay.

moist *adj. slightly wet*

He wiped the table with a moist cloth.
He wiped it with a damp cloth.

mom *n. informal*

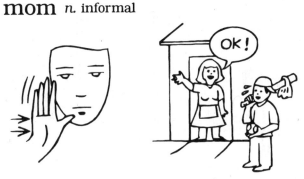

My mom let me go to the park.
My mother let me go there.

molasses *n. food*

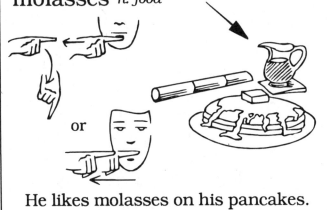

He likes molasses on his pancakes.

moment *n. minute*

Please wait a moment.
moment   moments

mold *n. mildew*

She saw mold on the cheese.

Monday *n. day of the week*

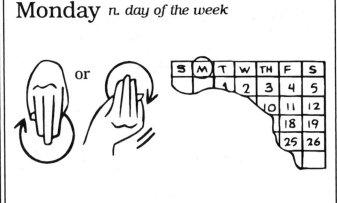

Monday comes before Tuesday.

296 money

money n. coins & bills

The man has a lot of money.

month n.

There are 12 months in a year.
month   months

monk n.

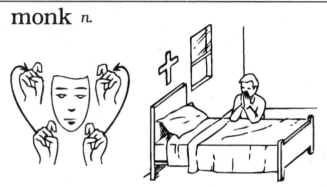

The man is a monk.
He lives in the monastery.

monthly adv.

He pays his insurance monthly.
He pays his insurance once a month.

monkey n. animal

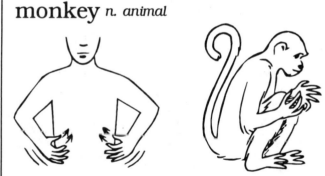

The monkey has a long tail.
monkey   monkeys

mood n.

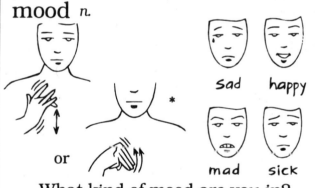

What kind of mood are you in?
What state of mind are you in?

monster n.

The monster frightened the children.
monster   monsters

moon n.

The astronaut landed on the moon.

most 297

moose n. animal
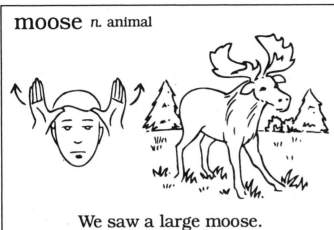
We saw a large moose.

more than

Asparagus costs more than a dollar.

mop n.
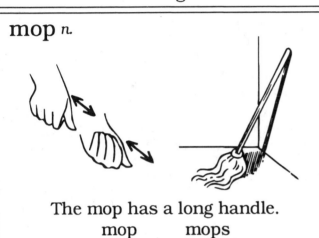
The mop has a long handle.
mop   mops

morning n. sunrise till noon

The sun comes up in the morning.
morning   mornings

mop v.

I mop the floor once a week.
mops   mopped   mopping

mosquito n. insect
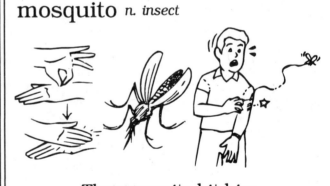
The mosquito bit him.
mosquito   mosquitoes/mosquitos

more adj.

The boy wants <u>more</u> cookies.
He wants <u>additional</u> cookies.

most n.

He ate most of the donuts.

298 motel

motel n.

We stayed at a nice motel.
motel   motels

motion n. movement

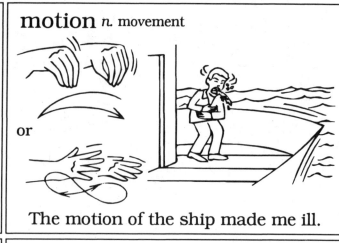

The motion of the ship made me ill.

moth n. insect

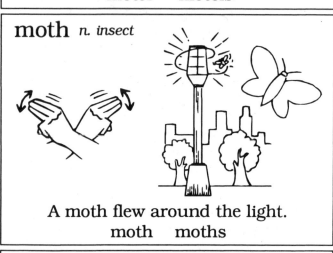

A moth flew around the light.
moth   moths

motor n.

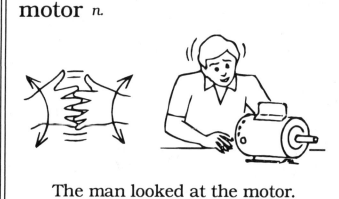

The man looked at the motor.
motor   motors

mother n. female parent

This is my mother.
mother   mothers

motorcycle n. vehicle

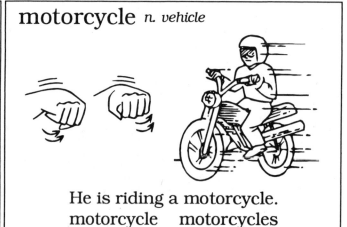

He is riding a motorcycle.
motorcycle   motorcycles

Mother's Day n.

Mother's Day is the
second Sunday in May.

mountain n.

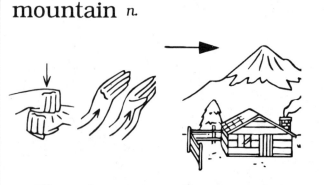

There is snow on the mountain.
mountain   mountains

movement 299

mouse n. rodent

The mouse has a long tail.
mouse   mice

mouthwash n.
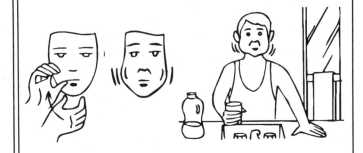
He rinsed his mouth with mouthwash.

mousetrap n.

I put cheese on the mousetrap.
mousetrap   mousetraps

move v.
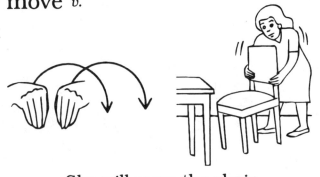
She will move the chair.
moves   moved   moving

moustache n. mustache
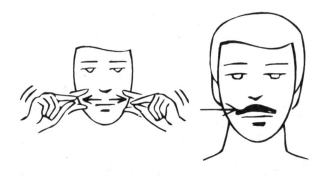
The man has a moustache.

move v.

Why did they move?

mouth n. body part
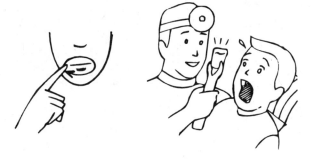
The boy's mouth is open.
mouth   mouths

movement n.

The ship's <u>movement</u> made him ill.
The ship's <u>motion</u> made him ill.

300 movie

movie n.
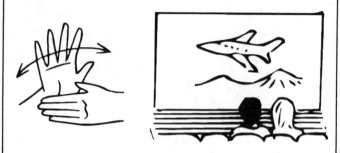
They enjoyed the movie.
movie   movies

much adj.

The boy ate much food.
The boy ate a lot of food.

mow v.
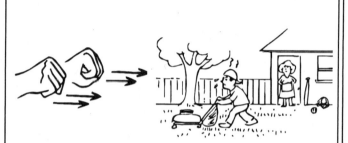
He has to mow the lawn.
He has to cut the grass.

mud n.
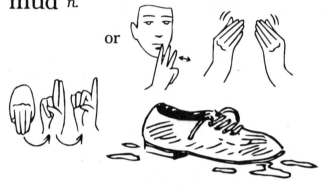
He got mud on his shoe.

Mr. n. Mister

This is Mr. Smith.
He is my husband.

muff n. clothing
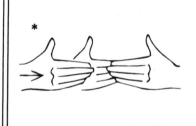 
The muff keeps her hands warm.
muff   muffs

Mrs. n. Missus

This is Mrs. Smith.
She is my wife.

muffin n. food

Do you like blueberry muffins?
muffin   muffins

museum 301

mug n.
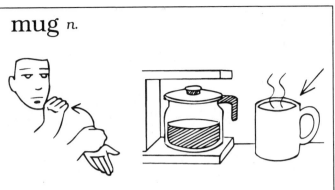
The mug is full of coffee.
mug   mugs

mummy n.

We saw a mummy in Egypt.
mummy   mummies

mule n. animal
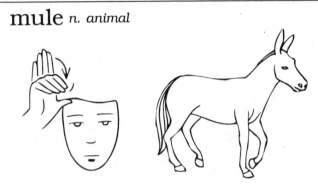
Mules can be stubborn.
mule   mules

mumps n. disease
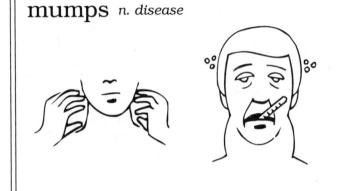
The man has the mumps.

multiply v.
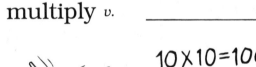
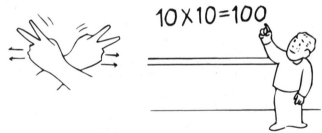
He can multiply by ten.
multiplies   multiplied   multiplying

muscle n.

He has strong muscles.
muscle   muscles

mull over

I'll have to turn over your offer in my mind. I'll think about it carefilly.

museum n.

We visited the museum.
museum   museums

302 mushroom

mushroom n. food

She is slicing the mushroom.
mushroom   mushrooms

mustard n.

He put mustard on the hot dog.

music n.

He enjoys listening to music.

my pron.

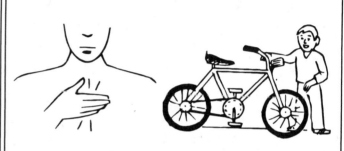

This is my bicycle.
This bicycle belongs to me.

must v.

You <u>must</u> keep that dog outside.
You <u>have to</u> keep it outside.

myself pron.

I drew this picture myself.
No one helped me.

mustache n. moustache

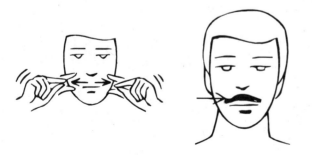

He grew a mustache.
mustache   mustaches

mystery n.

It's a mystery to me.
I can't explain it.

N n

nab *v. informal*

Did the officer <u>nab</u> the thief?
Did he <u>grab</u> the thief?

nail *v.*

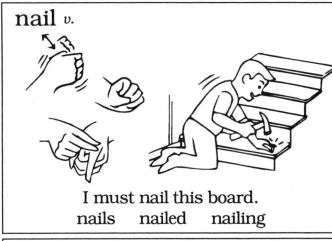

I must nail this board.
nails   nailed   nailing

nag *v.*

I nag my wife about the dog.
I always complain about the dog.

naked *adj. nude*

The girl is naked.
She isn't wearing any clothes.

nail *n. body part*

She is polishing her <u>nails</u>.
She's polishing her <u>fingernails</u>.

name *n.*

The man's name is Robinson Crusoe.
name   names

nail *n.*

He needs some nails.
nail   nails

name *v.*

I will name you "Fido."
names   named   naming

303

nap n.

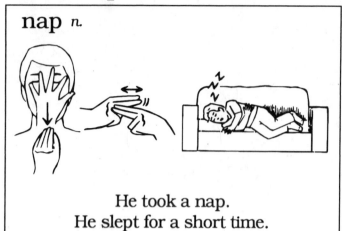

He took a nap.
He slept for a short time.

nation n. country

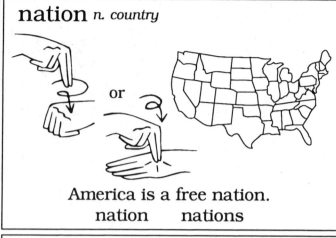

America is a free nation.
nation   nations

napkin n.

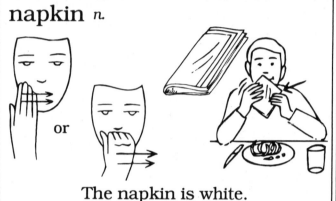

The napkin is white.
napkin   napkins

national adj.

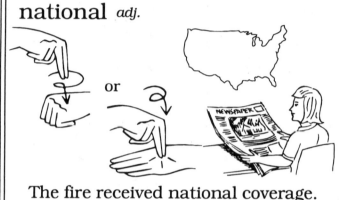

The fire received national coverage.
It was reported all over the nation.

narcotics n.

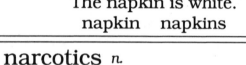

The man uses narcotics.
The man uses drugs.

natural adj.

She is a natural blond.
She was born with blond hair.

narrow adj.

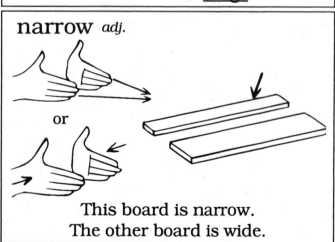

This board is narrow.
The other board is wide.

naughty adj.

She is a naughty girl.
She's a bad girl.

necessary 305

nauseate *v.*

The medicine will nauseate me.
It will make me feel sick.

nearly *adv.*

It is <u>nearly</u> 8:30.
It's <u>almost</u> 8:30.

navy *n.*

The man joined the navy.

nearly *adv.*

He <u>nearly</u> missed the bus.
He <u>almost</u> missed it.

near *adj.*

The store is <u>near</u>.
It's <u>close by</u>.

neat *adj.*

Her room is neat.
Her room is not a mess.

near *prep.*
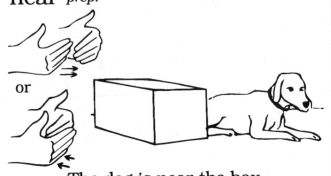
The dog is <u>near</u> the box.
It is <u>close to</u> the box.

necessary *adj.*

It is necessary to obey the law.
It's required that you obey the law.

306 necessity

necessity n.

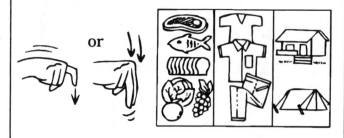

Food, clothing, and shelter are basic necessities.

necktie n.

The man is wearing a necktie.
necktie   neckties

neck n. body part

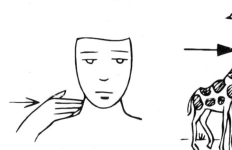

The giraffe has a long neck.
neck   necks

nectarine n. fruit

The nectarine is sweet and juicy.
nectarine   nectarines

neck v.

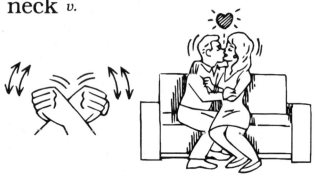

They often neck.
They often hug and kiss.

need v.

I need to study harder.
I ought to study harder.

necklace n. jewelry

The woman is wearing a necklace.
necklace   necklaces

need v. require

Plants need water.
They must have water.

neither 307

needle n.

The woman is threading the needle.
needle   needles

neighbor n.

The woman waved to her neighbor.
neighbor   neighbors

negative adj.

She gave a negative response.
She said no.

neither adj.

Neither answer is correct.
Both answers are wrong.

neglect v.

You neglect your work.
You ignore your work.

neither conj.

He isn't clean, and neither is she.

negligent adj.

The driver was negligent.
He was careless.

neither conj.
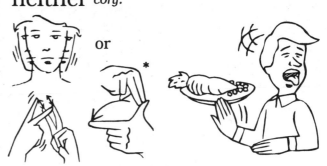
He likes neither carrots nor peas.
He doesn't like carrots or peas.

308 nephew

nephew n. male relative
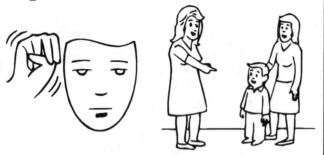
He is my nephew.
He's my sister's son.

nest n.

The baby birds are in the nest.
nest   nests

nerve n.

The noise got on his nerves.
It bothered him.

net n. tool
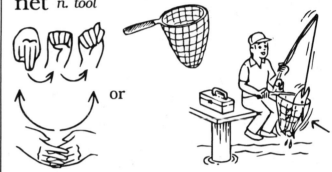
The boy is holding a net.
net   nets

nerve n.

She has a lot of nerve.
She is rude and bold.

Netherlands n. country

The Netherlands is
also called Holland.

nervous adj.

The man is very nervous.

never adv.

The boy is never rude.
He is always nice and polite.

New York 309

never mind

Mother finally said, "Never mind."
She finally said, "Forget it."

newspaper n.

She is reading the newspaper.
newspaper   newspapers

new adj.

Mary's book is new.
newer   newest

New Year's Day n.
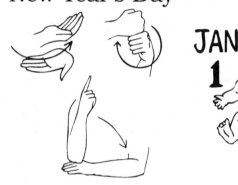
New Year's Day is January 1.

new adj.

She made a <u>new</u> pot of coffee.
She made a <u>fresh</u> pot of coffee.

New Year's Eve n.

They're celebrating New Year's Eve.

news n.

He watches the news on TV.

New York n. city

New York is a large city.

310 next

next *adj.*

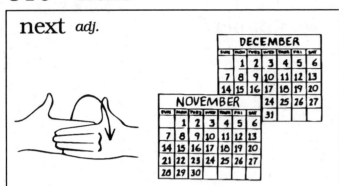

Next month is December.
The month after this is December.

nibble *v.*

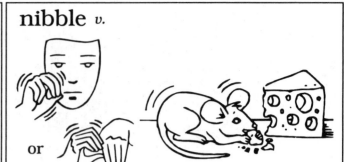

or

I saw the mouse nibble the cheese.
It took small bites of the cheese.

next *adj.*

He must take the next plane.

nice *adj.*

It will be a <u>nice</u> day today.
It'll be a <u>pleasant</u> day.

next door *adv.*

She lives next door.
She lives in the nearest house.

nice *adj.*

She is a nice girl.
She's thoughtful and friendly.

next week

His appointment is next week.

nice *adj.*

She is not a nice girl.
She has a bad temper.

nineteen 311

nickel *n. coin: 5 cents*

A nickle is worth 5 cents.
nickle   nickles

nightgown *n. clothing*

The girl is wearing a nightgown.
nightgown   nightgowns

nickname *n.*

His name is Bob, but
his nickname is Slim.

nightmare *n.*

The boy had a <u>nightmare</u>.
He had a <u>bad dream</u>.

niece *n. female relative*

She is my niece.
She's my sister's daughter.

nine *number: 9*

It is nine minutes after six.

night *n. after sunset*

The stars come out at night.
night   nights

nineteen *number: 19*

I have 80 cents. I need nineteen
cents more to buy some asparagus.

312 ninety

ninety *number: 90*

Grandmother is ninety years old.

no-good *adj.*

The car is no-good.
It is worthless.

ninth *n. 9th*

DECEMBER
1 2 3 4 5 6
7 8 ⑨ 10 11 12 13
14 15 16 17 18 19 20
21 22 23 24 25 26 27
28 29 30 31

Today is the ninth of December.

nobody *pron.*

Nobody came to the meeting.
No one came to the meeting.

no *adj.*

The man has no money.
He doesn't have any money.

noise *n.*

The noise bothers Father.
The loud sounds bother him.

no *adv.*

No, I didn't take the candy.

none *pron.*

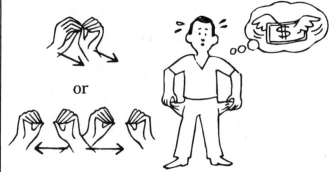

He needs money, but he has none.

North America 313

nonsense *n.*

Stop that nonsense!
Stop that foolish behavior!

normal *adj.*

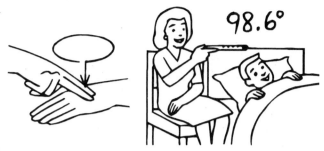

His temperature is normal.
His temperature is OK.

noodle *n. food*

I put noodles in my tuna casserole.
noodle   noodles

normally *adv.*

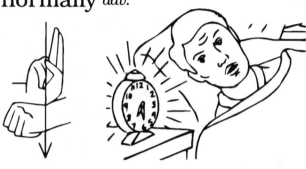

He normally gets up at 6:30.
He usually gets up then.

noon *n. 12:00 in the daytime*

We ate lunch at noon.
We ate lunch at 12 o'clock.

north *adv.*

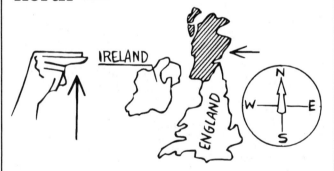

Scotland is north of England.

nor *conj.*

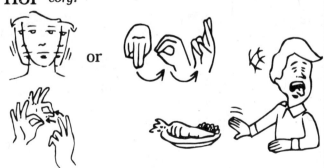

The boy likes neither peas nor carrots.
He doesn't like either peas or carrots.

North America *n. continent*

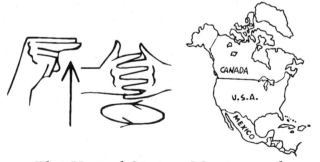

The United States, Mexico and
Canada are in North America.

314 Norway

Norway n. country

or

Norway is a country in Europe.

note n.
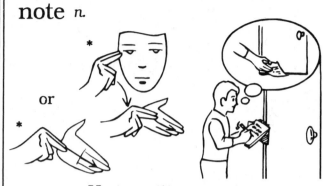
He is writing a note.
He's writing a short letter.

nose n. body part

The bee landed on his nose.
nose   noses

nothing n.
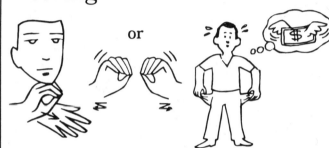
There is nothing in his pockets.
There isn't anything in his pockets.

nosy adj. nosey

She is a nosy person.
She's curious about my affairs.

for nothing n.

He got in for nothing.
He got in without paying.

not adv.

The man did not catch the plane.

notice n.

They put a notice on the wall.
notice   notices

numeral 315

notice *v.*

Did he notice the loose board?
Did he see it?

now and then *adv.*

He calls her now and then.
He calls her once in a while.

noun *n.*

The underlined words are nouns.
noun   nouns

nude *adj.* naked

The girl is nude.
She isn't wearing any clothes.

November *n. month*

Thanksgiving is in November.

number *n.*
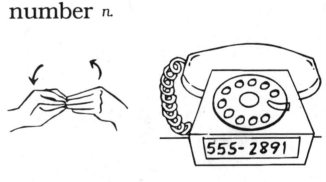
My telephone number is 555-2891.
number   numbers

now *adv.*
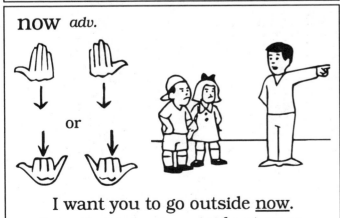
I want you to go outside now.
I want you to go outside at once.

numeral *n.*

I wrote some numerals on the board.
I wrote some numbers on the board.

numerator n.

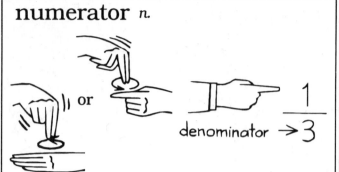

The numerator is above the line.
numerator   numerators

nut n. food

The squirrel has a nut.
nut   nuts

nun n.

The nun lives in a convent.
nun   nuns

nut n. slang

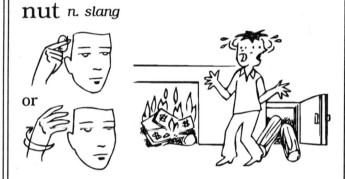

I think he's a nut.
I think he's crazy.

nurse n. worker

The nurse brought his medicine.
nurse   nurses

nut n.

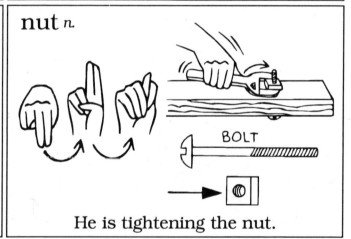

He is tightening the nut.

nursery n.

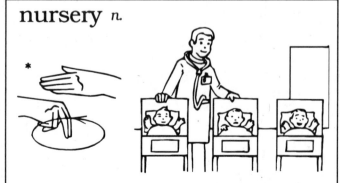

The babies are in the nursery.
nursery   nurseries

nutcracker n. tool

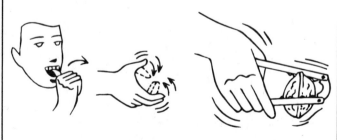

The woman is using a nutcracker.
nutcracker   nutcrackers

O o

oak *n. tree*

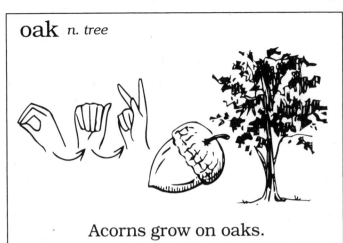

Acorns grow on oaks.

object *n.*

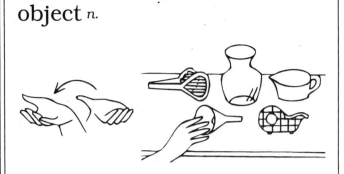

She put some <u>objects</u> on the table.
She put some <u>things</u> there.

oath *n.*

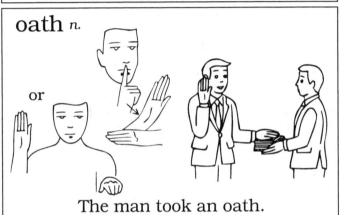

The man took an oath.
He promised to tell the truth.

object *v.*

I always <u>object</u> to the noise.
I always <u>complain</u> about it.

oatmeal *n. cereal*

I had oatmeal for breakfast.

observe *v.*

Did she <u>observe</u> the painting?
Did she <u>look at</u> it carefully?

obey *v.*

You must obey the traffic laws.
obeys   obeyed   obeying

occupation *n.*

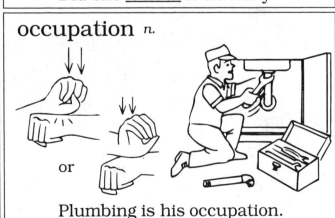

Plumbing is his occupation.
That's how he earns his living.

318 occur

occur *v.* happen

Where did the accident occur?
occurs   occurred   occurring

octopus *n.*

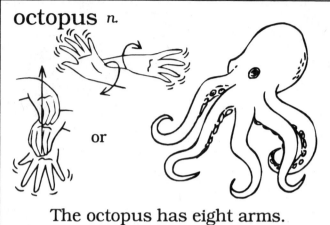

The octopus has eight arms.

ocean *n.* sea

We sailed across the ocean.
ocean   oceans

odd *adj.*

It's <u>odd</u> that the door is open.
It's <u>strange</u> that it is open.

o'clock *adv.*

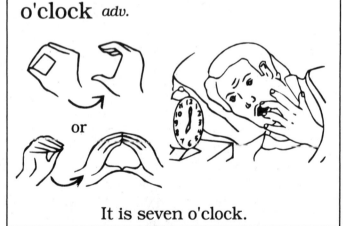

It is seven o'clock.

odd *adj.*

Five is an odd number. It has a
remainder of 1 if you divide by 2.

October *n.* month

Halloween is October 31st.

odor *n.*

The delicious odors made me hungry.
odor   odors

offer 319

of *prep.*

The boy is drinking a glass of water.

off *adj.*

The TV is off.
The TV is not on.

of *prep.*
or
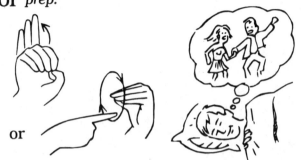
Bill is dreaming <u>of</u> the dance.
Bill is dreaming <u>about</u> the dance.

take **off** *v.*
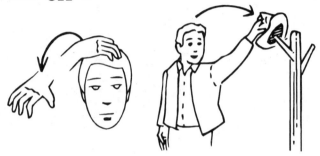
I must <u>take off</u> my hat.
I must <u>remove</u> it.

of *prep.*
or
or
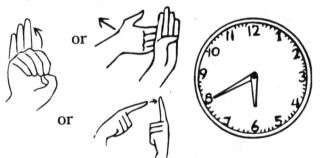
It's twenty minutes <u>of</u> six.
It's twenty minutes <u>to</u> six.

off *prep.*

He jumped off the train.

of course certainly, naturally
or
or
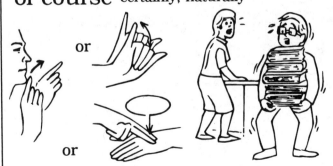
Will you help me?
Of course. Yes, I will.

offer *v.*

Bob will offer to help his brother.
offers   offered   offering

320 office

office n.

He works in an office.
office   offices

oil n.

The attendant is checking the oil.

officer n. worker

or
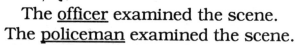
The officer examined the scene.
The policeman examined the scene.

OK adj. okay

or
He feels OK now.
He feels fine now.

often adv.

He often bothers that girl.
He frequently bothers her.

OK adj. okay

or
His grades are OK.
His grades are all right.

Oh! interjection
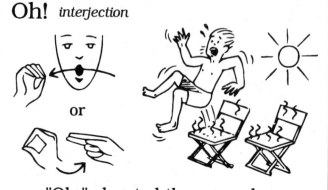
or
"Oh," shouted the man when he sat down in the hot chair.

okay adv. OK

or
I asked if I could go out, and she said,"Okay". She said, "Yes."

on and on 321

old *adj.*

Bob's book is old.
older   oldest

on *adv.*
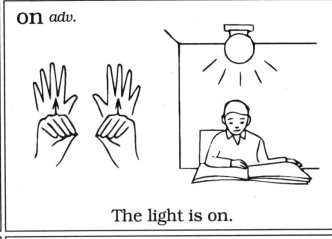
The light is on.

old *adj.*

Grandfather is old.

on *prep.*
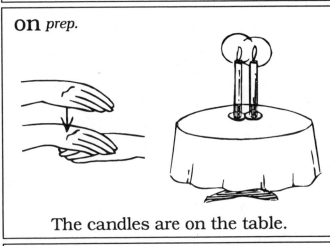
The candles are on the table.

Olympics *n.*
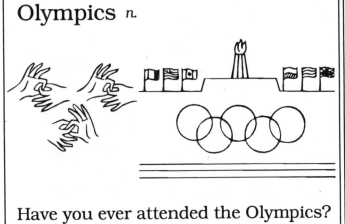
Have you ever attended the Olympics?

on and on *adv.*

or
She talked on and on.
She talked and talked and talked.

omit *v. leave out*

or
You always omit the comma.
omits   omitted   omitting

on and on *adv.*

or
He walked on and on.
He continued to walk and walk.

322 once

once *adv.*

Christmas comes <u>once</u> a year.
It comes <u>one time</u> each year.

one *adj.*

They have one son and one daughter.

once in a while *adv. phrase*

or

He calls her <u>once in a while</u>.
He calls her <u>now and then</u>.

one *pron.*

<u>One</u> must study to succeed.
<u>A person</u> must study to succeed.

once upon a time *adv. phrase*

<u>Once upon a time</u>, a girl was lonely.
<u>A long time ago</u>, a girl was lonely.

onion *n. vegetable*

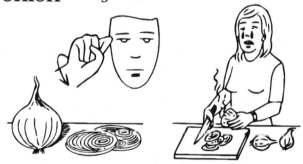

The onion made her eyes water.
    onion   onions

one *number: 1*

Add 1 and 1 and you have 2.
The sum of 1 and 1 is 2.

only *adj.*

or

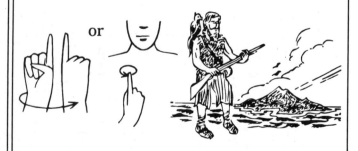

He is the only person on the
island. He is alone on the island.

operate 323

onto *prep.*

He tossed his coat <u>onto</u> the bed.
He tossed it <u>on</u> the bed.

open *v.*

Did she open her book?

Ooops! *interjection*

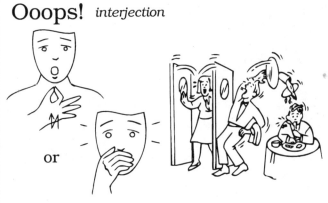

She said, "Ooops! Sorry about that."

operate *v.*

I <u>operate</u> every day.
I <u>perform surgery</u> every day.

open *adj.*

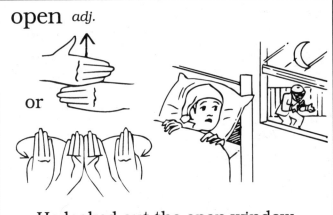

He looked out the open window.

operate *v.*

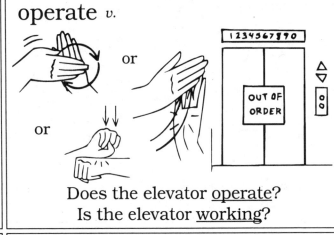

Does the elevator <u>operate</u>?
Is the elevator <u>working</u>?

open *v.*

I will open the door for our guests..
opens   opened   opening

operate *v.*

I <u>operate</u> an insurance business.
I <u>conduct</u> an insurance business.

324 opinion

opinion n.

He has a low opinion of her ability.
In his judgment, she lacks ability.

opposite n.

Short is the opposite of tall.

opossum n. animal
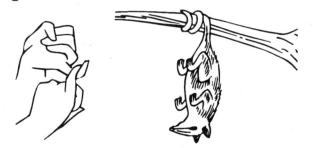
The opossum hangs by its tail.
opossum   opossums/opossum

or conj.
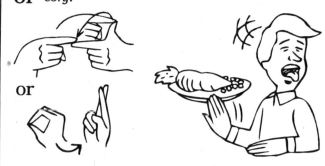
He doesn't like either
peas or carrots.

opportunity n.

She had no opportunity to rest.
She had no chance to rest.

orange adj. color
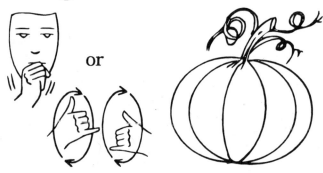
The pumpkin is orange.

oppose v.
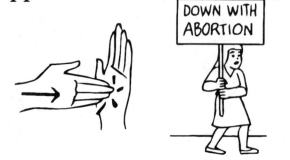
I oppose abortion.
I am against abortion.

orange n. fruit
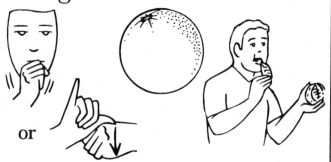
He is eating an orange.
orange   oranges

order 325

orbit v.

or

The satellite will orbit the earth.
It will travel around the earth.

order n.

or

Her room is in order.
It is neat.

orchard n.
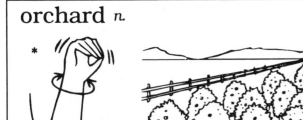

The orchard has many fruit trees.
orchard   orchards

order n.

or

His room is not in order.
It is not neat.

orchestra n.

or

The conductor leads the orchestra.
orchestra   orchestras

order v.
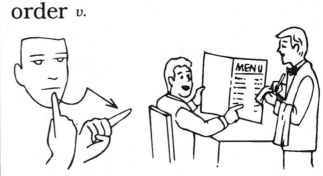

I will order my dinner now.
orders   ordered   ordering

order n.

She gave her order to the waiter.
She told him what she wanted.

order v.
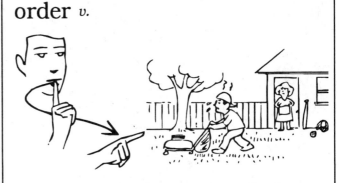

I have to order him to mow the lawn.
I have to tell him to mow the lawn.

326 organ

organ *n. musical instrument*
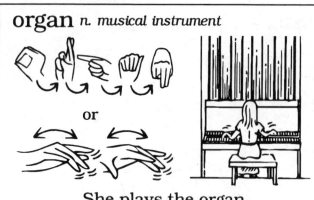
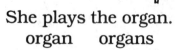
She plays the organ.
organ   organs

ostrich *n. bird*
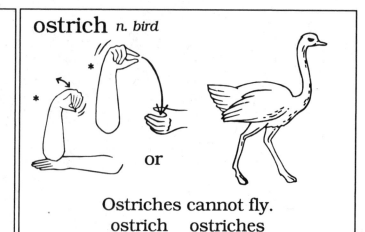
Ostriches cannot fly.
ostrich   ostriches

organize *v.*

She should organize her desk.
She should put her desk in order.

other *adj.*

She has a box under one arm
and a bundle under the other arm.

ornament *n.*

We hung ornaments on the tree.
ornament   ornaments

ouch *interjection*

"Ouch!" cried the boy.

orphan *n.*

Heidi was an orphan.
Her mother and father were dead.

ought to *v.*

He <u>ought to</u> study harder.
He <u>should</u> study harder.

ounce n.

There are 16 ounces in a pound.
ounce ounces

out adj.

The doctor is out.
The doctor is not in his office.

our pron.

This is our house.
We bought it.

out adj.

School is <u>out</u> for the day.
It is <u>finished</u> for the day.

ours pron.

This house is ours.
We own it.

out adv.

The boy went out.
He left the house.

ourselves pron.

We will make lunch ourselves.
We don't want you to help us.

come out v.

The sun may <u>come out</u>.
It may <u>appear</u>.

328 out

out *prep.*

He took the shirt out of the box.

oven *adj.*

The oven is empty.
oven   ovens

out of order
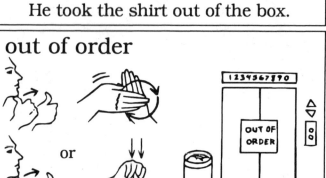
The elevator is <u>out of order</u>.
The elevator is <u>not working</u>.

over *adj.*

The meeting is <u>over</u>.
It has ended. It's <u>finished</u>.

outdoors *adv.*
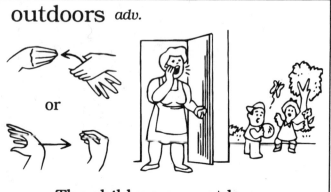
The children are outdoors.
They are not in the house.

over *adv.*

He did the paper <u>over</u>.
He did the paper <u>again</u>.

outside *adv.*

The boy is outside.
He is not in the house.

turn over *v.*

He will turn over the pancake.

overshoes 329

over *prep.*

The picture is over the couch.
It is above the couch.

overflow *v.*

Why did the tub overflow?
Why did it run over?

over *prep.*

Tijauna is over the border.
It's across the border.

overlook *v.*

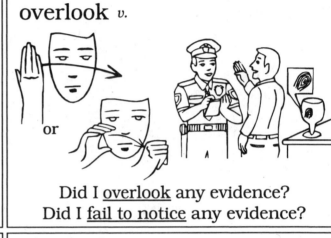

Did I overlook any evidence?
Did I fail to notice any evidence?

overalls *n. clothing*

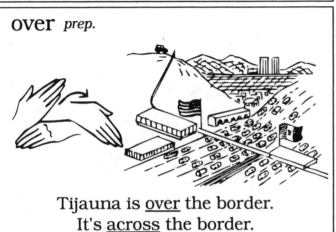

He's wearing a pair of overalls.

overnight *adv.*

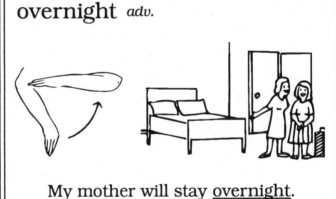

My mother will stay overnight.
She will stay all night.

overcoat *n. clothing*

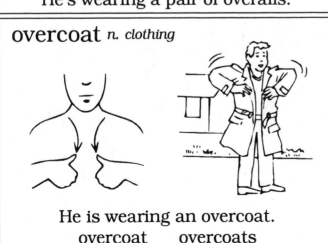

He is wearing an overcoat.
overcoat   overcoats

overshoes *n. clothing*

He's wearing a pair of overshoes.
overshoe   overshoes

330 Ow!

Ow! *interjection*
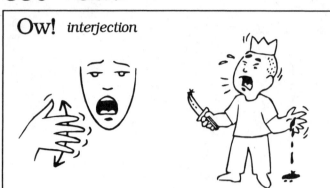
"Ow!" cried the boy.
He yelled because of the pain.

owner *n.*
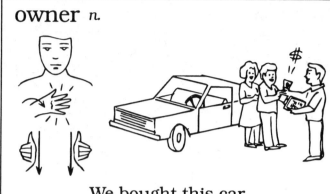
We bought this car.
We are the owners.

owe *v.*

I owe a lot of bills.
I have many debts.

ox *n. animal*

The ox is pulling the plow.
   ox   oxen

owl *n. bird*

The owl is in the tree.
   owl   owls

oxen *n. plural of* ox

The oxen are pulling the plow.

own *v.*
We own this house. We bought it.
  owns   owned   owning

oxygen *n.*
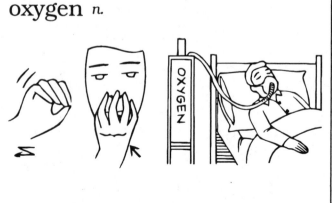
They are giving him oxygen.

P p

pack *n.*

We saw a <u>pack</u> of wolves.
We saw a <u>group</u> of wolves.

pack *v.*
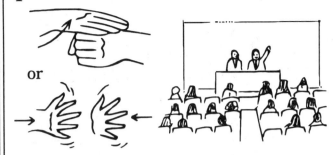
Good speakers <u>pack</u> the auditorium.
Good speakers <u>fill</u> the auditorium.

pack *n.*

He has a pack on his back.
pack   packs

package *n.*
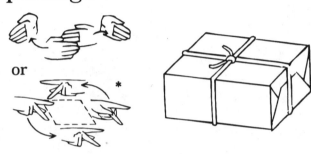
What's in that large package?
package   packages

pack *n.*
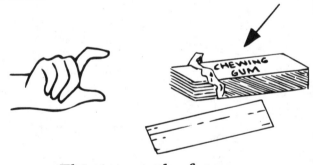
This is a <u>pack</u> of gum.
This is a <u>package</u> of gum.

pad *n.*

This is a pad of paper.
pad   pads

pack *v.*

I must pack my suitcase.
packs   packed   packing

padlock *n.*

He put a padlock on the toolbox.
padlock   padlocks

332 page

page n.

He is turning the page.
page pages

paint n.
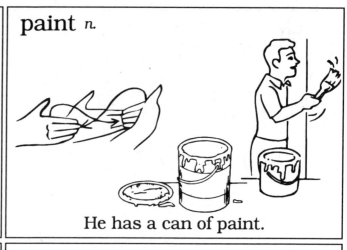
He has a can of paint.

paid pt. of pay

The woman paid for the cake.

paint v.

The artist will paint a picture.
paints painted painting

pail n. bucket

She's filling the pail with sand.
pail pails

painter n. worker

The painter is on the ladder.
painter painters

pain n.
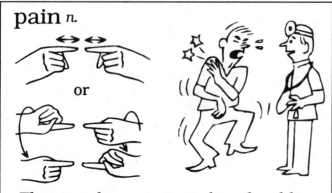
The man has a pain in his shoulder.
The man's shoulder hurts.

pair n.
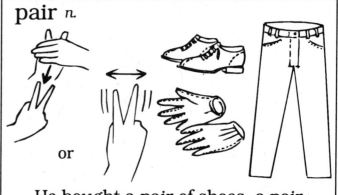
He bought a pair of shoes, a pair of pants, and a pair of gloves.

panda 333

pajamas n. clothing

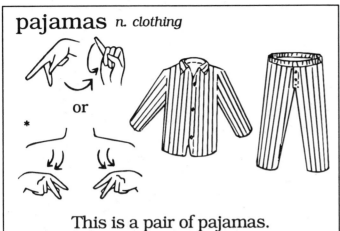

or

This is a pair of pajamas.

palm n. tree

or

Palms grow along the street.

pal n.

or

They are pals.
They're friends.

pan n.

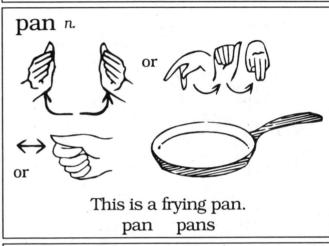

or

This is a frying pan.
pan   pans

palace n. castle

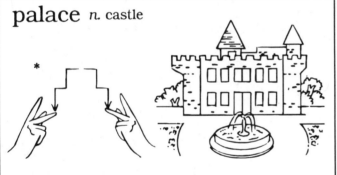

The king lives in the palace.
palace   palaces

pancakes n. hot cakes

He had pancakes for breakfast.
pancake   pancakes

palm n. body part

The key is in the palm of her hand.
palm   palms

panda n. animal

We saw a panda at the zoo.
panda   pandas

334 panther

panther n. animal

The panther is black.
panther   panthers

paper n.

She is reading the paper.
She's reading the newspaper.

pants n. clothing
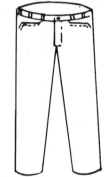
This is a pair of pants.
This is a pair of trousers.

paper n.

He needs more paper.

pants n. clothing
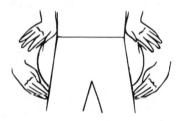
This is a pair of pants.
This is a pair of underpants.

paper v.
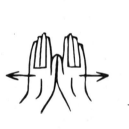
He will paper the wall.
papers   papered   papering

pantyhose n. clothing
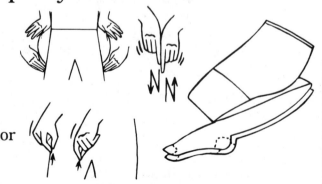
She bought a pair of pantyhose.

paperclip n.

This is a paperclip.
paperclip   paperclips

park 335

paper cutter n.

She's using a paper cutter.
paper cutter   paper cutters

pardon v.

Pardon me. Excuse me.
Please forgive me.

parachute n.
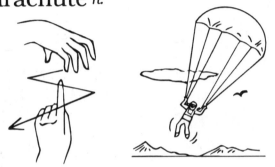
The parachute came down slowly.
parachute   parachutes

parent n. mother or father
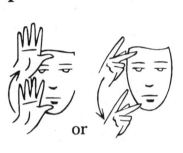
or
The children love their parents.
parent   parents

parade v.

or
We will parade around the room.
We'll march around the room.

park n.

or *
They are playing in the park.
park   parks

parakeet n. bird

The parakeet has a sharp beak.
parakeet   parakeets

park v.
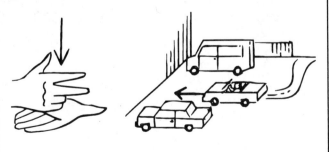
I park here every day.
parks   parked   parking

336 parking lot

parking lot n.

The parking lot is full.
parking lot   parking lots

part n.
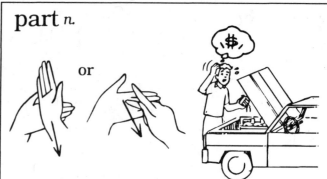
He needs a new part for his car.
part   parts

parrot n. bird

Robinson Crusoe had a pet parrot.
parrot   parrots

part v.
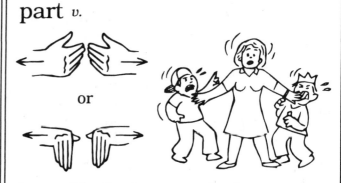
She had to part the boys.
She had to separate them.

part n.

She cut the pie into six parts.
She cut it into six pieces.

partner n.

They are partners.
They each own part of the business.

part n.

Part of the candy is missing.
Some of it is missing.

party n.
We had fun at the party.
party   parties

party n.

The hunting party walked slowly.
The group of hunters walked slowly.

pass v.

The car will pass the truck.
It will go by the truck.

pass v.

Please pass me the butter.
Please hand me the butter.

pass v.

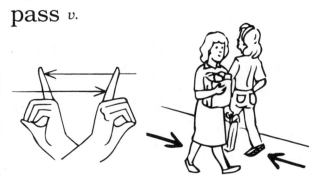

We often pass each other in the hall.
We often go by each other in the hall.

pass v.

I knew I would pass the test.
I knew I would get a good grade.

pass away v.

When did her husband pass away?
When did he die?

pass v.

The storm will pass soon.
It will end soon.

pass out v.

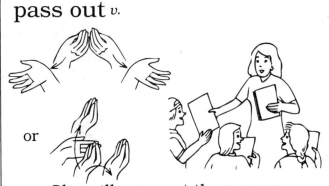

or

She will pass out the papers.
She'll distribute the papers.

338 pass out

pass out v. informal

Why did the woman pass out?
Why did she faint?

past prep.

It's half past three.
It's 30 minutes after three.

passenger n.

The man is the driver.
The woman is a passenger.

paste n.

The bottle of paste is on the table.

past n.

In the past, ships used sails.
Long ago, they used sails.

paste v.

I paste my pictures in my album.
pastes   pasted   pasting

past prep.

Tijuana is just past the border.
It is just across the border.

pastry n. food

She selected a pastry.
pastry   pastries

paw 339

pat v.
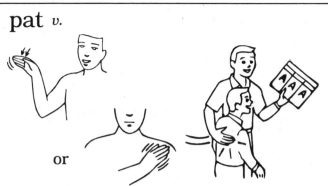
or

I had to pat my son on the back.
pats   patted   patting

patrol v.
Guards patrol the entrance.
They guard the entrance.

path n.
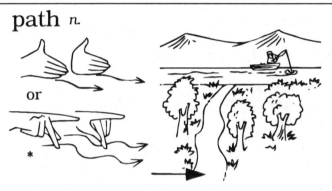
or
*

The path leads to the river.
path   paths

pattern n.

*

She pinned the pattern to the cloth.
pattern   patterns

patient adj.

The woman is very patient.
more patient   most patient

pavement n.

*

They are painting lines on the pavement.

patient n.
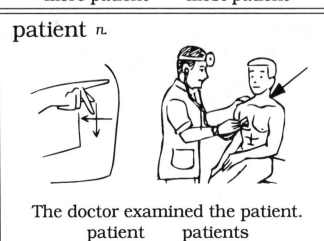

The doctor examined the patient.
patient   patients

paw n. body part

or
or
*

The cat is licking its paw.
paw   paws

340 pay

pay *v.*

The woman will pay for the cake.
pays   paid   paying

peace *n.*

The war ended and the country is at peace.

pay attention *v.*

Two students always pay attention.
One does not pay attention.

peach *n. fruit*

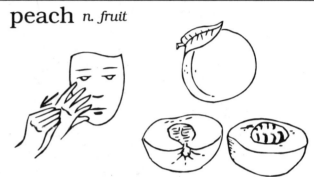

The peach is sweet and juicy.
peach   peaches

pea *n. vegetable*

or

I will cook some peas for dinner.
pea   peas

peacock *n. bird*

or

Peacocks have beautiful feathers.
peacock   peacocks/peacock

peace *n. quiet*

or

If you want peace in this family,
you must keep that dog outside.

peak *n. mountaintop*

The peak was covered with snow.
peak   peaks

pen 341

peanut *n. food*

He likes peanuts.
peanut   peanuts

pedal *v.*

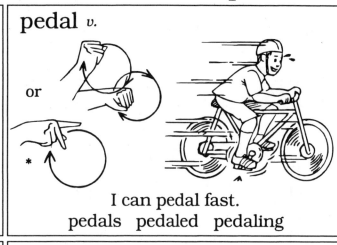

I can pedal fast.
pedals pedaled pedaling

peanut butter *n. food*

She is spreading the peanut butter.

peek *v.*

I will peek out the window.
peeks peeked peeking

pear *n. fruit*

The pear is sweet and juicy.
pear   pears

peel *v.*

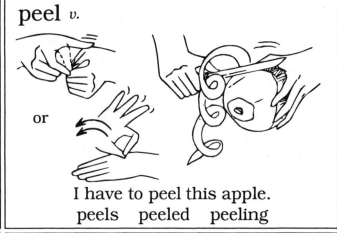

I have to peel this apple.
peels peeled peeling

pedal *n.*

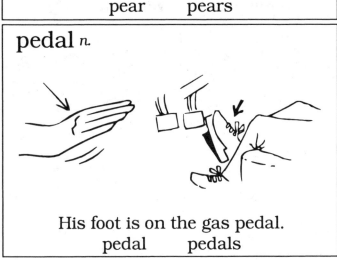

His foot is on the gas pedal.
pedal   pedals

pen *n.*

The pig is in a pen.
pen   pens

pen n.

He is writing with a pen.

penguin n. animal

The penguin is black and white.
penguin   penguins

penalty n. fine

The parking penalty is $50.00.
penalty   penalties

penny n. coin: 1 cent

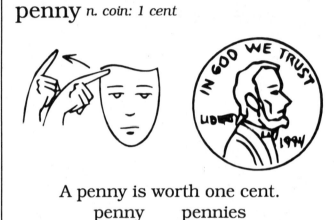

A penny is worth one cent.
penny   pennies

pencil n.

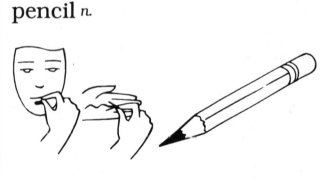

The pencil has a sharp point.
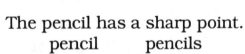
pencil   pencils

people n.

Many people were at the party.

pencil sharpener n.

They are using pencil sharpeners.
pencil sharpener   pencil sharpeners

pepper n. spice

He put pepper on his eggs.

permit 343

percent *adj.* per cent

The bank pays 8 <u>percent</u> interest.
The bank pays 8<u>%</u> interest.

period *n.*
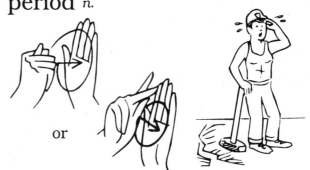
He rested for a short <u>period</u>.
He rested for a short <u>time</u>.

perfect *adj.*

He got a perfect score.
He didn't make any errors.

period *n. punctuation mark*

The sentence must end with a period.
period   periods

perfume *n.*

The woman likes this perfume.
perfume   perfumes

permission *n.*

Mother gave him <u>permission</u> to go.
She gave her <u>consent</u>.

perhaps *adv.*
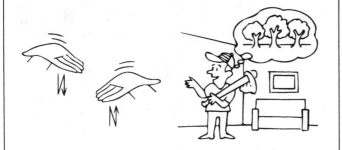
<u>Perhaps</u> I left my ball in the park.
<u>Maybe</u> I left it in the park.

permit *n.*
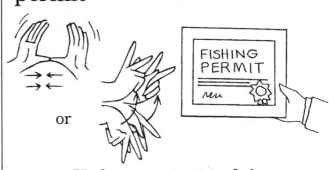
He has a permit to fish.
permit   permits

344 permit

permit v.

The sign does not permit hunting here.
It doesn't allow that.

perspire v.
I perspire in hot weather.
I sweat in hot weather.

person n.
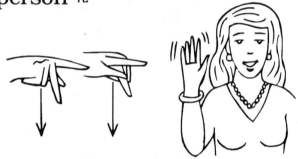
She is a very nice person.
She's a nice individual.

pet n.
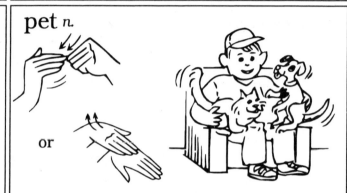
The boy has two pets.
pet   pets

personal adj.

or
This is a personal letter.
It contains private information.

pet n.

or
He is the teacher's pet.
He's her favorite.

personality n.
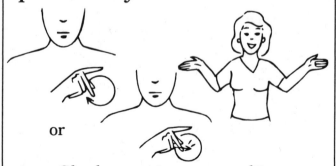
or
She has a nice personality.
She's always friendly and pleasant.

pet v.
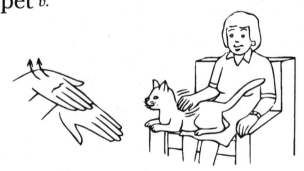
I often pet the cat.
pets   petted   petting

pick 345

pet v. informal

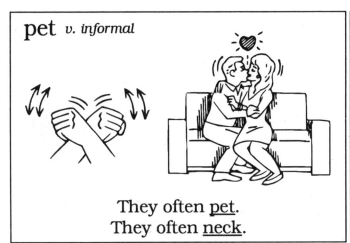

They often pet.
They often neck.

photograph n. picture, photo

He took some photographs.
photograph photographs

phone n.

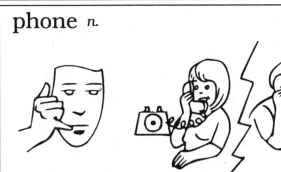

They are talking on the phone.
They're talking on the telephone.

physical n.

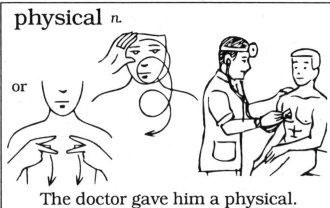

The doctor gave him a physical.
The doctor examined his body.

phonograph n.

He listened to the phonograph.
He listened to the record player.

piano n. musical instrument

She is playing the piano.
piano pianos

phony adj. informal: phoney

That is a phony gold brick.
That's a fake gold brick.

pick n. tool

The man is using a pick.
pick picks

346 pick

pick *v.*

He must pick a dessert.
He must choose a dessert.

pick out *v.*

Did the woman pick out a dress?
Did she select one?

pick *v.*

I always pick these flowers.
picks   picked   picking

pick up *v.*

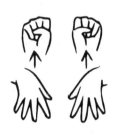

I will pick up the dog.
I'll lift the dog.

pick *v.*

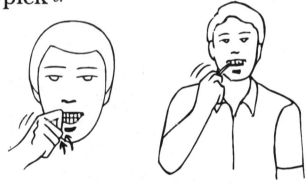

I must pick my teeth.

pickle *n. food*

The pickle is sour.
pickle   pickles

pick on *v. pester*

Why does he always pick on that girl?
Why does he always bother her?

pickpocket *n.*

The pickpocket stole his wallet.
pickpocket   pickpockets

pig 347

pickup n. truck

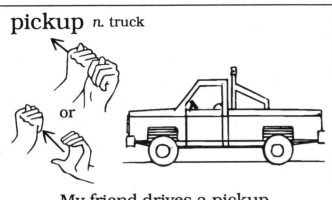

My friend drives a pickup.
pickup   pickups

piece n.

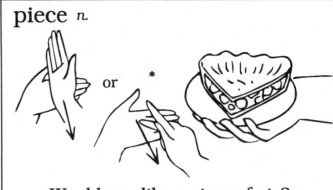

Would you like a piece of pie?
Would you like some pie?

picnic n.

We had a picnic in the park.
picnic   picnics

pier n.

He tied the boat to the pier.
pier   piers

picture n.

We hung a picture on the wall.
picture   pictures

pierce v.

She saw the arrow pierce the door.
She saw it come through the door.

pie n. food

She is cutting the pie.
pie   pies

pig n. animal

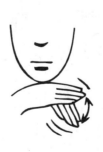

The pig is in the pen.
pig   pigs

348 piggy bank

piggy bank n.

He put money in his piggy bank.
piggy bank   piggy banks

Pilgrim n.
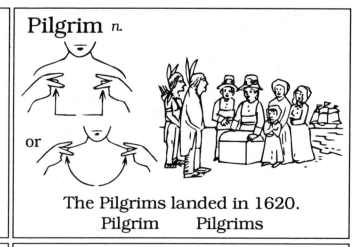
The Pilgrims landed in 1620.
Pilgrim   Pilgrims

pigtail n.
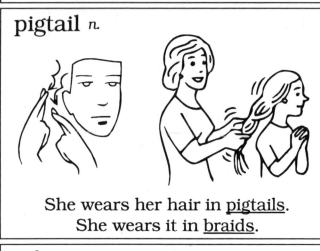
She wears her hair in pigtails.
She wears it in braids.

pill n. tablet
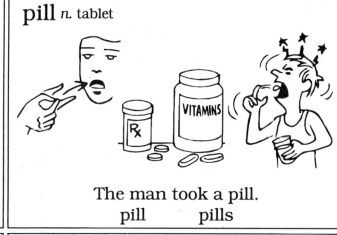
The man took a pill.
pill   pills

pile n.
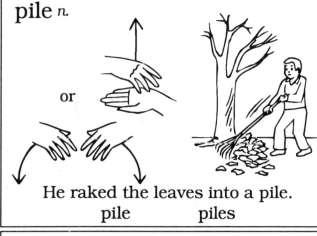
He raked the leaves into a pile.
pile   piles

pillow n.
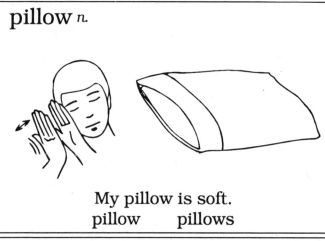
My pillow is soft.
pillow   pillows

pile v.
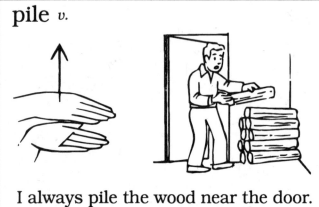
I always pile the wood near the door.
piles   piled   piling

pilot n. aviator
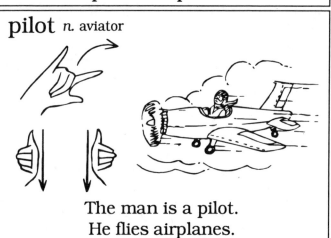
The man is a pilot.
He flies airplanes.

pint 349

pin n.

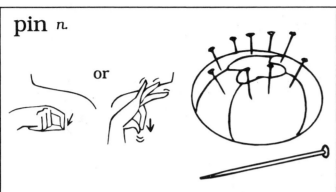

The pin has a sharp point.
pin   pins

pineapple n. fruit

Pineapples grow in Hawaii.
pineapple   pineapples

pin n. brooch

She wore a pretty pin.

Ping-Pong n. game

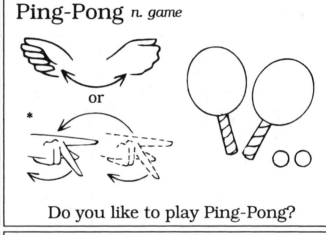

Do you like to play Ping-Pong?

pinch v.

Why did you pinch my cheek?
pinches   pinched   pinching

pink adj. color

She wore a pink dress.

pine n. tree

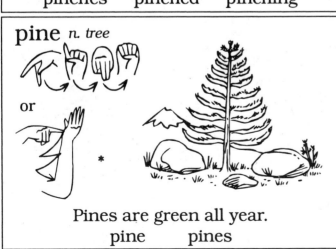

Pines are green all year.
pine   pines

pint n.

One pint equals two cups.
pint   pints

350 pipe

pipe n.

The plumber is fixing the pipe.
pipe   pipes

pitcher n.

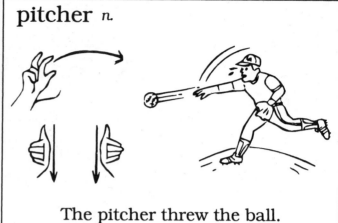

The pitcher threw the ball.

pipe n.

The man is smoking a pipe.

pitchfork n. tool

The farmer is using a pitchfork.
pitchfork   pitchforks

pirate n.

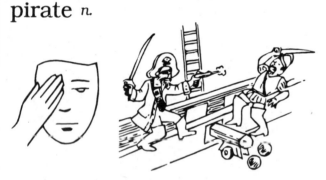

Pirates attack ships and rob them.
pirate   pirates

pity n.

She felt pity for the poor man.
She felt sorry for him.

pitcher n. container

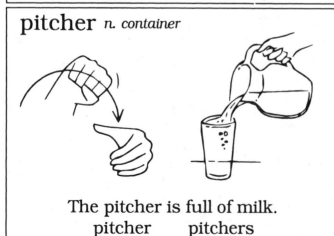

The pitcher is full of milk.
pitcher   pitchers

pizza n. food

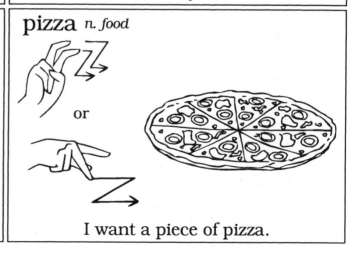

I want a piece of pizza.

plan 351

place n.

The girl found a place to hide.
place places

plain adj.

She likes the plain dress.
She likes the simple dress.

place n.
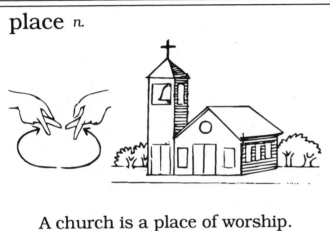
A church is a place of worship.

plan n.

The rain spoiled our plans.
plan plans

place v.

I usually place my hat on this shelf.
I usually put my hat on this shelf.

plan n.

He drew plans for the house.

plain adj. clear

It's plain that he broke the window.
It's obvious that he broke it.

plan v.

They plan to take a trip.
plans planned planning

352 plane

plane n. airplane

They are boarding the plane.
plane   planes

plastic n.
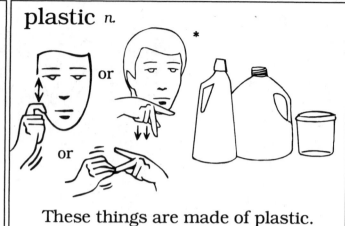
These things are made of plastic.

planet n.
 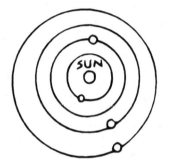
The planets move around the sun.
planet   planets

plate n. dish

She put the plate on the table.
plate   plates

plant n.

The plant is beautiful.
plant   plants

platter n.

The turkey is on the platter.
platter   platters

plant v.

He will plant a tree.
plants   planted   planting

play n.

We enjoyed the play.
play   plays

pliers 353

play v.

We often play in the park.
plays played playing

please adv.

Please take the dog outside.

player n.
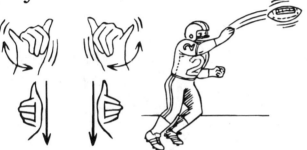
The player threw the ball.
player players

please v. satisfy

or
Nothing will please her.
pleases pleased pleasing

playground n.

The children are at the playground.
playground playgrounds

plenty adj.

The woman has plenty of money.
She has enough money.

pleasant adj.

She is a pleasant person.
She's a friendly person.

pliers n. tool
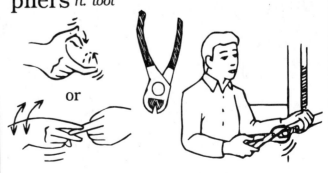
or
He's using a pair of pliers.

354 plow

plow v.

The farmer must plow the field.
plows plowed plowing

plumber n. worker

The plumber is fixing the sink.
plumber plumbers

plug n.
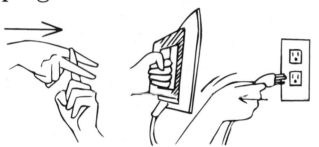
She pulled out the plug.
plug plugs

plunge v.

The boy plunged into the pool.
He jumped into the pool.

plug n.
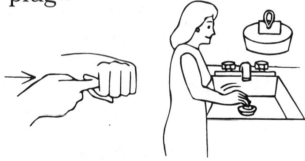
She put in the plug.
She put in the stopper.

plural n.

"Men" is the pural of man.
"Men" means more than one man.

plum n. fruit
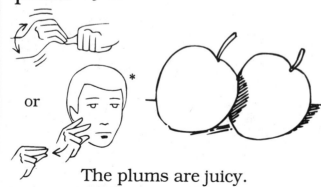
The plums are juicy.
plum plums

plus prep.

1 plus 1 equals 2.
1 added to 1 equals 2.

pole 355

pocket n.
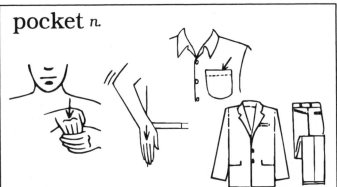
The shirt and suit have pockets.
pocket   pockets

poison n.

Keep poison away from children.
poison   poisons

pocketbook n.
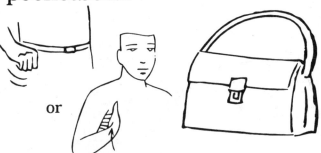
Her pocketbook is made of leather.
Her purse is made of leather.

poke v.

Why did she poke him in the ribs?
Why did she jab him in the ribs?

point n.
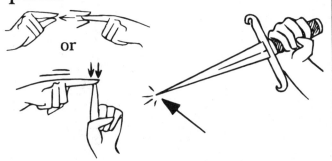
The point of the dagger is sharp.
The tip of the dagger is sharp.

Poland n. country

Poland is a country in Europe.

point v.

Did the man point to the dog?
points   pointed   pointing

pole n.
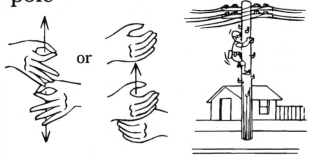
He is climbing the pole.
pole   poles

356 police

police n.

The woman called the police.

polite adj.

The boy is polite.
He has good manners.

policeman n. worker
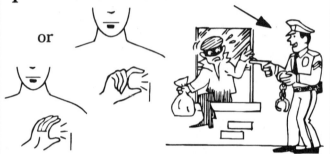
The policeman caught the burglar.
policeman   policemen

politics n.

He is involved in politics.

polish v.

I must polish these shoes.
polishes   polished   polishing

pond n.

The boy jumped into the pond.
pond   ponds

polish v.
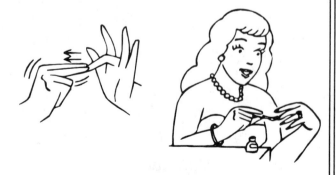
I polish my nails every week.

pony n. animal

The boy is riding a pony.
pony   ponies

pool n.

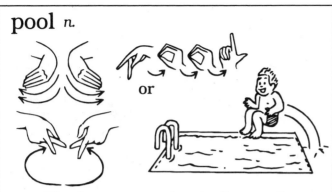

The boy jumped into the pool.
pool   pools

pool n. game

They are playing pool.

pool table n.

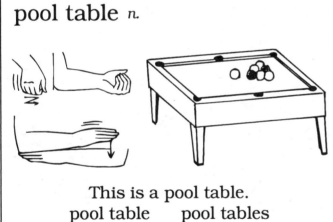

This is a pool table.
pool table   pool tables

poor adj.

The man is very poor.
He is very needy.

poor adj.

The poor girl is very sad.

poor adj.

He received poor grades.

pop n. beverage

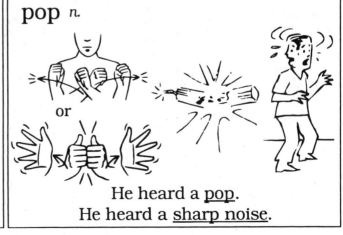

He drank some pop.

pop n.

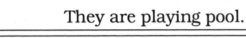

He heard a pop.
He heard a sharp noise.

358 pop

pop v.
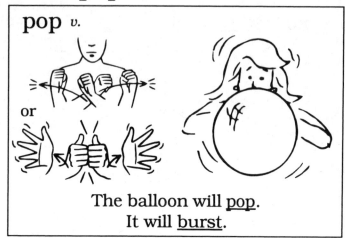
The balloon will pop.
It will burst.

popular adj.

She is very popular.
Everybody likes her.

pop up v.

Did the toast pop up?

porch n.
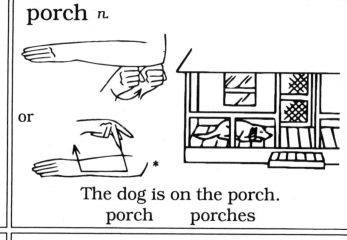
The dog is on the porch.
porch   porches

popcorn n. food

He bought a bag of popcorn.

porcupine n. animal
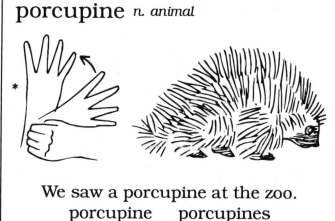
We saw a porcupine at the zoo.
porcupine   porcupines

popsicle n. food

She is eating a popsicle.
popsicle   popsicles

pork n. meat

Pork comes from pigs.

porpoise n.

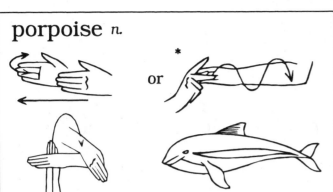

A porpoise is smaller than a whale.
porpoise   porpoises/porpoise

possible adj.

It is possible he will fall.
Maybe he'll fall.

port n.

The ship is in port.
It's in the harbor.

possible adj.

It is possible to improve your grades. You can improve your grades.

positive adj.

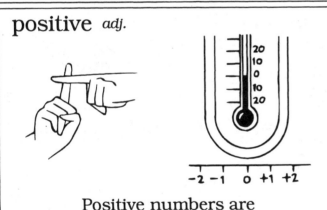

Positive numbers are greater than zero.

post n. pole

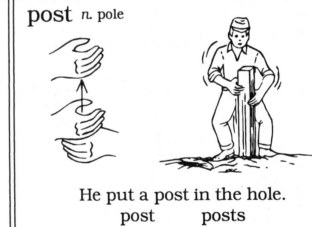

He put a post in the hole.
post   posts

positive adj.

I am positive that is the man.
I'm sure that's the man.

postcard n.

He bought some postcards.
postcard   postcards

360   postman

postman n. mailman

The postman delivers the mail.
postman   postmen

potato n. vegetable

She is peeling a potato.
potato   potatoes

post office n.

He went to the post office.
post office   post offices

potato chip n. food

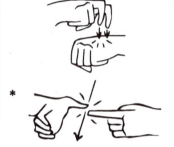 

He bought a bag of potato chips.
potato chip   potato chips

postpone v. put off, delay

We had to postpone our game.
We will play golf some other time.

potholder n.

The potholder protects her hand.
potholder   potholders

pot n. container

She made a pot of soup.
pot   pots

pound n.

There are 16 ounces in one pound.
pound   pounds

power 361

pound v.	powder n.
 You must pound a nail with a hammer. You must hit a nail with a hammer.	She put powder on her face.

pound v.	powder n.
Why did he pound on the door? Why did he bang on it?	She put talcum powder on the baby.

pour v.	power n. strength
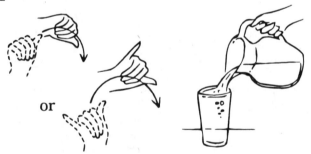 I will pour milk into the glass. pours poured pouring	 He pushed with all his power. He pushed with all his might.

poverty n.	power n.
 He lives in poverty. He is very poor.	 Police have the power to make arrests. They have that authority.

362 power

power *n.*
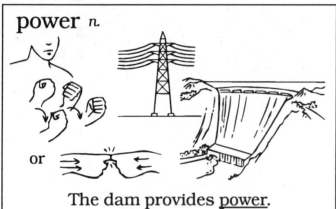
or
The dam provides power.
The dam provides energy.

prefer *v.*

or
I prefer apples to oranges.
I like apples better than oranges.

practice *v.*

You must practice for an hour.
practices   practiced   practicing

pregnant *adj.*
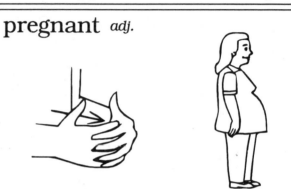
The woman is pregnant.
She will have a baby.

pray *v.*

I pray every day.
prays   prayed   praying

prejudice *n.*

Her prejudice is obvious.
prejudice   prejudices

predict *v.*

Did the weatherman predict rain?
Did he forcast rain?

prepare *v.*

or
She will prepare dinner.
She'll make dinner.

press 363

preposition n.
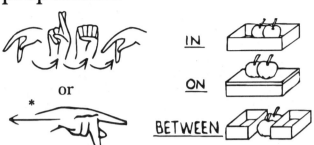
These words are prepositions.
preposition   prepositions

present n. gift

He gave me a present.
present   presents

prescription n.
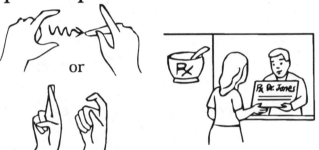
He will fill the prescription.
prescription   prescriptions

present v.

They will present him with an award.
They'll give him an award.

present adj.

One student is not present.
One student is not in class.

president n.

Washington was our first president.
president   presidents

present n.

At present, ships use engines.
Now, they use engines.

press v.

Did she press the button?
Did she push the button?

364 press

press v.

He will press the pants.
presses   pressed   pressing

pretend v.
or
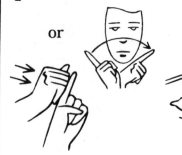
I often pretend to be asleep.
I'm not really asleep.

press v.
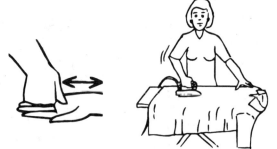
I have to press this dress.
I have to iron it.

pretty adj.

She is a pretty woman.
She's a beautiful woman.

pressure n. mental strain
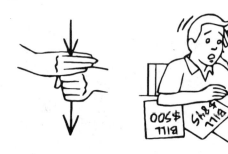
He is under a lot of pressure.
He's under a lot of stress.

pretzel n. food
or
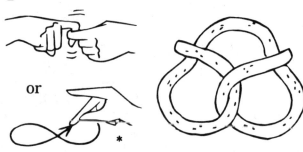
Do you like pretzels?
pretzel   pretzels

pretend v.
or
or
*

We can pretend to be pirates.
pretends   pretended   pretending

prevent v.

I hope I can prevent an accident.
I hope I can avoid one.

principal 365

price n. cost
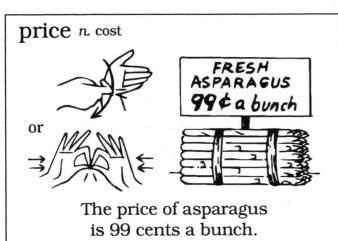
The price of asparagus is 99 cents a bunch.

primary adj.

He is in primary school.

pride n.

He takes pride in his work. It gives him pleasure and satisfaction.

prince n. royal male

The prince was the king's son.
prince   princes

priest n.
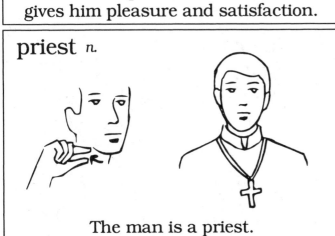
The man is a priest.
priest   priests

princess n. royal female

The king's daughter is a princess.
princess   princesses

primary adj.

Drinking is his <u>primary</u> problem.
Drinking is his <u>main</u> problem.

principal adj. chief

Cost is our <u>principal</u> concern.
Cost is our <u>most important</u> concern.

366 principal

principal *n. worker*

She is the principal of the school.
She's in charge of it.

prior *adj.*

He ate <u>prior to</u> the meeting.
He ate <u>before</u> the meeting.

print *v.*

I must print 1,000 copies.
prints   printed   printing

prison *n. jail, penitentiary*

or

The man is in prison.
prison   prisons

printer *n. worker*

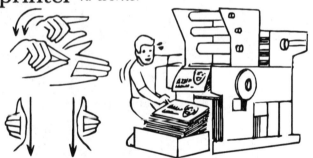

He works as a printer.
printer   printers

prisoner *n.*

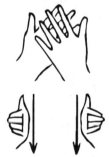 

The officer put handcuffs
on the prisoner.

printer *n.*

or

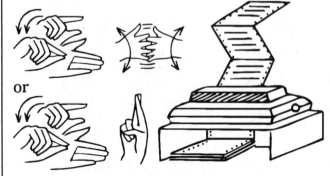

We bought a new printer.

private *adj.*

This letter is private.
You may not read it.

produce 367

prize n.

He won a prize.
prize   prizes

produce n.

He sells produce.
He sells fruits and vegetables.

probably adv.
or

The balloon will probably pop.
It will likely pop.

produce v.
or

They produce thousands of cars here.
They make thousands of them here.

problem n.

The woman has many problems.
She has many difficulties.

produce v.
or

Does the tree produce good apples?
Does it bear good apples?

problem n.
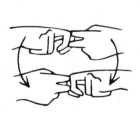

A
2 + 2 = 4
5 − 3 = 2
2 × 4 = 8
8 ÷ 2 = 4

The problems were easy.
problem   problems

produce v.
or
or

What did Edison's work produce?

368 produce

produce *v.*

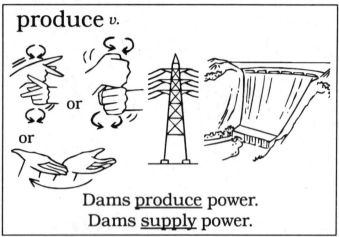

Dams produce power.
Dams supply power.

program *n.*

He looked at the program.
program   programs

produce *v.*

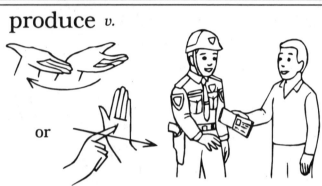

I had to produce my driver's license.
I took it out of my pocket.

program *n.*

We enjoyed the program.
We enjoyed the performance.

profession *n.*

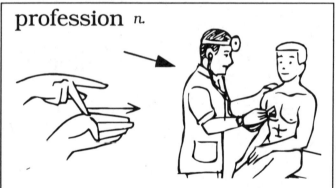

He is a doctor by profession.
He earns his living as a doctor.

prohibit *v.* forbid

Does the sign prohibit hunting?
prohibits   prohibited   prohibiting

profit *n.*

The man made a profit.
He took in more than he paid out.

projector *n.*

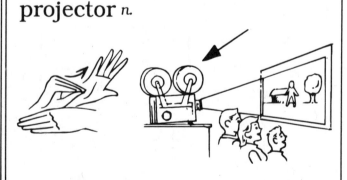

They have a movie projector.
projector   projectors

proud 369

promise *v.*

I promise to buy you a dog.
promises   promised   promising

not proper *adj.* improper

His behavior is not <u>proper</u>.
His behavior is not <u>right</u>.

promote *v.*

The army will promote the private - advance him to a higher rank.

protect *v.*

Don't worry. I will protect you.
protects   protected   protecting

pronoun *n.*

The underlined words are pronouns.
pronoun   pronouns

protest *v.*

I must <u>protest</u> the building plan.
I must <u>object to</u> it.

proof *n.*

He must show <u>proof</u> of citizenship.
He must show <u>evidence</u> of citizenship.

proud *adj.*

He is proud of his grades.
He's pleased with them.

370 prove

prove v.

I can prove where I was born.
I can show my birth certificate.

public adj.

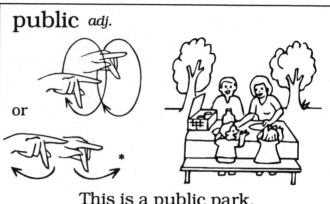

This is a public park.
Anyone may use it.

prove v.

Did he prove that he was innocent?
proves proved proving proved/proven

pudding n. food

She made some chocolate pudding.

prune n. food

Prunes are dried plums.
prune   prunes

puddle n.

He saw a puddle.
He saw a small pool of water.

pry v.

He had to pry the lid off.
He had to force the lid off.

pull v.

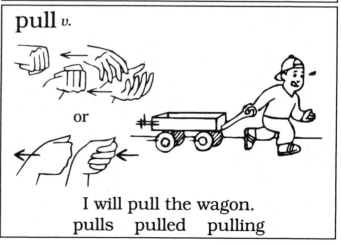

I will pull the wagon.
pulls   pulled   pulling

punctuate 371

pull v.

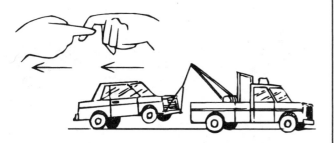
The truck will <u>pull</u> the car.
It will <u>tow</u> the car.

pumpkin n. fruit
The pumpkin is orange.
pumpkin   pumpkins

pulse n.
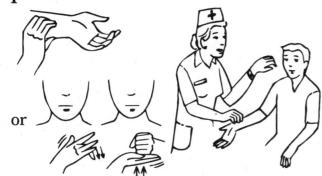
or
The nurse is taking his pulse.

punch n. beverage

or
She made some punch.

pump n.

He is using a pump.
pump   pumps

punch v.
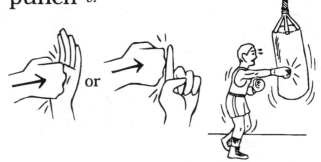
or
I punch the bag every day.
punches   punched   punching

pump v.

I must pump some water.
pumps   pumped   pumping

punctuate v.

You must punctuate your sentences.
You must use periods and commas.

372 punish

punish v.

Why did she punish her child?
punishes   punished   punishing

purchase v.

They will purchase a car.
They'll buy one.

pupil n. body part

The pupil is black.
pupil   pupils

pure adj.

He said the brick was pure gold -
not mixed with anything else.

pupil n.
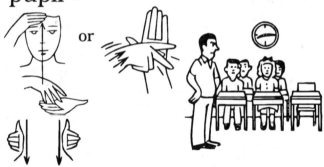
One pupil is absent.
One student is absent.

purple adj. color

The grapes are purple.

puppy n. young dog

The puppy is cute.
puppy   puppies

purpose n.

His purpose is to get a cookie.
His intention is to get one.

put down 373

on **purpose** deliberately

She broke the doll on purpose.
She meant to break it.

put *v.* set

I'll put the cookies on the table.
puts   put   putting

purse *n.* handbag

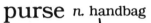

or

The purse is made of leather.
purse   purses

put *v.*

I will put the dish in the cupboard.
I'll place it in the cupboard.

push *v.*

He had to push the car.
pushes   pushed   pushing

put *v.*

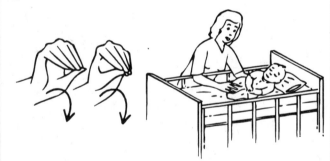

When did she put the baby to bed?

push *v.*

or

I must push through the crowd.
I must force my way through.

put down *v.*

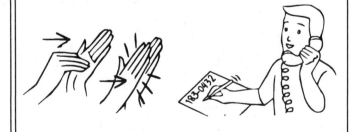

He will put down the numbers.
He'll write down the numbers.

374 put down

put down *v.*

I had to put down $300.00. I had to make a down payment of $300.00.

put out *v.*
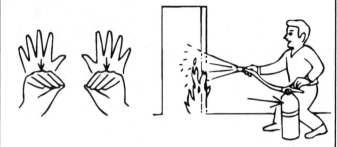
He will put out the fire. He'll extinguish it.

put off *v.*

We must put off our game. We must postpone it.

putty *n.*

He put putty in the hole.

put on *v.*
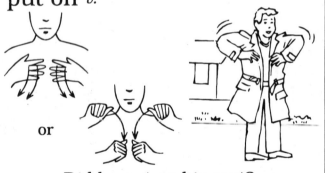
or
Did he put on his coat?
Did he put his coat on?

puzzle *n.*

He has a new puzzle.
puzzle   puzzles

put on *v.*

I always put on weight.
I always gain weight.

pyramids *n.*

The pyramids are in Egypt.
pyramid   pyramids

Q q

quarrel *v.*  They always <u>quarrel</u> about the dog. They always <u>argue</u> about the dog.	**quarter after** 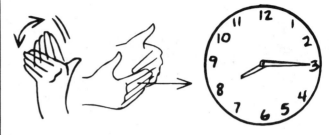 It is <u>quarter after</u> eight. It is <u>fifteen minutes after</u> eight.
quart *n.*  Four cups equal one quart. quart quarts	**quarter to** 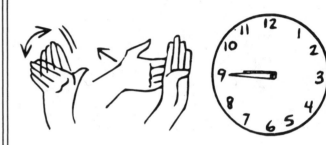 It is <u>quarter to</u> nine. It is <u>15 minutes</u> to nine.
quarter *n. coin: 25 cents*   He has a quarter. quarter quarters	**queen** *n. female ruler*   The queen is wearing a crown. queen queens
quarter *n.*  He ate a <u>quarter</u> of the pie. He ate a <u>fourth</u> of the pie.	**question** *n.*  The boy answered the question. question questions

376 question

question *v.* interrogate

The lawyer will question the witness.
questions   questioned   questioning

quiet *adj.*

It was very quiet outside.
There was no noise outside.

question mark *n.*

He forgot the question mark.
question mark   question marks

quiet *adj.*

He is a quiet boy.
He doesn't talk very much.

quick *adj.*

or

The driver made a quick stop.
He made a sudden stop.

quit *v.*

You must quit smoking.
You must stop smoking.

quickly *adv.*

The boy acted quickly.
He acted very fast.

quit *v.*

Why did he quit his job?
Why did he leave his job?

R r

rabbi *n.*

She spoke to the rabbi.
rabbi   rabbis

race *v.*

They will race each other.
races   raced   racing

rabbit *n. animal*

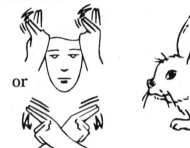 

The rabbit has long ears.
rabbit   rabbits

rack *n.*

He hung his hat on the rack.
rack   racks

raccoon *n. animal*

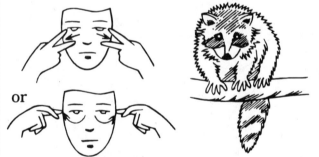

The raccoon has a bushy tail.
raccoon   raccoons

radio *n.*

He's listening to the radio.
radio   radios

race *n.*

Bob won the race.
race   races

radish *n. vegetable*

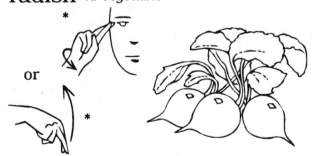

Radishes are red outside
and white on the inside.

377

378 raft

raft n.
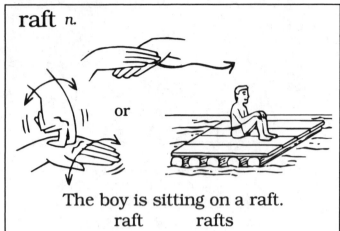
The boy is sitting on a raft.
raft   rafts

rain n.

The rain spoiled their picnic.

rag n.

He used a rag to wipe the car.
He used an old piece of cloth.

rain v.

It may rain all day.
rains   rained   raining

rail n.
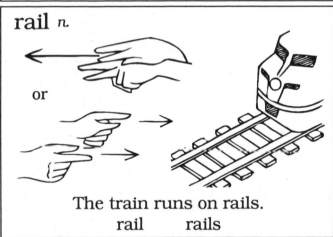
The train runs on rails.
rail   rails

rainbow n.
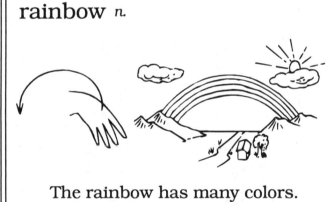
The rainbow has many colors.
rainbow   rainbows

railroad n.
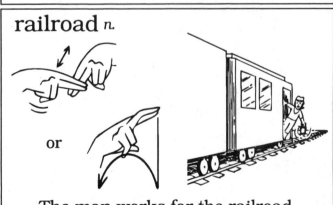
The man works for the railroad.
railroad   railroads

raincoat n.

She is wearing a raincoat.
raincoat   raincoats

rake 379

rainy adj.

It is a rainy day.
rainier   rainiest

raise v.

Parents raise their children.
Parents bring up their children.

raise n.

He got a raise in pay.
He got an increase in pay.

raised v.

The boy was raised in England.
He grew up there.

raise v. lift

Why did he raise the hood?
raises   raised   raising

raisins n. food

Raisins are dried grapes.
raisin   raisins

raise v.

I raise corn and wheat.
I grow corn and wheat.

rake n. tool

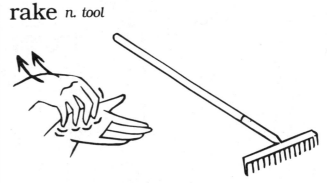

The rake has a long handle.
rake   rakes

380 rake

rake *v.*

I have to rake the leaves.
rakes   raked   raking

rapid *adj.*

He is a rapid worker.
He works very fast.

ran *pt. of* **run**

The boy ran to school.

rash *n.*
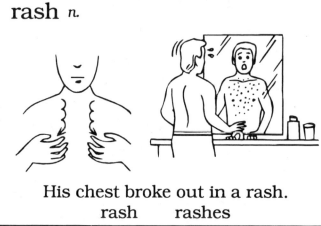
His chest broke out in a rash.
rash   rashes

ranch *n.*

They raise cattle on the ranch.
ranch   ranches

raspberry *n. fruit*
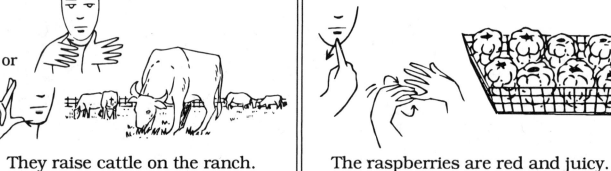
The raspberries are red and juicy.
raspberry   raspberries

rang *pt. of* **ring**

rat *n.*
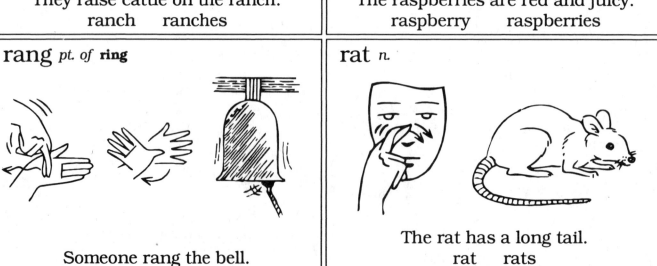
Someone rang the bell.

The rat has a long tail.
rat   rats

read 381

rather adv.

The boy would rather play baseball.
He'd prefer to do that.

razor n.
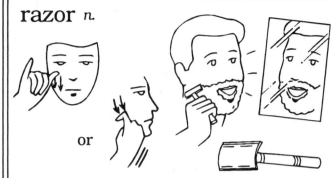
He shaves with a razor.
razor razors

rattle n. toy
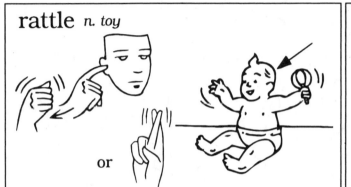
The baby is shaking the rattle.
rattle rattles

reach v.

He can't reach the cookies.
reaches reached reaching

rattlesnake n.

Rattlesnakes are poisonous.
rattlesnake rattlesnakes

reach v.

When did she reach home?
When did she arrive home?

raw adj.

The meat is raw.
It's not cooked.

read v.
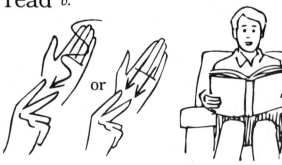
I often read in the evening.
reads read reading

382 ready

ready *adj.* prepared

The girl is ready for bed.
readier readiest

rear *adj.*

The children sat in the rear seat.
They sat in the back seat.

real *adj.* genuine

The man said the brick
was made of real gold.

reason *n.*

What is your reason for being late?
What caused you to be late?

realize *v.*

We didn't realize Father was home.
We weren't aware that he was home.

rebel *v.*

I always rebel when she
asks me to mow the lawn.

really *adv.* truly

The man said the brick was gold,
but I didn't really believe him.

recall *v.*

He can't recall the number.
He can't remember it.

record 383

receive v. get

I always receive several letters.
receives   received   receiving

reckless adj.

He drove in a <u>reckless</u> manner.
He drove in a <u>careless</u> manner.

recently adv.

They <u>recently</u> moved.
They moved <u>a short while ago</u>.

recognize v.

She can <u>recognize</u> the robber.
She can <u>identify</u> him.

recess n.

They took a recess at 10 o'clock.
recess   recesses

record n.

He played a record.
record   records

recipe n.

She looked at the recipe.
recipe   recipes

record v.

He must <u>record</u> the information.
He must <u>write down</u> the facts.

384 record player

record player n.

He has a record player.
He has a phonograph.

red adj. color
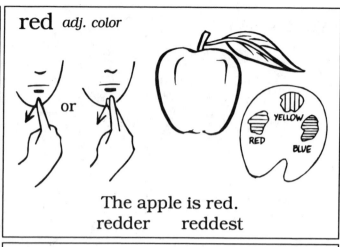
The apple is red.
redder   reddest

recover v.
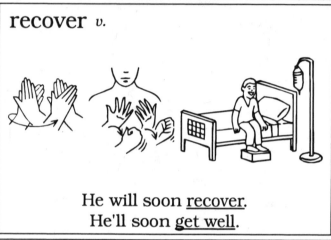
He will soon recover.
He'll soon get well.

reduce v.

Did the store reduce the price?
Did the store lower it?

recover v.

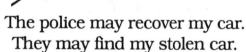
The police may recover my car.
They may find my stolen car.

refrigerator n.
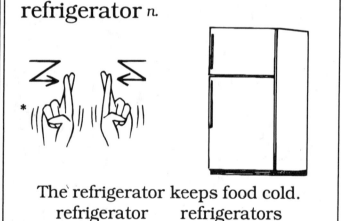
The refrigerator keeps food cold.
refrigerator   refrigerators

rectangle n. shape
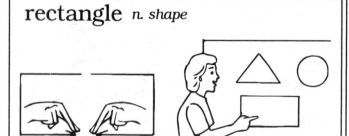
She drew a rectangle on the board.
rectangle   rectangles

refuse v.

I refuse to mow the lawn.
I will not mow it. I won't do it.

remain 385

register *v.*

They must register at the hotel.
registers registered registering

release *v.*

Did they release the prisoners?
Did they set them free?

regular *adj.*

I expect regular attendance.
I expect students to be here every day.

reliable *adj.*

He is a <u>reliable</u> person.
He's a <u>dependable</u> person.

reindeer *n. animal*
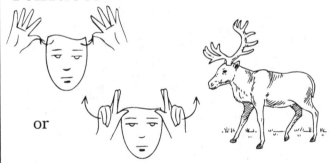
or
Reindeer have antlers.
reindeer   reindeer/reindeers

religion *n.*

What is your religion?
What faith do you belong to?

relax *v.*
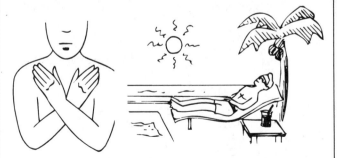
I will <u>relax</u> in the sun.
I'll <u>rest</u> in the sun.

remain *v.*
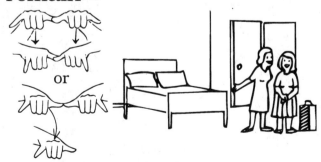
She will <u>remain</u> with us for a week.
She'll <u>stay</u> with us for a week.

386 remainder

remainder *n.*

She ate one donut and he ate <u>the remainder</u>. He ate <u>all the others</u>.

remove *v.*

He should <u>remove</u> the trash.
He should <u>get rid of</u> it.

remember *v.*

The man can't remember where he put his money.

remove *v.*

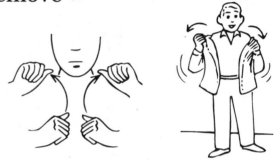

I will <u>remove</u> my coat.
I'll <u>take off</u> my coat.

remind *v.*

I had to remind mom about the cake.
reminds   reminded   reminding

rent *n.*

The rent is $500 a month.
It costs $500 a month to live here.

remove *v.*

He must remove the dirty dishes.
removes   removed   removing

rent *v.*

I will rent a small apartment.
rents   rented   renting

require 387

repair v.
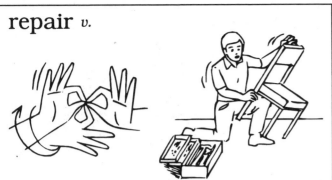
The man will repair the chair.
He'll fix it.

report v.

I report to work at 8 o'clock.
I show up at 8 o'clock.

reply v.

He could reply to the question.
He could answer it.

report card n.

He is proud of his report card.
report card   report cards

report n.

He wrote a report of the burglary.
He wrote an account of the burglary.

request n.

She made a request.
She asked him to do something.

report v.

She will report the accident.
She'll inform the police.

require v.

The plants require water.
They must have water.

388 rescue

rescue v.

The man had to rescue the girl.
He had to save her.

respond v.

Did the boy respond to the question?
Did he answer it?

reservation n.

She made hotel reservations.
reservation   reservations

responsible adj.
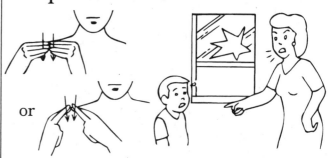
You are responsible for breaking the window. That is your fault.

reside v.

They reside in this house.
They live in it.

rest n.

She ate one donut and he ate the rest. He ate the remainder.

respect v.

We respect Edison's work.
We think highly of it.

rest v.
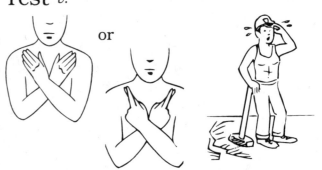
I must rest for a minute.
I have to relax for a minute.

reverse 389

restaurant n.

They had dinner at a restaurant.
restaurant   restaurants

return v.

Did she <u>return</u> from her trip?
Did she <u>come back</u> from her trip?

restless adj.

The boy is restless.
more restless   most restless

return v.
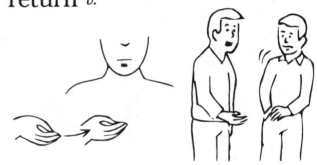
You must <u>return</u> my money.
You must <u>give back</u> my money.

rest room n.

The girls are in the rest room.
rest room   rest rooms

return address n.
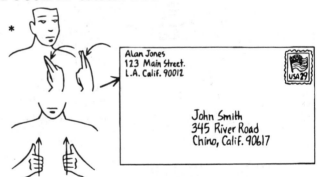
Don't forget the return address.

result n.

Illness can be the result of smoking.
Illness can be caused by smoking.

reverse n.

She put the car in reverse.
She wants to back up.

reward n.

The police offered a reward.
reward   rewards

rich adj. wealthy

She is a rich woman.
She has a lot of money.

rhinoceros n. animal

or

The rhinoceros has thick skin.
rhinoceros   rhinoceros/rhinoceroses

ridden pp. of ride

She has never ridden on a motorcycle.

ribbon n.
*

or

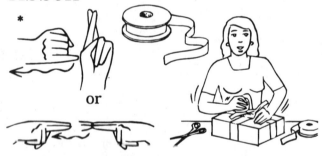

She tied the gift with ribbon.
ribbon   ribbons

ride n.

or

The family took a ride in the car.
ride   rides

rice n. grain

or

The bowl is full of rice.

ride n.

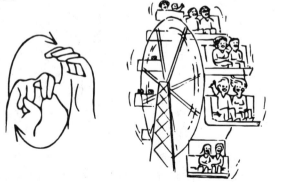

We took a ride on the Ferris wheel.

right 391

ride v.
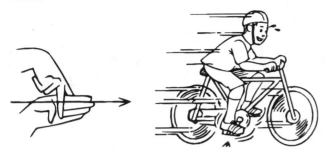
He likes to ride his bicycle.
rides   rode   riding   ridden

rifle n. weapon

The hunter has a rifle.
rifle   rifles

ride v.

I ride my horse every day..

right adj.
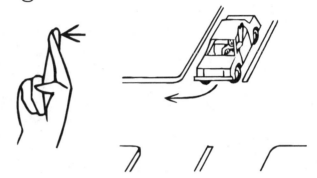
The car is making a right turn.

ridicule v.
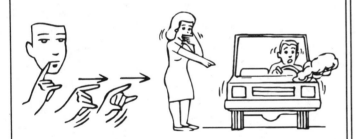
I always <u>ridicule</u> his car.
I always <u>make fun of</u> it.

right adj.

The answer is <u>right</u>.
It's <u>correct</u>.

ridiculous adj.

She wore a <u>ridiculous</u> hat.
She wore a <u>silly</u> hat.

right n. privilege

Citizens have a right to vote.

392 right away

right away *adv.*

I want you to leave right away.
I want you to leave immediately.

riot *n.*

The police controlled the riot.
They controlled the disturbance.

ring *n.*

She showed us her ring.
ring   rings

rip *v.*

Why did he rip the paper?
Why did he tear it?

ring *v.*

He must ring the doorbell.
rings   rang   ringing   rung

ripe *adj.*

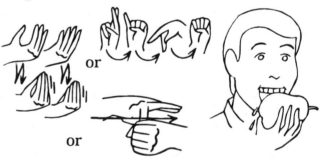

The pear is ripe.
It's ready to eat.

ring *v.*

Did the bell ring?

rise *v.* come up

The sun will soon rise.
rises   rose   rising   risen

roaster 393

rise *v.*

Please rise.
Please stand up.

road *n.*

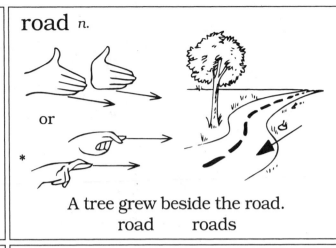

A tree grew beside the road.
road   roads

rise *v.*

I usually rise at 6:30.
I usually get up then.

roam *v.*

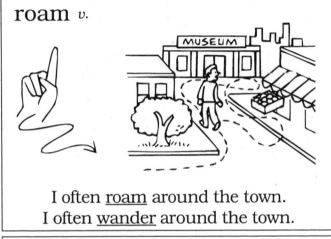

I often roam around the town.
I often wander around the town.

risen *pp. of* **rise**

The sun has risen.

roast *n. food*

The roast was delicious.
roast   roasts

river *n.*

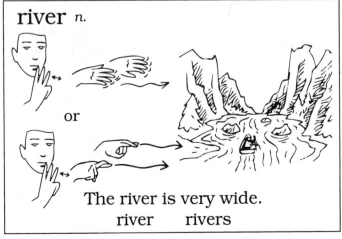

The river is very wide.
river   rivers

roaster *n.*

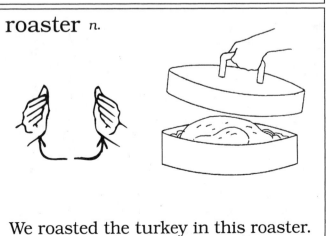

We roasted the turkey in this roaster.

394 robe

robe n. clothing
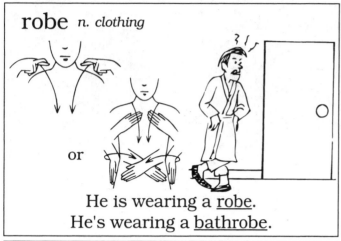
He is wearing a robe.
He's wearing a bathrobe.

rock n.

There are two rocks near the pond.
There are two stones there.

robin n. bird
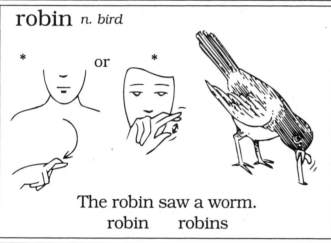
The robin saw a worm.
robin   robins

rock v.

Please don't rock the boat.
rocks   rocked   rocking

Robinson Crusoe

Have you read this book about Robinson Crusoe?

rock v.
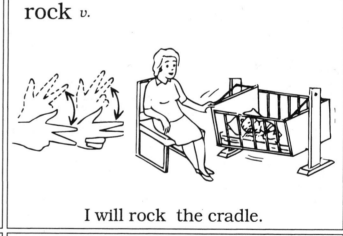
I will rock the cradle.

robot n.

The boy played with the robot.
robot   robots

rocket n.
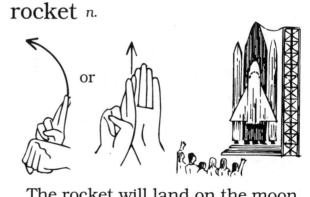
The rocket will land on the moon.
rocket   rockets

roller 395

rocking chair n. furniture

I sat in the rocking chair.
rocking chair   rocking chairs

rodeo n.

We enjoyed the rodeo.
rodeo   rodeos

rocking horse n. toy

The boy has a rocking horse.
rocking horse   rocking horses

roll n. food
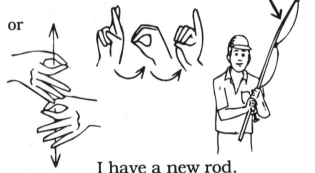
I made some rolls for dinner.
roll   rolls

rod n.
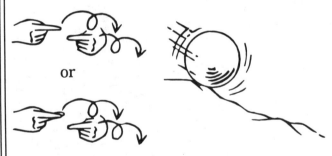
I have a new rod.
rod   rods

roll v.

The ball will roll down the hill.
rolls   rolled   rolling

rode pt. of ride

Yesterday, he rode the horse.

roller n.
She does her hair up in rollers.
roller   rollers

396 roller coaster

roller coaster n.

We rode the roller coaster.
roller coaster   roller coasters

roof n.
The antenna is on the roof.
roof   roofs/rooves

roller skate n. toy

He has a pair of roller skates.
roller skate   roller skates

room n.

The living room is the largest room in the house.

rolling pin n.

She is using a rolling pin.
rolling pin   rolling pins

roommate n.

They are roommates.
They share this room.

Rome n. city

We visited the ruins in Rome.

rooster n.

The rooster crowed at dawn.
rooster   roosters

row 397

root n.

The tree has long roots.
root   roots

rotten adj.

The fruit is rotten.
It's not fit to eat.

rope n.

or
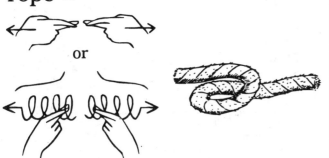
The rope is thick and strong.
rope   ropes

rough adj.
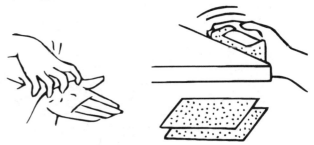
Sandpaper is rough.
Sandpaper is not smooth.

rose n. flower

The rose is red.
rose   roses

round adj.

The table is round.

rose pt. of rise
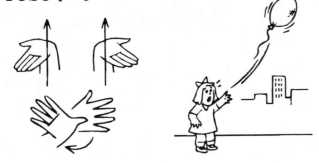
The balloon rose.
It went up.

row n.

The boy sat in the first row.
row   rows

398 row

row n.
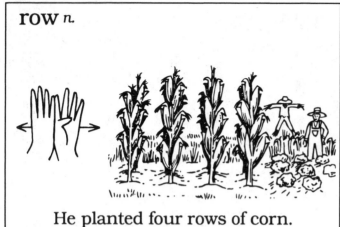
He planted four rows of corn.

rubber n.
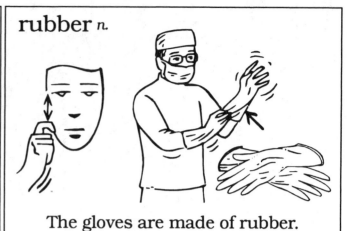
The gloves are made of rubber.

row v.

We must row faster.
rows   rowed   rowing

rubber band n.
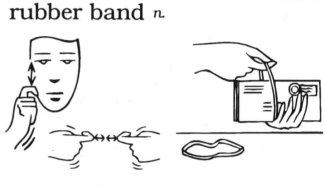
I put a rubber band around the letters.
rubber band   rubber bands

rowboat n.

The rowboat has two oars.
rowboat   rowboats

rude adj.
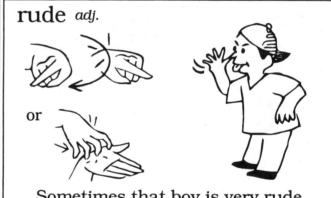
Sometimes that boy is very rude.
Sometimes he's not polite.

rub v.
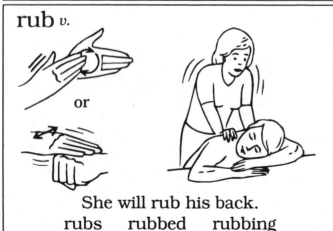
She will rub his back.
rubs   rubbed   rubbing

rug n.

We bought a new rug.
rug   rugs

run 399

ruin v.

Drought can ruin the crops.
Dry weather can destroy them.

run v.

The elevator will not run.
The elevator won't work.

rule n.

You must follow the rules.
    rule   rules

run v.

I run the business.
I manage it.

ruler n.
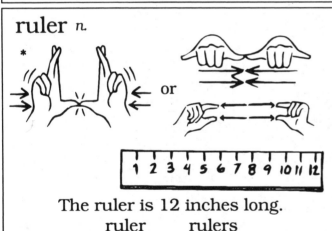
The ruler is 12 inches long.
    ruler   rulers

run v.
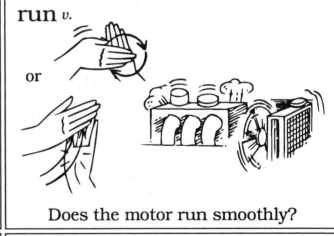
Does the motor run smoothly?

run v.

I always run to school.
  runs ran running

run v.
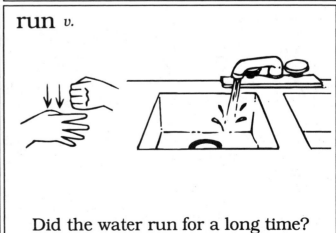
Did the water run for a long time?

400 run after

run after *v.* chase

The children always run after the ice-cream truck.

rung *pp. of* **ring**

The mailman has rung the doorbell.

run out of *v.*

Did he run out of milk?
Did he use up all the milk?

runway *n.*

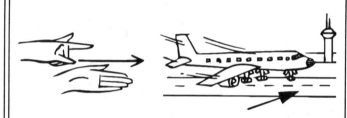

The plane will land on the runway.
runway   runways

run over *v.*

Why did the tub run over?
Why did it overflow?

rush *v.* hurry

I had to rush to catch my plane.
rushes   rushed   rushing

run over *v.*

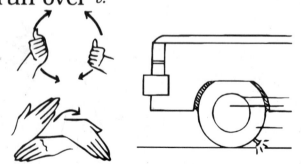

What did he run over?
What did he drive over?

Russia *n.* country

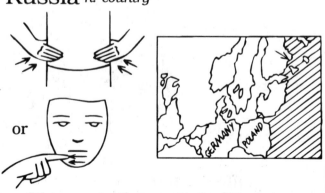

or

Moscow is the capital of Russia.

S s

sack *n.*

The sack is empty.
The bag is empty.

saddle *v.*

I will saddle my horse.
saddles　saddled　saddling

sack *n.*

She bought a sack of potatoes.
sack　sacks

saddle *v.*

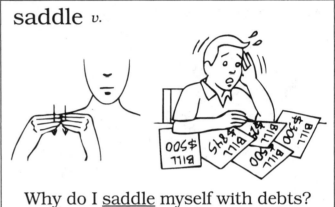

Why do I saddle myself with debts?
Why do I burden myself with them?

sad *adj.*

The young woman is sad.
She's unhappy.

safe *adj.*

It is not safe to skate on thin ice.
safer　safest

saddle *n.*

He bought a new saddle.
saddle　saddles

safety *n.*

He carried the girl to safety.
He carried her to a safe place.

402 safety pin

safety pin n.

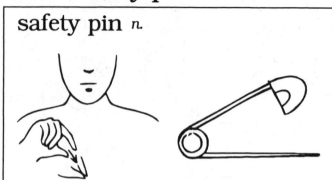

This is a safety pin.
safety pin   safety pins

sailor n. worker

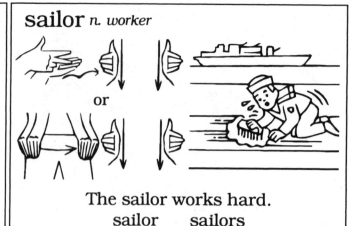

The sailor works hard.
sailor   sailors

said pt. of say

The man said it was his book.

Saint Patrick's Day n.

Saint Patrick's Day is March 17.

sail v.

I can sail the boat.
sails   sailed   sailing

salad n. food

I will make a salad.
salad   salads

sailboat n.

The sailboat has three sails.
sailboat   sailboats

salad dressing n. food

I need some salad dressing.
salad dressing   salad dressings

same 403

salary n. wage

His salary is small.
salary salaries

saltshaker n.

He is filling the saltshaker.
saltshaker saltshakers

sale n.

or
The store is having a sale.
sale sales

salute v.
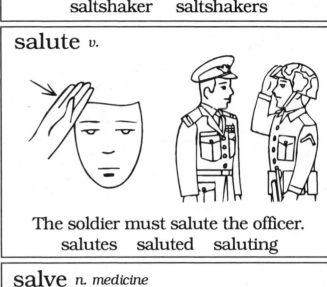
The soldier must salute the officer.
salutes saluted saluting

salesman n. worker

The salesman sells vacuum cleaners.
salesman salesmen

salve n. medicine

Mother put salve on the burn.

salt n. seasoning

She put some salt in the soup.

same adj.
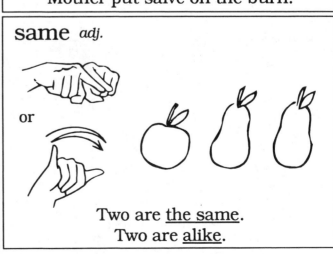
or
Two are the same.
Two are alike.

404 sample

sample n.

He showed samples of his work.

sandbox n. toy

The girl played in the sandbox.
sandbox   sandboxes

sample v.

I must <u>sample</u> the soup.
I must <u>taste</u> it.

sandwich n. food

I had a sandwich for lunch.
sandwich   sandwiches

sand n.

He is playing in the sand.

sane adj.
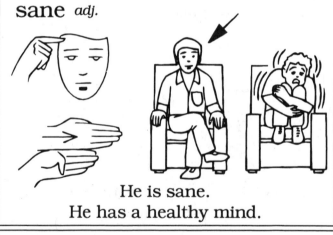
He is sane.
He has a healthy mind.

sandal n. shoe
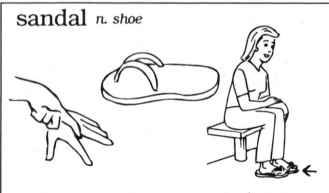
She is wearing a pair of sandals.
sandal   sandals

sang pt. of **sing**

The choir sang a song.

satisfactory 405

sanitary *adj.*

Her kitchen is sanitary.
It is not dirty and filthy.

sat *pt. of* sit

He sat in the chair and read.

sank *pt. of* sink

The ship sank.
The ship went under the water.

Satan *n.* devil

Satan is an evil spirit.

Santa Claus *n.*

The children visited Santa Claus.

satellite *n.*
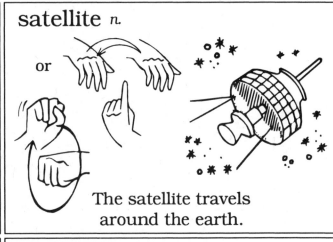
The satellite travels around the earth.

sassy *adj. informal*

She is a <u>sassy</u> child.
She is an <u>impudent</u> child.

satisfactory *adj.*

Her work is not satisfactory.
He isn't pleased with her work.

406 satisfy

satisfy v.

Did the food satisfy him?
Is he hungry now?

savage adj.

Lions are savage beasts.
They are not tame and gentle.

Saturday n. day of the week
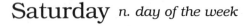

Saturday comes after Friday.

save v.
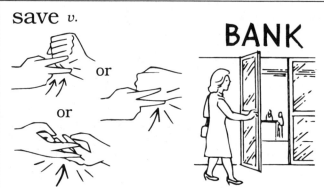
I save some money each month.
I put money in the bank each month.

saucer n.

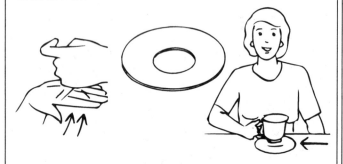
She put the cup on the saucer.
saucer   saucers

save v.

The man had to <u>save</u> the little girl.
He had to <u>rescue</u> her.

sausage n. meat

He had sausages with his eggs.
sausage   sausages

saw n. tool
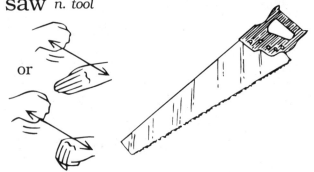
The saw has a wooden handle.
saw   saws

scarf 407

saw *pt. of* **see**

He saw the fire and ran for help.

scale *v.*

He will scale the mountain.
He'll climb up the mountain.

saw *v.*

or

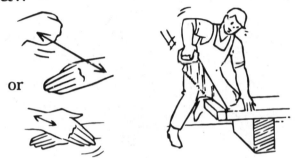

I have to saw this board.
saws   sawed   sawing   sawed/sawn

scare *v. frighten*

or

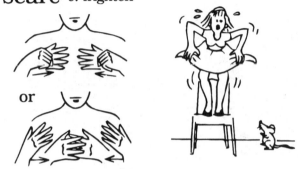

Mice always scare me.
scares   scared   scaring

say *v.*

What did the man say?
says   said   saying

scarecrow *n.*

The scarecrow frightens birds away.
scarecrow   scarecrows

scale *n.* scales

or   or

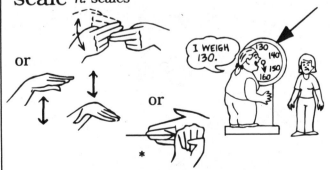

She is using the scale.
She is weighing herself.

scarf *n. clothing*

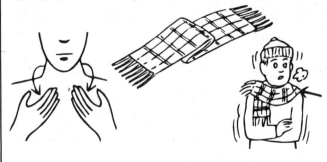

He is wearing a scarf.
scarf   scarves

408 scarf

scarf n.

She tied a scarf around her neck.

schedule n.

He studied the bus schedule.
schedule schedules

scarves n. pural of **scarf**

She looked at the scarves.

school n.

He goes to school every day.
school schools

scat v. informal

He told the children to scat.
He told them to go away.

science n.

He is studying science.

scatter v.

I scatter things around the house.
I leave things here and there.

scissors n.

This is a pair of scissors.

scour 409

scold v.

Why did she scold the boy?
scolds   scolded   scolding

scorpion n. spider

Scorpions are poisonous.
scorpion   scorpions

scoop n.

or

He wanted two scoops of ice cream.
scoop   scoops

Scotch tape

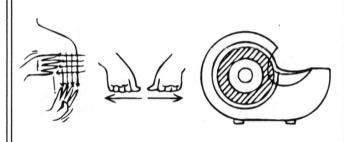

I seal packages
with Scotch tape.

scooter n. toy

The scooter has 2 wheels.
scooter   scooters

Scotland n.

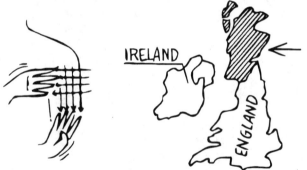

Scotland is north of England.

score n.

Our team had the highest score.
score   scores

scour v.

I must <u>scour</u> this pot.
I must <u>scrub</u> it.

410 scour

scour v.

I will scour the park for my ball.
I'll look everywhere.

scrape v.
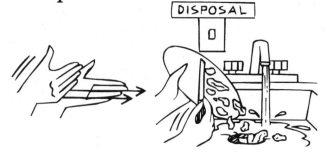
She has to scrape the plate.
scrapes   scraped   scraping

scout n.

He is a scout.
scout   scouts

scratch v.
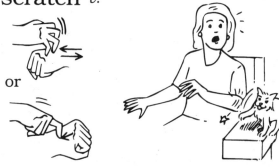
Did the cat scratch her arm?
scratches   scratched   scratching

scramble v.

She will scramble the eggs.
scrambles   scrambled   scrambling

scratch v.

I must scratch my
arm because it itches.

scrapbook n.

He showed me his scrapbook.
scrapbook   scrapbooks

scream v. yell, holler, call

I screamed when I saw the mouse.
screams   screamed   screaming

scythe 411

screen n.

He put a screen on the window.
screen   screens

screwdriver n. tool
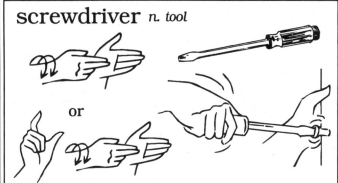
The man is using a screwdriver.
screwdriver   screwdrivers

screen n.
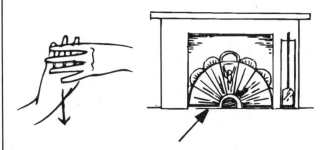
We have a screen around the fireplace.

scribble v.

Don't scribble in the book.
scribbles   scribbled   scribbling

screen n.

He is setting up the screen.

scrub v.

I have to scrub the tub.
scrubs   scrubbed   scrubbing

screw n.
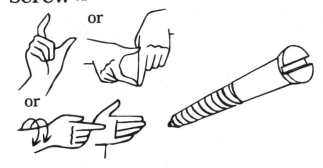
The man needs a screw.
screw   screws

scythe n.

The man is using a scythe.
scythe   scythes

412 sea

sea n.

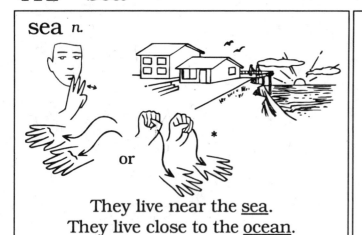

They live near the sea.
They live close to the ocean.

seal v.

She must seal the letter.
seals   sealed   sealing

sea n.

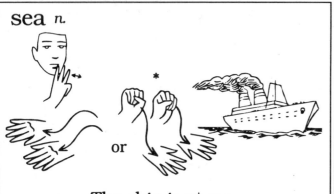

The ship is at sea.
It is out on the ocean.

search v.

I will search for my ball.
I'll look for my ball.

seal n. animal

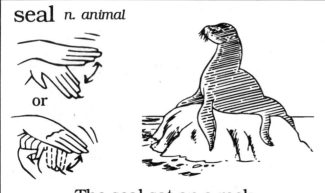

The seal sat on a rock.
seal   seals

season n. period

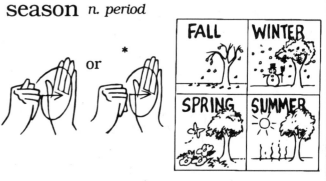

Winter is the coldest
season of the year.

seal n.

This is the seal of the
President of the United States.

season v.

I have to season the soup.
I have to add spices to the soup.

secret 413

seat n.
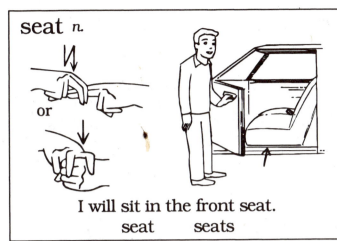
I will sit in the front seat.
seat   seats

second n.
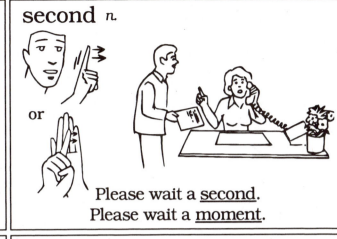
Please wait a <u>second</u>.
Please wait a <u>moment</u>.

seat belt n.
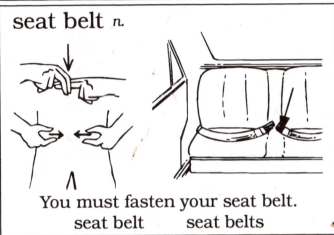
You must fasten your seat belt.
seat belt   seat belts

second hand n.
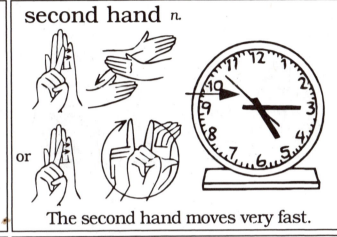
The second hand moves very fast.

second adj. 2nd

The woman is second in line.

secondhand adj.
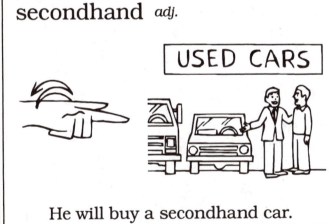
He will buy a secondhand car.

second n. 1/60 of a minute
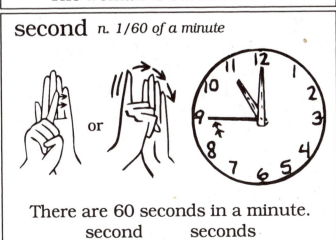
There are 60 seconds in a minute.
second   seconds

secret n.

She is telling him a secret.
secret   secrets

414 secretary

secretary n. worker

She is a good secretary.
secretary   secretaries

secure v.

He will <u>secure</u> a loan from the bank.
He'll <u>get</u> a loan from the bank.

section n. part, region

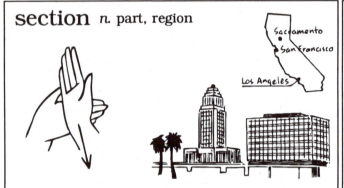

Los Angeles is in the
southern section of the state.

see v.

I see a loose board.
sees   saw   seeing   seen

secure adj.

The woman feels <u>secure</u>.
She feels <u>safe</u>.

seed n.

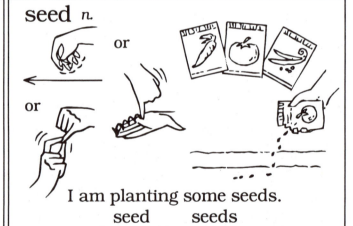

I am planting some seeds.
seed   seeds

secure adj.

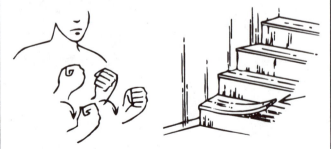

The board is not secure.
It isn't fastened firmly.

seek v. look for

He had to seek another job.
seeks   sought   seeking

sell 415

seek *v.*

He will seek advice.
He'll look for help to solve his problem.

seldom *adv.*

He <u>seldom</u> takes a drink.
He <u>rarely</u> takes one.

seem *v.*

Does the man <u>seem</u> to be angry?
Does he <u>appear</u> to be angry?

select *v.*

or
Did she <u>select</u> a dress?
Did she <u>pick out</u> one?

seen *pp. of* see

Have you seen my ball?

selfish *adj.*

or
The man is selfish.
He won't share with others.

seesaw *n. toy*

The girls like the <u>seesaw</u>.
They like the <u>teeter-totter</u>.

sell *v.*

He will sell her a vacuum.
sells   sold   selling

416 Senate

Senate *n.*

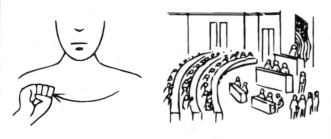

The Senate is the upper house of Congress.

sense *n.*

The locks give her a <u>sense</u> of security - a <u>feeling</u> of security.

send *v.*

I will send a letter to my friend.
sends sent sending

sent *pt. of* **send**

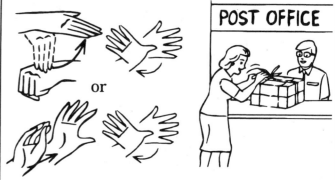

She sent a package to her mother.

sense *n.*

Dogs have a keen sense of hearing.
They have excellent ability to hear.

sentence *n.*

He wrote a sentence on the paper.
sentence   sentences

sense *n.*

The boy showed good sense.
He acted wisely.

sentence *n.*

He received a short <u>sentence</u>.
He received a short <u>term in jail</u>.

service 417

separate adj.
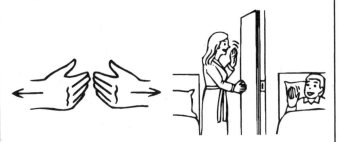
They have separate rooms.
They don't sleep in the same room.

serve v.
 or
I will serve the roast.
serves   served   serving

separate v.

The teacher had to separate the boys.
She had to push them apart.

serve v.
 or
I <u>serve</u> the customers.
I <u>wait on</u> them.

September n. month
 or

School starts in September.

serve v.
 or
He will <u>serve</u> time in jail.
He will <u>spend</u> some time in jail.

serious adj.

This is a <u>serious</u> matter.
It's an <u>important</u> matter.

service n.

May I be of service?
May I help you?

418 service

service *n.*

They went to the early service last Sunday.

set *v.*

The sun will <u>set</u> in the west.
It will <u>go down</u> in the west.

service station *n.* gas station

He drove to the service station.
service station   service stations

set *v.*

or

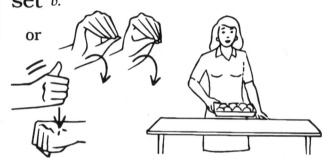

I will <u>set</u> the cookies on the table.
I'll <u>put</u> them on the table.

set *n.*

or

She bought a set of dishes.
set   sets

set *v.*

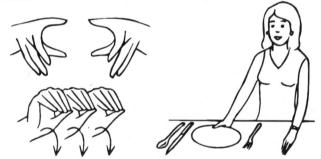

I must set the table.
sets   set   setting

set *v.*

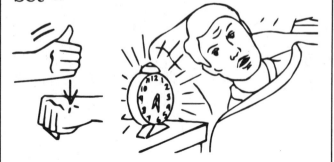

I set the alarm for 6:30.
sets   set   setting

set up *v.*

They <u>set up</u> the tent.
They <u>put up</u> the tent.

seventh 419

set up v.

We must set up the next meeting.
We must plan the next meeting.

settle v. resolve

We always settle our arguments.
We always solve the problem.

settle v.

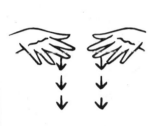

The sugar will settle to the bottom.
It will sink slowly to the bottom.

seven number: 7

 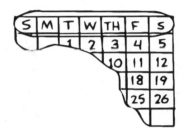

A week has seven days.
There are seven days in a week.

settle v.

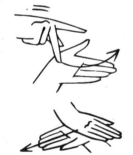

He will settle his bill.
He'll pay it.

seventeen number: 17

or

She is seventeen years old.

settle v.

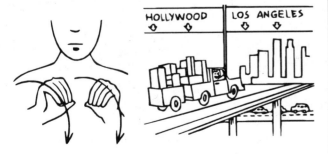

They will settle in Los Angeles.
They plan to live in Los Angeles.

seventh n. 7th

He arrived on the seventh of May.

420 seventy

seventy *number*: 70

Sixty plus ten equals seventy.

sewing machine *n.*

She is using a sewing machine.
sewing machine   sewing machines

several *adj.*

We had <u>several</u> guests for dinner.
We had <u>two or three</u> guests.

sewn *pp. of* sew

She has sewn on the button.

severe *adj.*

He has a <u>severe</u> headache.
He has a <u>terrible</u> headache.

sex *n.*
 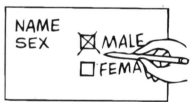
He recorded the baby's sex.

sew *v.*

or
I will sew this by hand.
sews   sewed   sewing   sewed/sewn

shade *n.*
*

He is resting in the shade.
He's resting out of the sun.

shampoo 421

shade n.
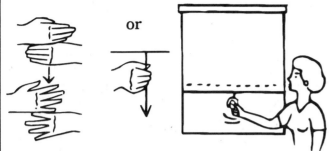
She pulled down the shade.
She pulled down the blind.

shall v.

I shall plant this tree.
I will plant it.

shadow n.
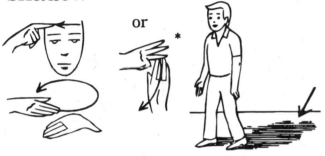
I saw the man's shadow.
shadow   shadows

shallow adj.

The water is shallow.
It is not deep.

shake v.

The baby is shaking the rattle.
shakes   shook   shaking   shaken

shampoo n.

This is a bottle of shampoo.

shaken pp. of shake

The table was shaken by the boy.

shampoo v.

I must shampoo this rug.
shampoos   shampooed   shampooing

422 shampoo

shampoo v.

She will shampoo her hair.

sharp adj.
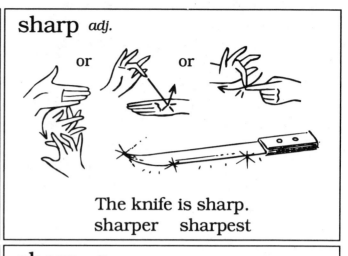
The knife is sharp.
sharper   sharpest

shape n.
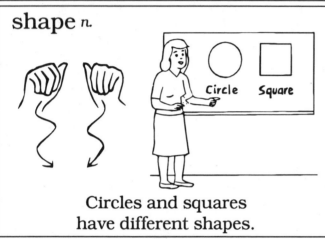
Circles and squares have different shapes.

sharp adj.

The boy is very sharp.
He is very smart.

share v.

I share my cookies with my friend.
shares   shared   sharing

shave n.
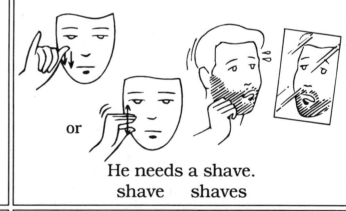
He needs a shave.
shave   shaves

shark n.
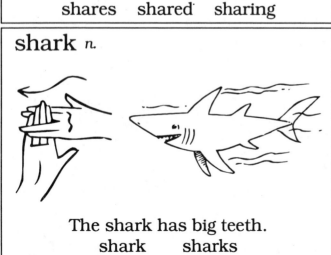
The shark has big teeth.
shark   sharks

shave v.

He has to shave every day.
shaves   shaved   shaving

shell 423

she *pron.*

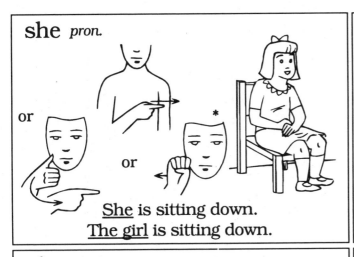

She is sitting down.
The girl is sitting down.

shelf *n.*

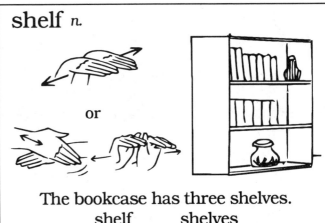

The bookcase has three shelves.
shelf   shelves

sheep *n. animal*

They raise sheep for wool.
one sheep   many sheep

shell *n.*

The turtle has a hard shell.
shell   shells

sheet *n.*

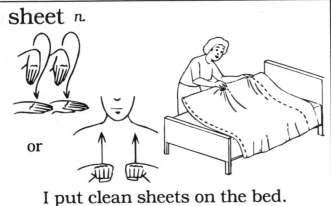

I put clean sheets on the bed.
sheet   sheets

shell *n.*

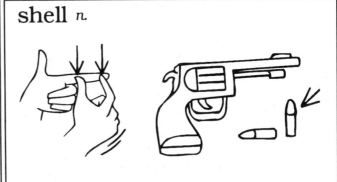

You have to put shells in a gun.
You must put bullets in a gun.

sheet *n.*

He picked up a sheet of paper.
He picked up a piece of paper.

shell *n.*

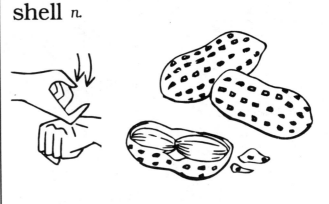

Peanuts have soft shells.

424 shell

shell v.

They will shell the enemy.
They'll bombard the enemy.

shield n.

The soldier is carrying a shield.
shield   shields

shelves *plural of* shelf

The shelves are full of books.

shield v.

I must shield the girl.
I must protect her from harm.

shepherd n. worker

The shepherd takes
care of the sheep.

shift v.

He has to shift gears.
shifts shifted shifting

sheriff n. officer
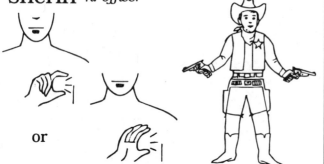
or
The sheriff carries a gun.
sheriff   sheriffs

shine v.

or
The sun will shine all day.
shines shined/shone shining shone

shock 425

shine *v.* polish

I must shine these shoes.
shines   shined   shining

shirt *n. clothing*

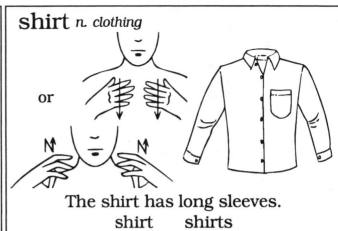

The shirt has long sleeves.
shirt   shirts

ship *n. boat, vessel*

The ship sailed across the ocean.
ship   ships

shiver *v.*

Why did he shiver?
shivers   shivered   shivering

ship *v. send*

We ship the boxes by train.
ships   shipped   shipping

shock *n.*

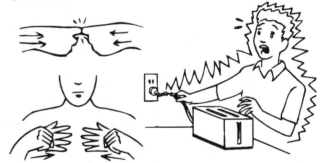

He got an electric shock.
shock   shocks

shirk *v.*

I always shirk my duties.
I always try to avoid working.

shock *v.*

Does his behavior shock his mother?
shocks   shocked   shocking

426 shoe

shoe n. clothing

I bought a new pair of shoes.
shoe   shoes

shoestring n. shoelace

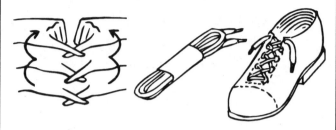

He bought a pair of shoestrings.

shoebrush n.

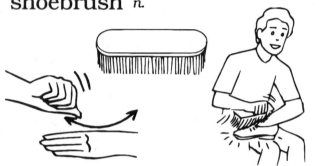

He is using a shoebrush.
shoebrush   shoebrushes

shone pp. of **shine**

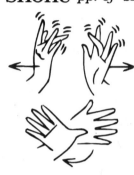

Her face had shone with happiness.

shoelace n. shoestring

He needs a new shoelace.
shoelace   shoelaces

shone pt. of **shine**

The sun shone brightly.

shoe polish n.

He bought some shoe polish.

shook pt. of **shake**

The boy shook the table.

shore 427

shoot *v.* fire

The man will shoot the gun.
shoots   shot   shooting

shop *v.*

I shop here all the time.
shops   shopped   shopping

shoot *v.*

Did he shoot the deer?
Did his bullet hit the deer?

shoplifter *n.*

The guard watched the shoplifter.
shoplifter   shoplifters

shoot *v.*

I will <u>shoot</u> several pictures.
I'll <u>take</u> several pictures.

shopping bag *n.*

The shopping bag is empty.
shopping bag   shopping bags

shop *n.*

She went to the candy <u>shop</u>.
She went to the candy <u>store</u>.

shore *n.*

We walked along the <u>shore</u>.
We walked along the <u>coast</u>.

428 short

short *adj.* not tall

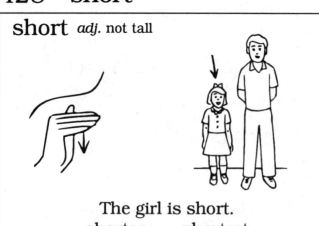

The girl is short.
shorter   shortest

shot *n.* injection

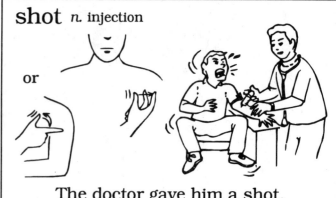

The doctor gave him a shot.
shot   shots

short *adj.*

I'll be ready in a short time.
I'll be ready soon.

shot *pt. of* **shoot**

The man shot the gun.

short *adj.*

He is short of money.
He doesn't have much money.

should *v.*

He should study harder.
He ought to study harder.

shorts *n.* clothing

She is wearing a pair of shorts.

shoulder *n.* body part

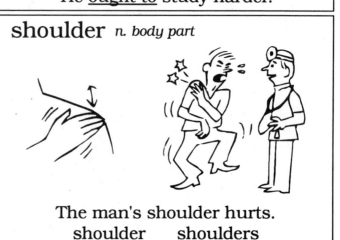

The man's shoulder hurts.
shoulder   shoulders

shown 429

shout v. yell, holler

I must shout for help.
shouts   shouted   shouting

show v. display

I can show examples of my work.
shows   showed   showing

shove v. push

Did he shove the girl?
shoves   shoved   shoving

show v. demonstrate

I'll show you how the vacuum works.

shovel n. tool

He used a shovel to dig the hole.
shovel   shovels

shower n.

He's taking a shower.
shower   showers

show n.

We enjoyed the <u>show</u>.
We enjoyed the <u>performance</u>.

shown pp. of show

She has shown us her ring.

430 shrimp

shrimp n. food

She ordered shrimp.
shrimp   shrimp/shrimps

shut off v.

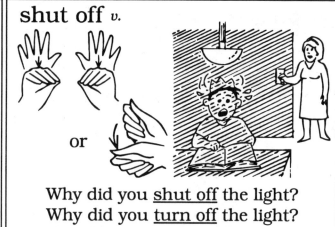

Why did you shut off the light?
Why did you turn off the light?

shrug v.

Why did he shrug his shoulders?
shrugs   shrugged   shrugging

shut up v.

I shut up the store at night.
I lock up the store at night.

shut v.

The boy will shut the window.
He will close it.

shut up v.

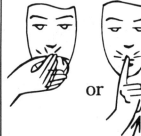 

Please shut up.
Please be quiet.

shut v.

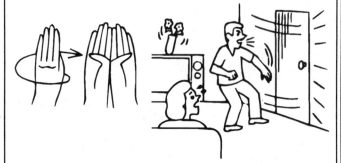

Why did he shut the door like that?
Why did he close it with a bang?

shy adj.

The girl is shy.
She's bashful.

sight 431

sick *adj.*
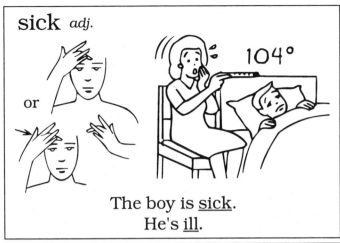
The boy is sick.
He's ill.

sidewalk *n.*

The sidewalk is clean.
sidewalk   sidewalks

side *n.*

Our side won the game.
Our team won it.

sight *n.*

I've never seen such an awful sight.

side *n.*
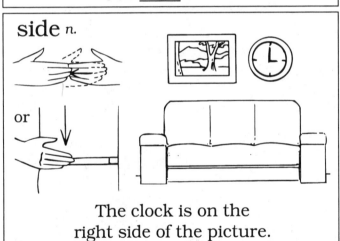
The clock is on the
right side of the picture.

sight *n.*

The man lost his sight.
He lost his vision. He can't see.

side *n.*
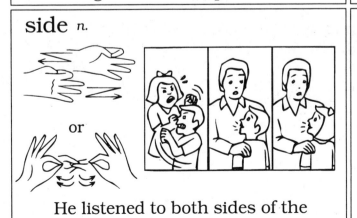
He listened to both sides of the
story - to both explanations.

out of sight

She put the gifts out of sight -
where they couldn't be seen.

432 sight

sight *v.*

Did the man <u>sight</u> a ship?
Did he <u>see</u> a ship?

sign *v.*

I must <u>sign</u> the check.
I must <u>write my name on</u> the check.

sign *n.*

She stopped at the stop sign.
    sign   signs

sign language *n.* ASL

They are learning sign language.

sign *n.*

He looked at the signs.

signal *n.*

He didn't stop at the <u>signal</u>.
He didn't stop at the <u>traffic light</u>.

sign *n.*

He knows some signs.
He knows some sign language.

signal *v.*

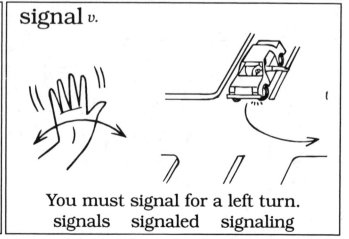

You must signal for a left turn.
  signals   signaled   signaling

simple 433

signature n.

He put his signature on the check.
He signed the check.

silver n. precious metal

The tea set is made of silver.

silently adv.

Father entered the room silently.
He entered without making any noise.

silverware n. eating utensils
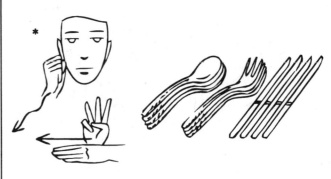
She bought some silverware.

silly adj.

He is a silly boy.
sillier   silliest

similar adj.

The dresses are similar.
They're almost the same.

silo n.
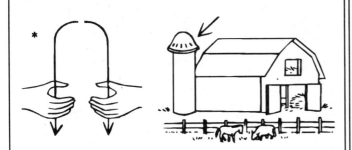
Food for the farm animals
is stored in the silo.

simple adj.
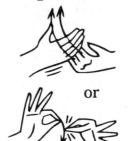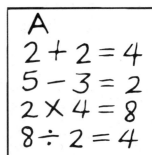
The problems were <u>simple</u>.
They were <u>easy</u>.

434 simple

simple *adj.*

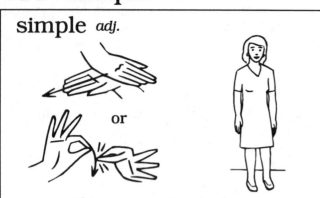

She wore a <u>simple</u> dress.
She wore a <u>plain</u> dress.

sing *v.*

The choir will sing.
sings sang/sung singing sung

sin *n.*

Stealing is a sin.
It's against the laws of God.

single *adj.*

Only a <u>single</u> person showed up.
Only <u>one</u> person showed up.

since *prep.*

I have been looking for my ball
since yesterday afternoon.

single *adj.*

He is <u>single</u>.
He is <u>not married</u>.

sincere *adj.* honest

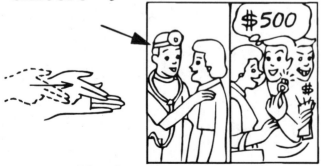

The doctor is sincere.
The other man is not sincere.

sink *n.*

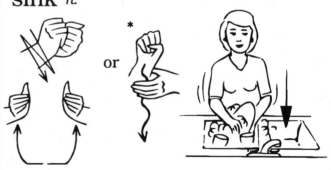

She washes dishes in the sink.
sink   sinks

six 435

sink *v.* go down

The ship will sink.
sinks   sank/sunk   sinking   sunk

sister *n.*

She is my sister.
sister   sisters

sinus *n. body part*

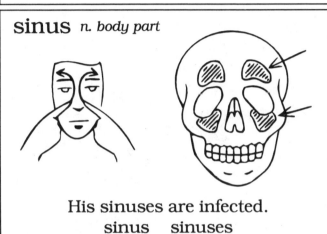

His sinuses are infected.
sinus   sinuses

sit *v.*

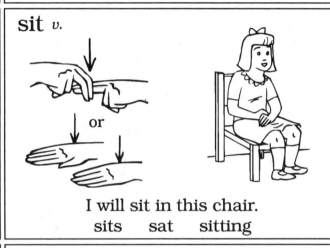

I will sit in this chair.
sits   sat   sitting

sip *v.*

I always sip hot tea.
sips   sipped   sipping

sit down *v.*

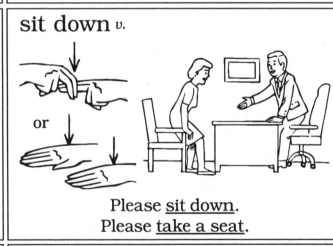

Please <u>sit down</u>.
Please <u>take a seat</u>.

siren *n.*

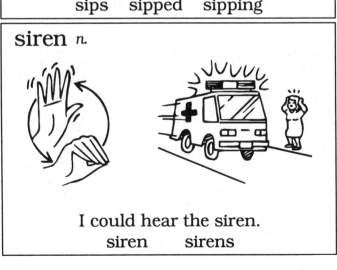

I could hear the siren.
siren   sirens

six *number: 6*

She is six years old.

436 sixteen

sixteen *number:* 16

There are sixteen ounces in a pound.

skate *n.* roller skate

He lost one skate.
skate   skates

sixth *n.* 6th

My appointment is the sixth of May.

skate *n.* ice skate

This is a pair of skates.

sixty *number:* 60

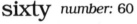

Fifty plus ten equals sixty.

skateboard *n.* toy

He is riding his skateboard.
skateboard   skateboards

size *n.*

The dress is the wrong size.
The woman needs a larger size.

skeleton *n.*

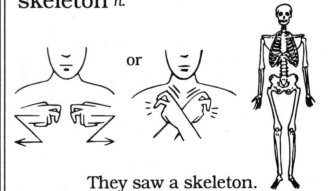

They saw a skeleton.
skeleton   skeletons

skip 437

ski n.
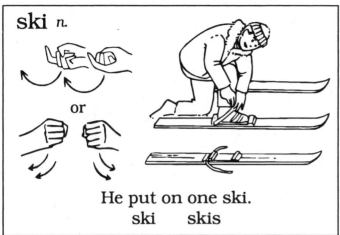
He put on one ski.
ski   skis

skillful adj.

He is a skillful worker.
He is an expert worker.

skid v.
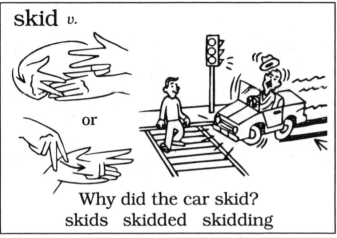
Why did the car skid?
skids   skidded   skidding

skin n. body part
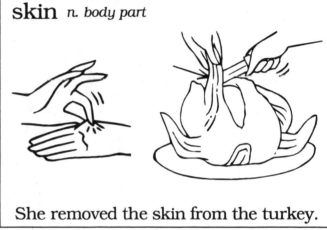
She removed the skin from the turkey.

skill n.

He has a lot of skill.
He has a lot of ability.

skinny adj.
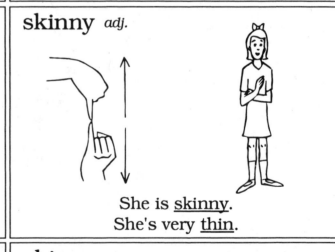
She is skinny.
She's very thin.

skilled adj.

He is a skilled worker.
He has had training and experience.

skip v.

I will skip down the path.
skips   skipped   skipping

438 skip

skip v.

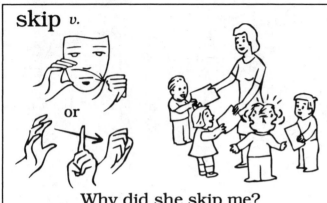

Why did she skip me?
Why didn't she give me a paper?

skunk n. animal

The skunk is black and white.
skunk   skunks

skip v. informal

He will skip class.
He will not go to his class today.

sky n.

The sun is in the sky.
sky   skies

skirt n. clothing

She bought a new skirt.
skirt   skirts

slacks n. clothing

He bought a new pair of slacks.

skull n. body part

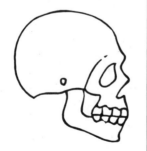

They found a skull.
skull   skulls

slam v.

Why did he slam the door?
Why did he close it with a bang?

sleeve 439

slap v.

Why did she slap his face?
slaps   slapped   slapping

sleep v.

He may sleep all day.
sleeps   slept   sleeping

slave n.

Long ago, slaves had to obey their masters. They had to obey their owners.

sleeping bag n.
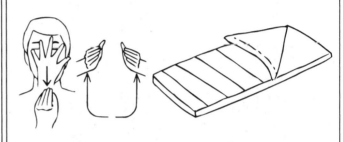
He has a new sleeping bag.
sleeping bag   sleeping bags

slave v.

He had to slave away.
He had to work very hard.

sleepy adj.

The boy is tired and sleepy.
sleepier   sleepiest

sled n.
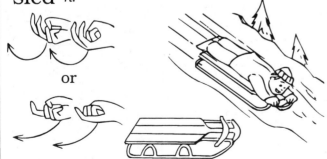
The boy is riding his sled.
sled   sleds

sleeve n.
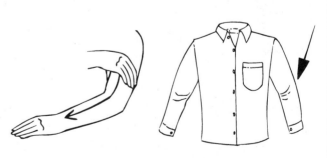
The shirt has long sleeves.
sleeve   sleeves

440 sleigh

sleigh *n. vehicle*

They're riding in a sleigh.
sleigh   sleighs

slice *v.*

I have to slice the cucumber.
slices   sliced   slicing

slender *adj.*
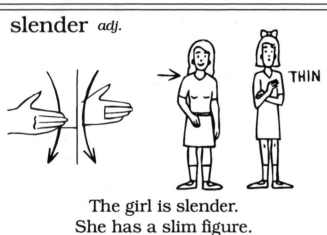
The girl is slender.
She has a slim figure.

slick *adj.*

The sidewalk is slick.
It is slippery.

slept *pt. of* sleep
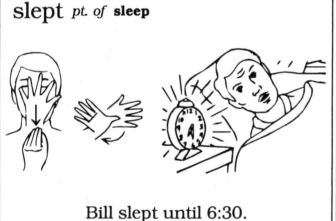
Bill slept until 6:30.

slid *pt. of* slide
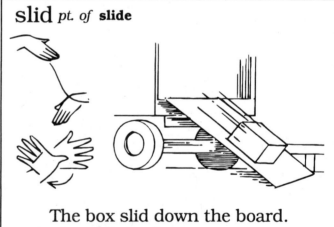
The box slid down the board.

slice *n.*

He's eating a slice of bread.
slice   slices

slidden *pp. of* slide

She has slidden down the pole.

slipper 441

slide n.

The children ran to the slide.
slide   slides

slip n. clothing
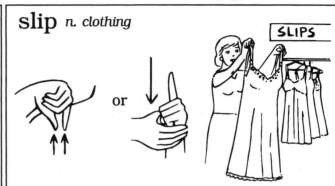
She bought a new slip.
slip   slips

slide v.

She will slide down the slide.
slides   slid   sliding

slip v.

You can slip on ice.
slips   slipped   slipping

slim adj.
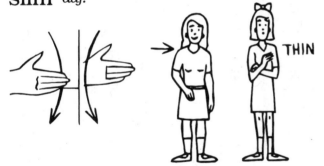
She has a <u>slim</u> figure.
She has a <u>slender</u> figure.

slip v.

I will slip a note under the door.

sling n.

She has her arm in a sling.
sling   slings

slipper n. clothing

He can't find his other slipper.
slipper   slippers

442 slippery

slippery *adj.*

The sidewalk is slippery.

slow *adj.*

My watch is slow.
It doesn't keep the correct time.

sliver *n. splinter*

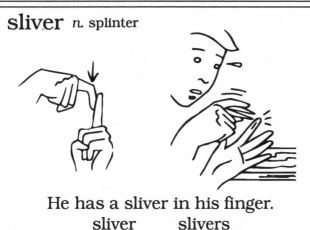

He has a sliver in his finger.
sliver   slivers

slow *adj.*

Business is slow.
There are not enough customers.

sloppy *adj.*

He did a sloppy job.
He did the work carelessly.

small *adj.*

One bear is small.
One bear is little.

slow *adj.*

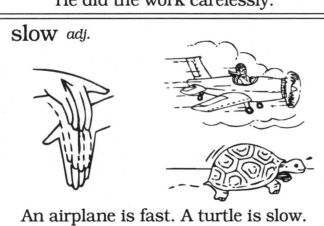

An airplane is fast. A turtle is slow.
slower   slowest

smallpox *n. illness*

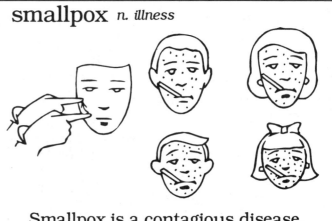

Smallpox is a contagious disease.

smog 443

smart *adj.*

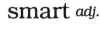

The boy is smart.
He is bright.

smart *adj.*

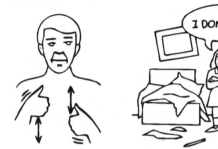

The girl was smart with her mother.
She was sassy.

smart *adj.* chic, neat, well-dressed

She looks smart in that suit.
She looks good in that suit.

smart *v.*

Her eyes smart because of the smoke.
Her eyes sting because of the smoke.

smash *v.* or

I will smash the jar.
I'll break it to pieces.

smell *v.*

The man could smell the food.
smells   smelled/smelt   smelling

smile *v.*

Did the girl smile?
smiles   smiled   smiling

smog *n.*

The smog made his eyes smart.

444 smoke

smoke n.
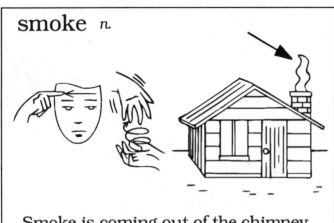
Smoke is coming out of the chimney.

snail n.

I saw a snail in the garden.
snail   snails

smoke v.

You can't smoke here.
smokes   smoked   smoking

snake n. reptile
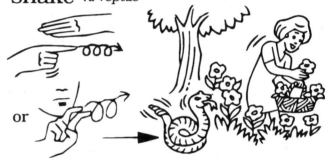
The woman didn't see the snake.
snake   snakes

smooth adj.

The road is smooth.
There are no bumps in the road.

snap n.
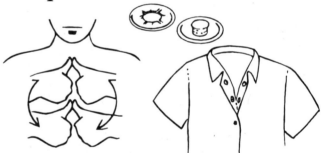
The shirt has snaps.
snap   snaps

snack n.

We had a snack at 3 o'clock.
We had a little bit of food.

snap n.
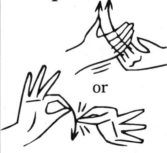
The test was a snap.
It was easy.

snow 445

snap v.

I will snap my fingers.
snaps   snapped   snapping

sneak v.

I will sneak into the movie.
sneaks   sneaked   sneaking

snap v.

Why did the clothesline snap?
Why did it break?

sneeze v.

The man had to sneeze.
sneezes   sneezed   sneezing

snap v.

or

I often snap at my wife.
I often speak angrily to her.

snore v.
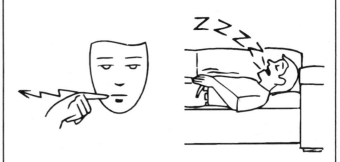
Does the man snore?
snores   snored   snoring

snap v.

He will snap a picture.
He'll take a picture.

snow n.

or
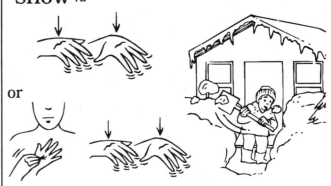
He is shoveling the snow.

446 snow

snow v.

It may snow all day.
snows   snowed   snowing

so conj.

My husband plays golf on Saturday; so I have my hair done then.

snowflake n.

Each snowflake is different.
snowflake   snowflakes

so far adv. up to this time
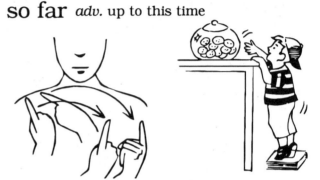
So far, he has not been able to reach the cookie jar.

snowman n.

The children made a snowman.
snowman   snowmen

so long interjection: goodby

Grandpa said, "So long."

snowshoe n.
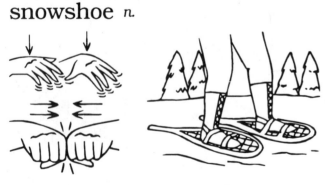
He is wearing snowshoes.
snowshoe   snowshoes

soak v.
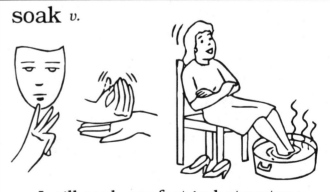
I will soak my feet in hot water.
soaks   soaked   soaking

socket 447

soaking adv.

He got soaking wet in the rain.
All of his clothes were wet.

Social Security n.

He has a Social Security card.

soap n.

He is holding a bar of soap.

socialize v.

I don't socialize with tough boys.
I don't enjoy associating with them.

sob v. cry
or
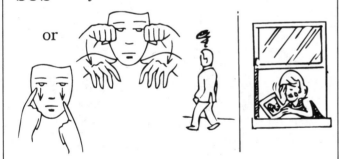
Why did the woman sob?
sobs   sobbed   sobbing

sock n.

He has a hole in his sock.
sock   socks

sober adj. not drunk
or

The women are sober.
The man is not sober.

socket n.

She's plugging the iron into the socket.

448 soda

soda n. beverage

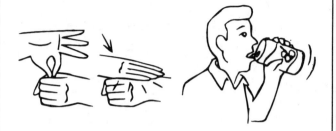

He drank some soda.
He drank some pop.

soil v.

How did he soil his clothes?
How did he get his clothes dirty?

sofa n. furniture

We bought a new sofa.
We bought a new couch.

sold pt. of **sell**

The man sold the woman a vacuum.

soft adj. not hard

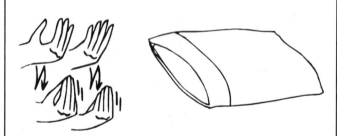

The pillow is very soft.
softer   softest

solder v.

He will solder the wire.
solders   soldered   soldering

soil n.

The soil was damp after the rain.
The earth was damp after the rain.

soldier n.

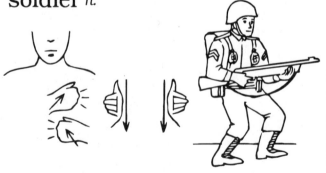

The soldier has a gun.
soldier   soldiers

some 449

sole *adj.*

He's the sole person on the island.
He's the only person there.

sole *n. bottom of the foot*

I got a thorn in the sole of my foot.
sole   soles

sole *n. shoe bottom*

The shoe needs a new sole.

solid *adj.*

Water becomes solid when it freezes.

solid *adj.*

This log is solid.
It is not hollow.

solution *n.*

He found a solution.
He found a way to solve his probelm.

solve *v.*

He can't solve the problem.
He can't figure it out.

some *adj.*

The boy wants some juice.

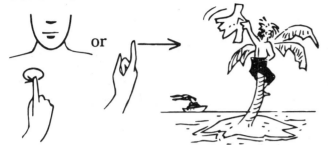

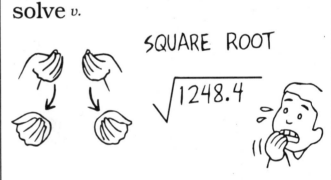

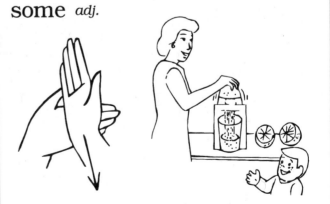

450 somebody

somebody pron.

Somebody took his clothes.
Someone took them.

something pron.

Something happened to my baseball.
It was either stolen or lost.

someday adv. in the future

They plan to take a trip someday.

sometimes adv.

Sometimes that boy is very rude.
He's rude now and then.

someone pron.

Someone ate the candy.
Somebody ate it.

son n. male child

The man and woman have one son.
son   sons

somersault n. summersault

He did a somersault.

song n.

The choir is singing a song.
song   songs

sought 451

soon *adj.*

It will soon be 8:30.
It'll be 8:30 in a short time.

sorry *adj.*

I'm sorry that I broke the window.
I didn't mean to break it.

sore *adj.*

His shoulder is sore.
It hurts.

sort *n.* type

What sort of seeds are you planting?
What kind of seeds are you planting?

sore throat *n.*

He has a sore throat.
His throat hurts.

sort *v.*

He must sort the mail.
sorts   sorted   sorting

sorrow *n.*

His death caused great sorrow.
It caused much sadness.

sought *pt. of* **seek**

He sought another job.
He looked for another job.

452 sound

sound *adj.*
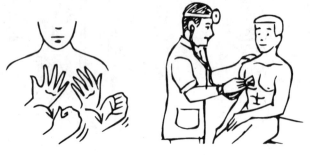
He is in sound condition.
He is healthy.

sound *n.*

The firecracker made a loud sound.
It made a loud noise.

sound *adj.*

He gave me some sound advice.
He gave me some good advice.

sound *v.*

"Write" and "right" sound the same.

sound *adj.*

She has a sound business.
Her business is making money.

sound *v.*

I must sound the alarm.
I must warn people of the danger.

sound *adv. deeply*

The man is sound asleep.

soup *n. food*

The soup is hot.

spaghetti 453

sour adj.

The lemon is sour.
more sour   most sour

space n.

The moon is in outer space.

south adv.
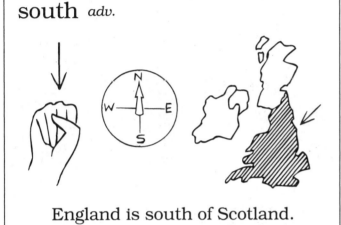
England is south of Scotland.

spaceship n.
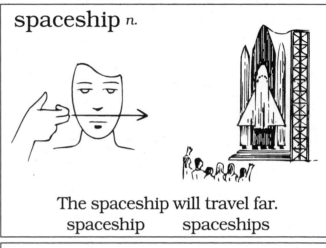
The spaceship will travel far.
spaceship   spaceships

South America n. continent

Brazil is in South America.

spade n. tool
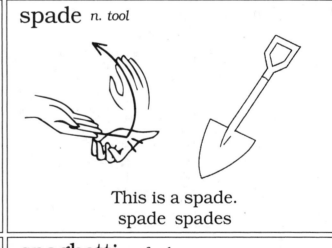
This is a spade.
spade spades

space n.
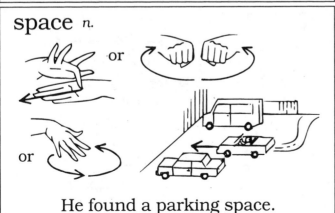
He found a parking space.
He found a place to park.

spaghetti n. food

We had spaghetti for dinner.

454 Spain

Spain *n. country*

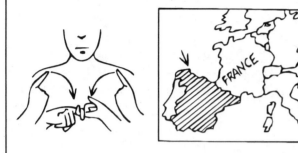

Spain is a country in Europe.

speaker *n.*

The speaker was interesting.
speaker   speakers

spank *v.*

Why did she spank her son?
spanks   spanked   spanking

speaker *n.*

The stereo has two speakers.

spatula *n. utensil*

They are using spatulas.
spatula   spatulas

spear *n. weapon*

The native is carrying a spear.
spear   spears

speak *v.*

He must speak into the mike.
speaks   spoke   speaking   spoken

spear *n.*

This is a spear of asparagus.

spend 455

spear v.

He can spear fish.
spears   speared   spearing

speed v.

I often speed. I often drive too fast.
speeds   sped/speeded   speeding

special adj.

The baby eats special food.

spell v.

The boy can spell the word.
spells   spelled   spelling

sped pt. of speed

He sped down the road.
He speeded down the road.

spend v.

She will spend some money.
She'll buy something.

speech n.

She thought the speech was boring.
speech   speeches

spend v.
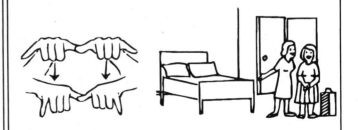
Mother will spend the night here.
She'll stay here tonight.

456 spent

spent *pt. of* spend

She spent $10.30 for the cake.

spill *v.*
or

How did I spill my milk?
spills   spilled   spilling

spice *n. seasoning*
or

She bought some spices.
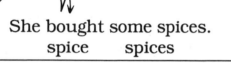

spin *n.*
or
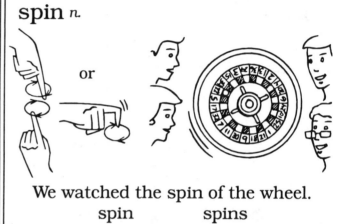
We watched the spin of the wheel.
spin   spins

spider *n. insect*
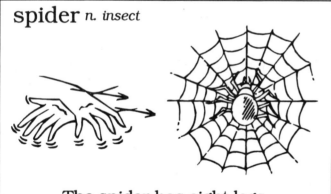
The spider has eight legs.
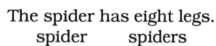

spin *n.*
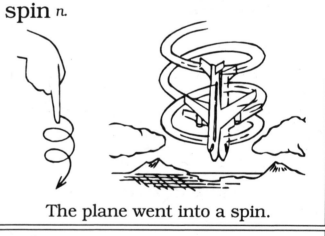
The plane went into a spin.

spider web *n. spider's web, cobweb*
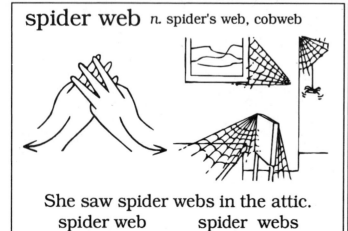
She saw spider webs in the attic.
spider web   spider webs

spin *v.*
or
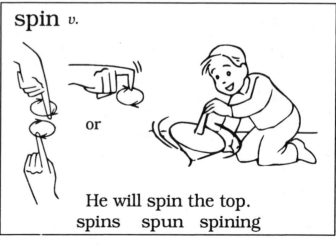
He will spin the top.
spins   spun   spining

split up 457

spin v.

The spider will spin a web.

splinter n. sliver

or

He has a splinter in his finger.
splinter   splinters

spin v.

What made her head spin?
What made her feel dizzy?

split v.

He has to split the log.
splits   split   splitting

spinach n. vegetable

Do you like spinach?

split v.

or

We will split the bill.
We'll each pay half of the bill.

splash v.

The baby likes to splash the water.
splashes   splashed   splashing

split up v.

We will split up the marbles.
We'll divide them evenly.

458 split up

split up v.

We will split up.
We won't be sweethearts any longer.

spoken pp. of speak
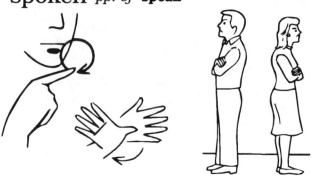
They haven't spoken for days.

spoil v. ruin

The rain will spoil our picnic.
spoils   spoiled/spoilt   spoiling

sponge n.

The sponge is on the drainboard.
sponge   sponges

spoil v.

Hot weather can spoil the fruit.
It can cause it to decay.

spool n.
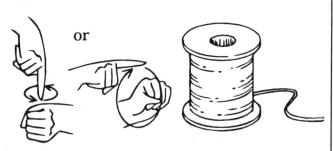
This is a spool of thread.
spool   spools

spoke pt. of speak

The man spoke into the mike.

spoon n.
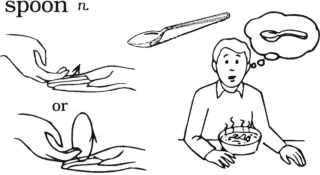
I need a spoon to eat my soup.
spoon   spoons

spread 459

sport *n.*

Baseball is his favorite sport.
sport   sports

spotless *adj.*

The room was spotless.
It was very clean.

spot *n.*

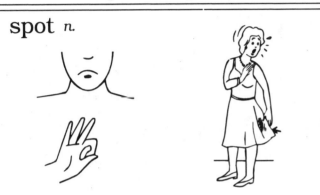

There is a spot on her dress.
There's a mark on it.

sprain *v.*

How did he sprain his ankle?
sprains   sprained   spraining

spot *n.*

She found a spot to hide the gifts.
She found a place to hide them.

spray *v.*

He will spray the paint.
sprays   sprayed   spraying

spot *v.*

Did he spot a ship?
Did he see one?

spread *n.*

I bought a new spread.
I bought a new bedspread.

460 spread

spread v.

I have to spread the butter.
spreads   spread   spreading

sprinkle v.

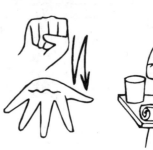 

She must sprinkle the clothes.
sprinkles   sprinkled   sprinkling

spread v.

She will spread news of her engagement.
She'll tell everyone about it.

sprinkle v.

It began to sprinkle.
It began to rain lightly.

spring n. season

In the spring the trees
bloom and the snow melts.

spun pp. of **spin**

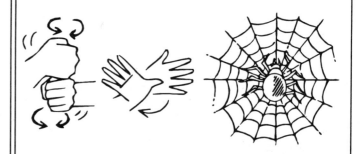

The spider has spun a web.

spring v. leap

Why did he spring out of bed?
springs sprang/sprung springing sprung

spun pt. of **spin**

The boy spun the top.

square 461

spy n.

He's a spy.
He secretly gathers information.

square n. shape

She drew a square on the board.
square   squares

spy v.
or
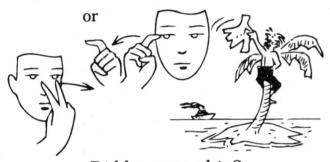
Did he <u>spy</u> a ship?
Did he <u>see</u> one?

square n. tool

The man is using a square.

square adj.

He needs a <u>square</u> meal.
He needs a <u>good</u> meal.

square n. slang
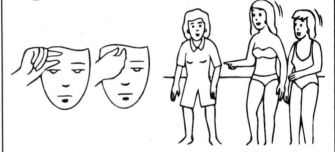
She is a <u>square</u>.
She's <u>old-fashioned</u>.

square adj.
or

He got a <u>square</u> deal.
It was <u>fair and just</u>.

square v.
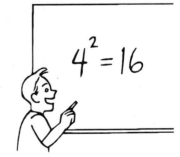
He can square the number.
squares   squared   squaring

462 square

square v.

I will square my debts.
I'll pay all of my bills.

squeeze v.

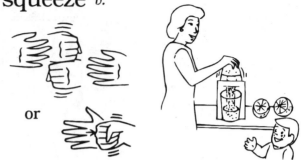

or

She will squeeze some oranges.
squeezes   squeezed   squeezing

squash n. vegetable

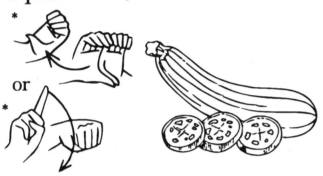

or

She bought some squash.

squeeze v.

Did the man squeeze her?
Did he hug her?

squash v. crush

Did she squash the banana?
squashes   squashed   squashing

squeeze v.

He had to squeeze through the crowd.
He had to force his way through.

squat v.

We will squat near the fire.
squats   squatted/squat   squatting

squirrel n. animal

The squirrel has a bushy tail.
squirrel   squirrels

stamp 463

stable n.

The horses are in the stable.

stairs n.

The boy can't get up the <u>stairs</u>.
He can't get up the <u>steps</u>.

stack n. pile

He has a stack of money.
stack   stacks

stale adj.

This loaf of bread is <u>stale</u>.
This loaf is <u>not fresh</u>.

stack v. pile

I have to stack the boxes here.
stacks   stacked   stacking

stamp n.

He needs a stamp.
stamp   stamps

stagecoach n. vehicle
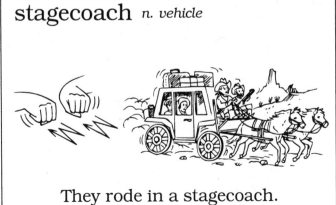
They rode in a stagecoach.
stagecoach   stagecoaches

stamp v.

He will stamp the bill.
stamps   stamped   stamping

464 stand

stand v.

He tried to stand on the fence.
stands   stood   standing

stapler n.
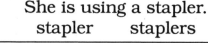
She is using a stapler.
stapler   staplers

stand up v.

I stand up while I file.

star n.

One star was very bright.
star   stars

stank pt. of stink
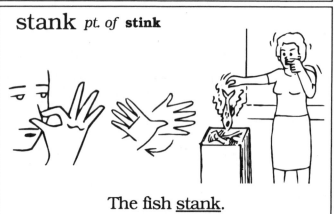
The fish stank.
The fish stunk.

start v.

I knew it would start to rain.
I knew it would begin to rain.

staple v.

She had to staple the papers.
staples   stapled   stapling

startle v.
or

Did the noise startle him?
Did it frighten him.?

stationery 465

starve v.

The man may starve.
He may die from hunger.

station n.

I drove to the station for gas.
station   stations

state n.
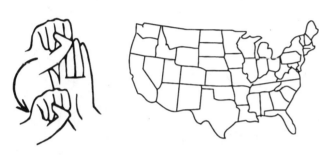
Do you know the names of the states?
state   states

station n.

The train pulled into the station.

state n.

The kitchen is in an awful state.
It's in an awful condition.

stationary adj.
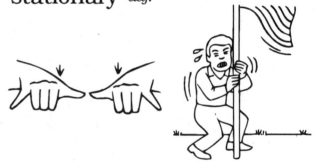
The flagpole is stationary.
It cannot be moved.

state v.

PLEASE STATE YOUR NAME.
Please state your name.
Please tell me your name.

stationery n.
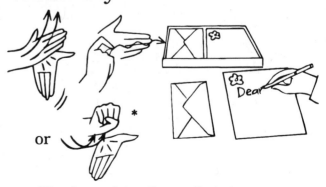
or
She bought a box of stationery.

466 station wagon

station wagon n. vehicle

She drives a station wagon.
station wagon   station wagons

steak n. meat
or

He ordered a steak.
steak   steaks

statue n.
or

There was a statue in the park.
statue   statues

steal v.
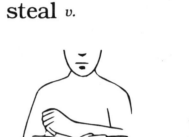
He will steal some money.
steals   stole   stealing   stolen

stay v. remain
or

My mother will stay for a week.
stays   stayed   staying

steam n.
or
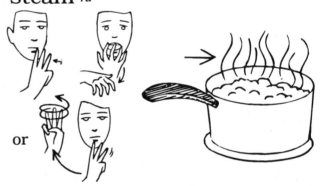
Boiling water makes steam.

stay v.
or
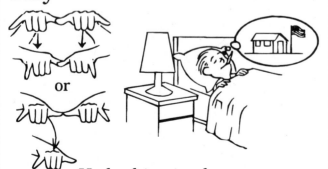
He had to stay home.
He had to remain at home.

steer n. animal
or

They raise steer for beef.

stew 467

steer v.
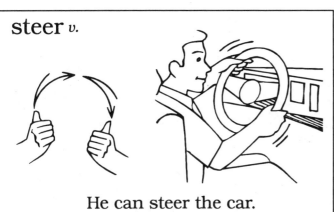
He can steer the car.
steers   steered   steering

watch one's step

She must watch her step.
She must be very careful.

steer v. guide
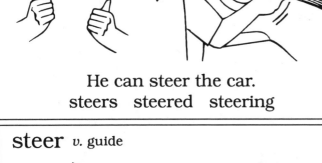
I must steer the patient to the bed.
I must lead the patient to the bed.

stereo n.

The stereo has two speakers.
stereo   stereos

step n.
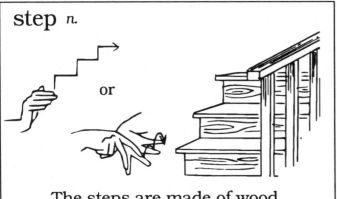
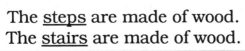
The steps are made of wood.
The stairs are made of wood.

stethoscope n.
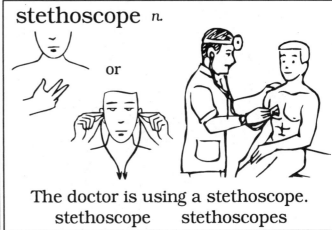
The doctor is using a stethoscope.
stethoscope   stethoscopes

step v.

Did she step on the banana?
steps   stepped   stepping

stew n. food

I will make some stew.
stew   stews

468 stick

stick *n.*

He is carrying a stick.
He's carrying a piece of wood.

sticky *adj.*

His fingers are sticky.
stickier stickiest

stick *n.*
or

This is a stick of gum.

still *adj.*

It is very still outside.
It's very quiet outside.

stick *v.*

I will stick the picture in my album.
I'll paste it in my album.

still *adv.*

He is still looking for his ball.
He continues to look for it.

stick *v.*
or

Why did the drawer stick?
Why wouldn't it open?

still *adv.*

I told the children to sit still.
I told them to sit quietly.

stomach 469

sting v.

Did the bee sting the boy?
stings   stung   stinging

stocking n. clothing
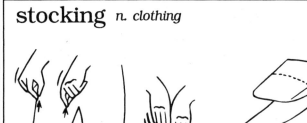
She bought a pair of stockings.
stocking   stockings

stingy adj.

The man is stingy.
He's selfish.

stole pt. of steal

He stole the money.

stink v.

Why does the kitchen stink?
stinks   stank/stunk   stinking   stunk

stolen pp. of steal

He has stolen a wallet.

stir v.

I have to stir the pudding.
stirs   stirred   stirring

stomach n. body part
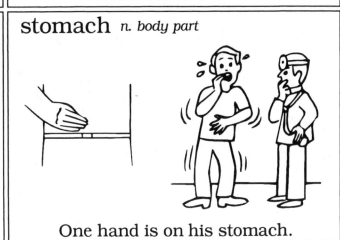
One hand is on his stomach.

470 stomachache

stomachache n.

He has a stomachache.
His stomach hurts.

stool n.
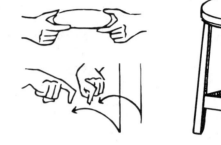
The stool has four legs.
stool   stools

stone n. rock

There are two stones near the pond.
stone   stones

stop v.

I hope I can stop in time.
stops   stopped   stopping

stood pt. of stand

The boy stood on a book and
tried to reach the cookies.

stopper n. plug
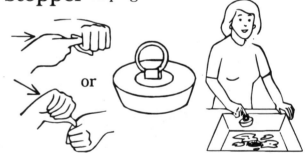
She pulled out the stopper.
stopper   stoppers

stood up pt. of stand up

She stood up while she filed.

store n.

The store is having a sale.
store   stores

straight 471

stories *plural of* **story**	**stove** *n.*
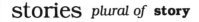  He likes adventure stories.	She wants a new stove. stove stoves

storm *n.*	**straight** *adj.*
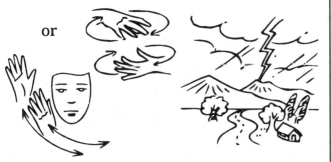 There was an awful storm yesterday. storm storms	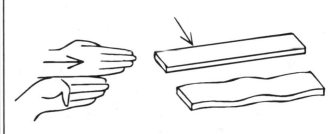 This board is <u>straight</u>. It's <u>not crooked</u>.

story *n.* tale	**straight** *adj.*
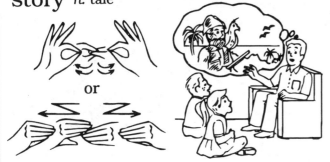 He is telling the children a <u>story</u>.	 I want a <u>straight</u> answer. I want an <u>honest</u> answer.

story *n.*	**straight** *adj.*
 The building has three <u>stories</u>. It has three <u>floors</u>.	 He kept a straight face. He showed no emotion.

472 straight

straight adv.

He ran straight to the plane.
He ran directly to it.

strain v.

I have to strain the broth.

strain n. stress, pressure
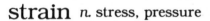
He is under a lot of strain.
strain   strains

strand v.

He was stranded on the island.
He had no way to get home.

strain v. injure

How did you strain your back?
strains   strained   straining

strange adj. unfamiliar

We visited some strange places.
stranger   strangest

strain v.

He had to strain to lift the box.
He had to try hard to lift it.

stranger n.

The man is a stranger.
I don't know him.

streetcar 473

straw n.

The horse sleeps on the straw.

stream v.

I saw people stream out of the building.
I saw people pour out.

straw n.

He is drinking through a straw.
straw   straws

stream v.

Tears began to stream down her face.
Tears began to run down her face.

strawberry n. fruit

The strawberry is sweet.
strawberry   strawberries

street n.

This street is not very wide.
street   streets

stream n.
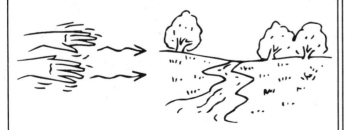
A stream is smaller than a river.
stream   streams

streetcar n. vehicle
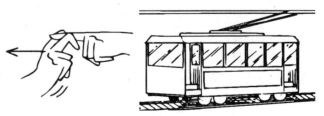
He rides the streetcar to work.
streetcar   streetcars

474 strength

strength n.

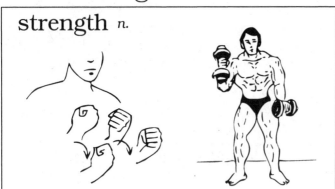

He has a lot of strength.
He is very strong.

stretch v.

I need to stretch.
stretches   stretched   stretching

stress n. pressure, strain

He is under a lot of stress.
He feels a lot of pressure.

stretch v.

Don't stretch that rubber band.

stress v. emphasize

I must stress the need for caution.
stresses   stressed   stressing

stretch out

I often stretch out under the tree.

stretch n.

There was no rain for a long stretch - for a long period of time.

stretcher n.

Two men are carrying the stretcher.
stretcher   stretchers

string 475

stricken pp. of strike

His name was stricken from the list.
It was crossed off the list.

strike n.

Three strikes and the player is out.

strict adj.

The teacher is very strict.
She expects us to study and behave.

strike v.

or

I will strike him with my umbrella.
I'll hit him with my umbrella.

strike n.

The workers are on strike.
    strike   strikes

strike v.

The clock began to strike 12 o'clock.
strikes struck striking struck/stricken

strike n.

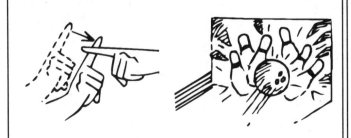

She made a strike.
All of the pins fell down.

string n.

or

He tied the package with string.
    string   strings

476 string

string n.

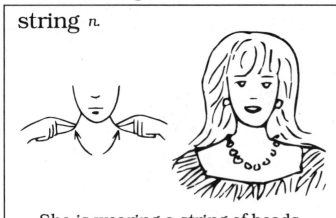

She is wearing a string of beads.

stripe n.

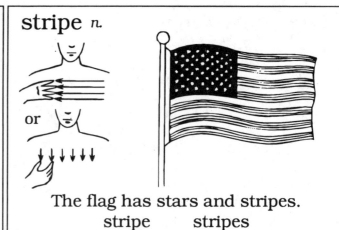

The flag has stars and stripes.
stripe   stripes

string n.

A string of people were waiting.
A line of people were waiting.

strong adj.

The man is very strong.
stronger   strongest

string v.

They will string the rope
from the tree to the house.

struck pp. of **strike**

The clock has struck 12.
The clock has stricken 12.

string bean n. vegetable

I will cook some string beans.
string bean   string beans

struck pt. of **strike**

He struck the door with his fist.

study 477

struggle v.

Did he <u>struggle</u> with the burglar?
Did he <u>fight</u> with the burglar?

stuck pt. of **stick**

The drawer stuck.

struggle v.

I had to <u>struggle</u> through the crowd.
I had to <u>work hard</u> to move forward.

student n. pupil

One student answered the question.
    student   students

stubborn adj.

The boy is stubborn.
He won't obey his mother.

study v. try to learn

You must study hard.
  studies studied studying

stuck pp. of **stick**

She had stuck a flower in her hair.

study v.

He has to <u>study</u> the evidence.
He must <u>examine</u> it carefully.

478 stuff

stuff n.

She bought some <u>stuff</u>.
She bought some <u>things</u>.

stung pt. of **sting**

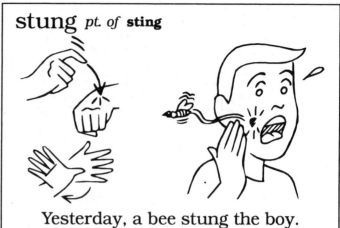

Yesterday, a bee stung the boy.

stuff v.

She will stuff the turkey.
stuffs   stuffed   stuffing

stunk pt. of **stink**

The fish <u>stunk</u>.
It <u>stank</u>.

stuff v.

I always stuff myself.
I always eat too much.

stupid adj.

or

I did a stupid thing.
I didn't study hard.

stumble v.

Why did he <u>stumble</u> and fall?
Why did he <u>trip</u> and fall?

sturdy adj.

or

He has a <u>sturdy</u> body.
He has a <u>strong</u> body.

suddenly 479

submarine n.

Submarines travel under water.
submarine submarines

success n.

Edison made a success of his life.
He made a good life for himself.

subtract v.

He can subtract 6 from 8.
subtracts subtracted subtracting

sucker n. candy
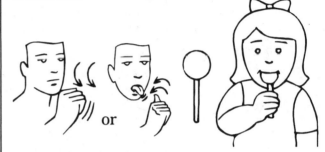
She is eating a sucker.
She's eating a lollipop.

subway n. vehicle
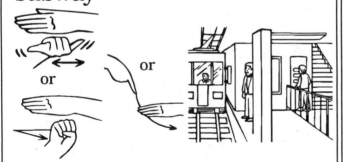
He takes the subway to work.
subway subways

sudden adj.

A sudden noise startled him.
An unexpected noise startled him.

succeed v.

The attack did succeed.
It was successful.

suddenly adv.

He jumped up suddenly.
He jumped up quickly.

480 suffer

suffer v.
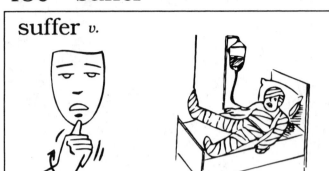
I suffer a lot of pain.
suffers   suffered   suffering

suit n. clothing

The man bought a new suit.
suit   suits

sugar n. food

He uses sugar in his coffee.

suit v. be agreeable to

Does the price suit you?
Is the price satisfactory?

suggest v.

I suggest you stop smoking.
I'm telling you that you should stop.

not suitable adj. unsuitable

Your manners are not suitable.
Your manners are not appropriate.

suggestion n.

She made a suggestion.
She offered a plan.

suitcase n.
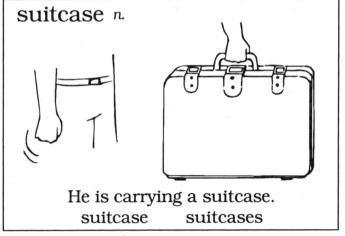
He is carrying a suitcase.
suitcase   suitcases

sunk 481

sum *n.* total

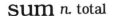

The sum of 1 and 1 is 2.

Sunday *n. day of the week*

They go to church every Sunday.
Sunday   Sundays

summer *n. season*

We get a vacation every summer.
summer   summers

sung *pp. of* **sing**

The choir has sung a song.

sun *n.*

or

The sun comes up in the morning
and goes down in the evening.

sunglasses *n.*

She's wearing a pair of sunglasses.

sundae *n.*

She ordered a sundae.
sundae   sundaes

sunk *pp. of* **sink**

The boat has sunk.

482 sunk

sunk pt. of sink

The boat sunk.
The boat sank.

super adj. informal

My new bike is super.
My new bike is wonderful.

sunny adj.

or

It is a sunny day.
sunnier sunniest

Superman n.

Superman is very strong.

sunrise n. dawn

or

The sun comes up at sunrise.
sunrise sunrises

supervise v.

I supervise the work.
I see that it's done correctly.

sunset n. nightfall

or

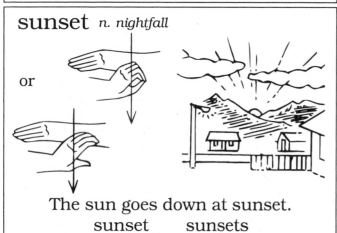

The sun goes down at sunset.
sunset sunsets

supper n. evening meal

We had roast beef for supper.
supper suppers

surgery 483

support *v.*

The prop will support the branch.
supports   supported   supporting

sure *adj.*

I am sure that's the thief.
I'm certain that's him.

support *v.*

I support the peace movement.
I am in favor of it.

surface *n.*

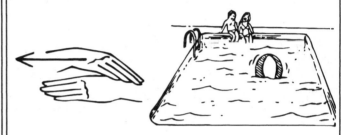

The ball floats on
the surface of the water.

suppose *v.*

I suppose it will rain.
I think it will rain.

surface *v.*

The submarine will surface.
It will rise to the surface of the water.

supposed to

You are supposed to do your homework.
You're expected to do it.

surgery *n.*

He had surgery.
He had an operation.

484 surprise

surprise n.
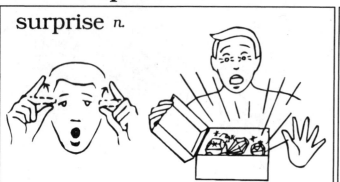
Imagine my surprise when I saw jewels.
surprises   surprised   surprising

suspicious adj.

She is suspicious of him.
She suspects he is dishonest.

surrender v.

We surrender.
We give up.

swallow v.
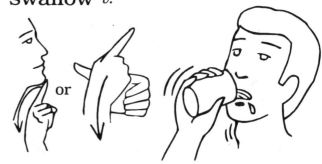
The man will swallow some water.
swallows   swallowed   swallowing

surround v. circle

Why did they surround the cabin?
surrounds   surrounded   surrounding

swam pt. of swim

Yesterday, they swam in the ocean.

suspect v.

I suspect the man is dishonest -
that he's trying to cheat that woman.

swan n. bird

The swan is swimming in the lake.
swan   swans

swell 485

sweat v.
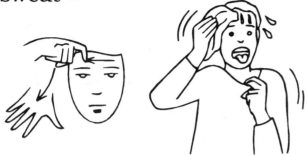
I <u>sweat</u> in hot weather.
I <u>perspire</u> in hot weather.

sweet adj.

Pie and candy are sweet.
sweeter   sweetest

sweater n. clothing
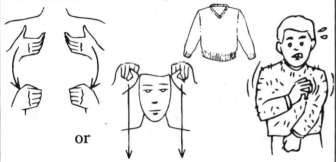
or
The sweater makes him itch.
sweater   sweaters

sweethearts n.

They are sweethearts.
They love each other.

Sweden n. country
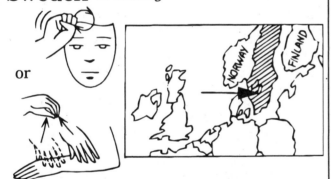
or
Sweden is a country in Europe.

swell adj. informal

We had a <u>swell</u> time.
We had a <u>wonderful</u> time.

sweep v.

She will sweep the floor.
sweeps   swept   sweeping

swell v.

My ankle began to swell.
swells   swelled   swelling   swelled/swollen

486 swept

swept *pt. of* **sweep**

The woman swept the floor.

swimming *n.*

They like swimming in the ocean.

swift *adj.*

or

She is <u>swift</u> to lose her temper.
She's <u>quick</u> to lose her temper.

swimming pool *n.*

or

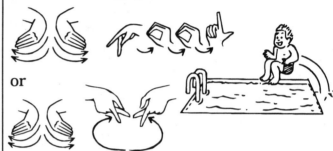

He enjoys the swimming pool.
swimming pool   swimming pools

swim *v.*

I swim every day.
swims   swam   swimming   swum

swimsuit *n. clothing*

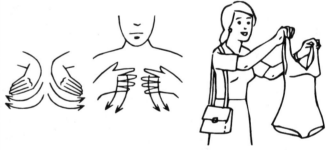

She bought a new <u>swimsuit</u>.
She bought a new <u>bathing suit</u>.

swim *v.*

Her head began to swim.
She began to feel dizzy.

swing *n.*

The girl ran to the swing.
swing   swings

swollen 487

swing *v.*

They swing at school every day.
swings swung swinging

switch off *v.*

Don't <u>switch off</u> the light.
Don't <u>turn off</u> the light.

switch *n.*
 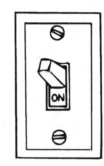
The switch is on the wall.
switch switches

switch on *v.*
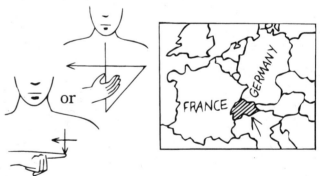
Did Father <u>switch on</u> the light?
Did he <u>turn on</u> the light?

switch *v. exchange, trade*

They'll switch sandwiches.
switches switched switching

Switzerland *n. country*

Switzerland is a country in Europe.

switch *v.*

I could switch you, but maybe it's better to give you some time-out.

swollen *adj.*

He has a swollen jaw.

488 swollen

swollen pp. of **swell**

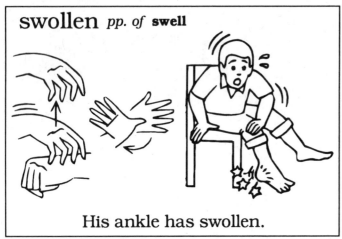

His ankle has swollen.

symbol n.

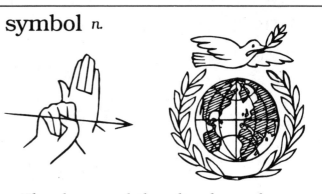

The dove and the olive branch are peace symbols. They represent peace.

sword n. weapon

He is holding his sword.
sword   swords

sympathy n.

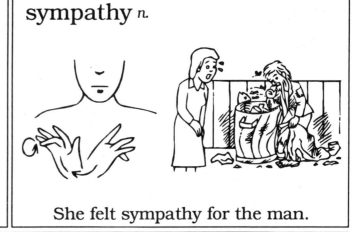

She felt sympathy for the man.

swum pp. of **swim**

He has swum for an hour.

syrup n. food

He poured syrup on his pancakes.

swung pt. of **swing**

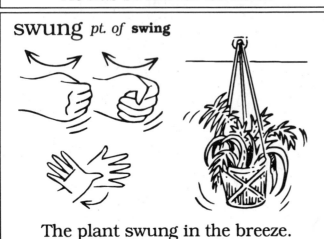

The plant swung in the breeze.

system n.

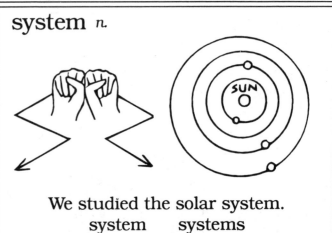

We studied the solar system.
system   systems

T t

table *n. furniture*

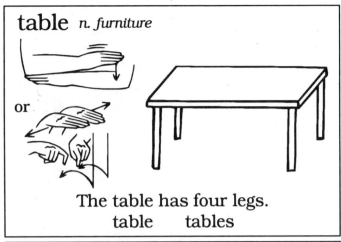

The table has four legs.
table   tables

tablet *n.*

She wrote on the tablet.
tablet   tablets

table *n.*

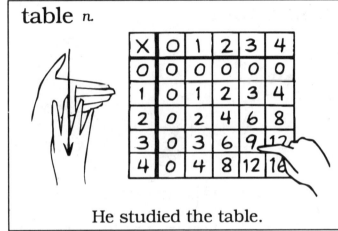

He studied the table.

tack *n.*

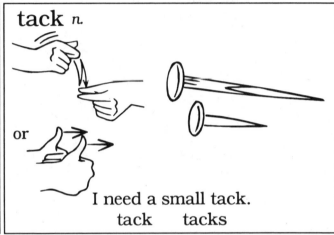

I need a small tack.
tack   tacks

tablecloth *n.*

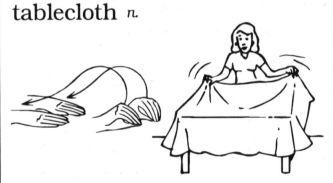

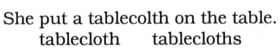

She put a tablecolth on the table.
tablecloth   tablecloths

taco *n. food*

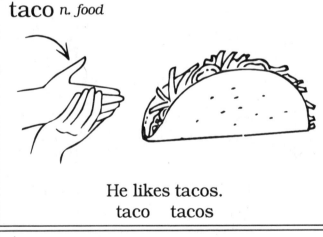

He likes tacos.
taco   tacos

tablet *n.*

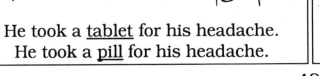

He took a <u>tablet</u> for his headache.
He took a <u>pill</u> for his headache.

tag *n.*

She looked at the price tag.
tag   tags

490 tag

tag *n. game*

They are playing tag.

take *v.*

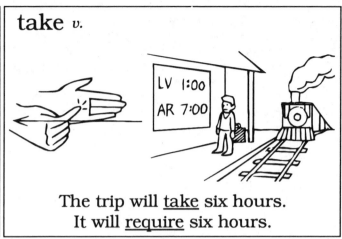

The trip will <u>take</u> six hours.
It will <u>require</u> six hours.

tail *n. animal body part*

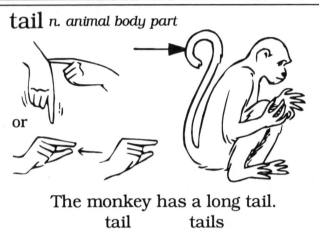

or

The monkey has a long tail.
tail   tails

take advantage of *v.*

You always take advantage of me.
You always cheat me.

tailor *n. clothes maker*

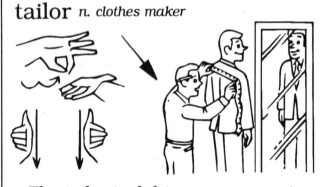

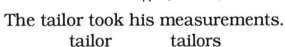

The tailor took his measurements.
tailor   tailors

take away *v. subtract*

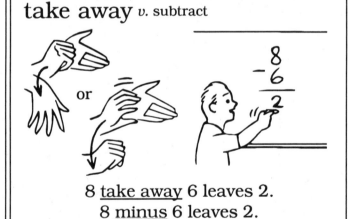

or

8 <u>take away</u> 6 leaves 2.
8 <u>minus</u> 6 leaves 2.

take *v.*

or

Don't take my ball.
takes   took   taking   taken

take care of *v.*

I take care of the baby.

tall 491

take off v.

The plane will take off.
It will leave the ground.

take turns v.

They take turns using the swing.

take off v.

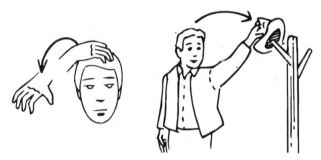

He has to take off his hat.
He has to remove his hat.

taken pp. of **take**

He has taken a cupcake.

take off v. informal

I saw the burglar take off.
I saw him rush away.

talk v.

The man will talk about the storm.
talks   talked   talking

take place v.

When did the accident take place?
When did it happen?

tall adj.

The boy is tall.
taller   tallest

492 tamale

tamale n. food

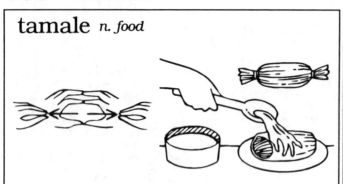

She fixed tamales for dinner.
tamale   tamales

tap n.

The tap leaks.
The faucet leaks.

tame v. train

The man will tame the lion.
tames   tamed   taming

tap v.

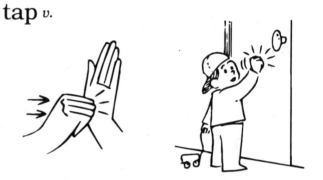

I will just tap on the door.
I'll just knock lightly.

tan n. color

She got a tan at the beach.

tap v.

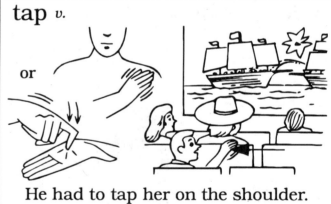

He had to tap her on the shoulder.
taps   tapped   tapping

tank n. weapon

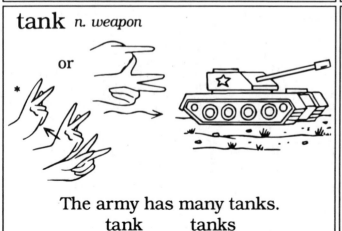

The army has many tanks.
tank   tanks

tape n.

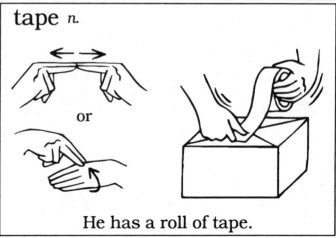

He has a roll of tape.

tax 493

tape measure n.
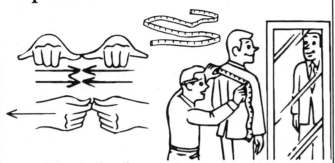
The tailor has a tape measure.
tape measure   tape measures

taste v.

The cook must taste the soup.
tastes   tasted   tasting

tape recorder n.
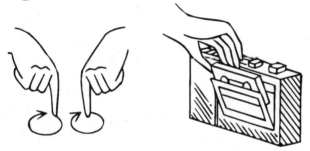
He has a tape recorder.
tape recorder   tape recorders

tattletale n.

He's a tattletale.
He runs and tells Mother everything.

tardy adj.

The boy was tardy.
He was late.

taught pt. of teach
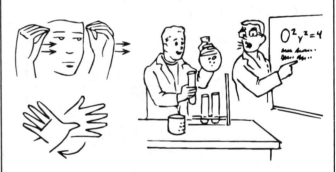
The man taught the class.

target n.

He hit the target.
target   targets

tax n.

She forgot to add the tax.
tax   taxes

494 taxi

taxi n. vehicle
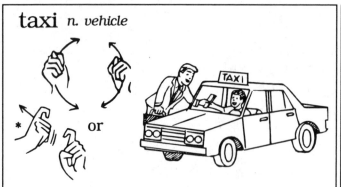
He took a taxi to the airport.
He took a cab to the airport.

teacher n. worker
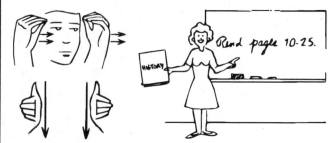
She is a good teacher.
teacher   teachers

TDD n. TTY

He called his friend on the TDD.

teakettle n.

I heat water in the teakettle.
teakettle   teakettles

tea n. beverage

Father drinks tea.

team n.

Our team won the game.
team   teams

teach v.
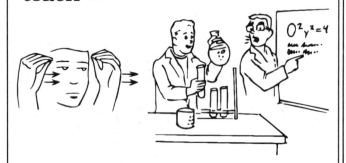
I teach this class every year.
teaches   taught   teaching

tear n.
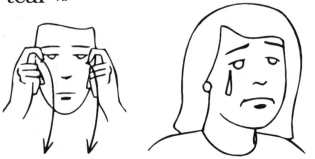
There is a tear on her cheek.
tear   tears

telegram 495

tear v.
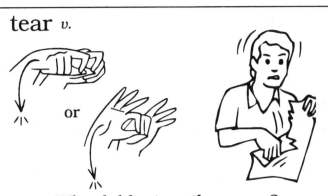
Why did he tear the paper?
tears   tore   tearing   torn

teenager n.

They are teenagers.
They're between 13 and 19 years old.

tease v.

The boy likes to tease that girl.
teases   teased   teasing

teeter-totter n.

The girls like the teeter-totter.
They like the seesaw.

technical adj.

The instructions contain technical words that he doesn't understand.

teeth plural of tooth
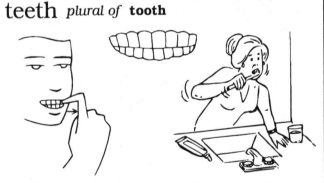
She brushes her teeth every day.
tooth   teeth

teddy bear n. toy

The boy loves his teddy bear.
teddy bear   teddy bears

telegram n.
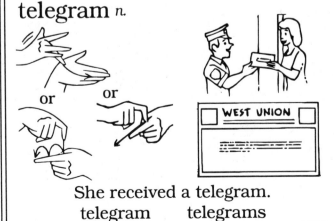
She received a telegram.
telegram   telegrams

496 telephone

telephone n. phone

They are talking on the telephone.
telephone   telephones

temper n.

She has a bad temper.
She becomes angry easily.

telescope n.

He is looking through the telescope.
telescope   telescopes

temperature n.
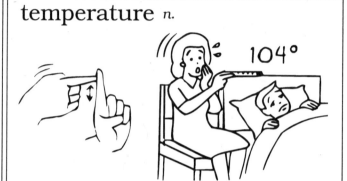
He has a high temperature.
temperature   temperatures

television n. TV

He is watching television.

temperature gauge n.
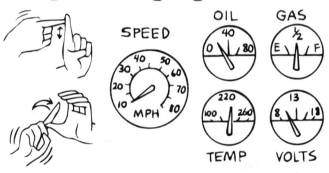
The temperature gauge is on the dashboard.

tell v.

I will tell you a story.
tells   told   telling

temple n. synagogue, synagog

They go to the temple on Saturday.
temple   temples

tennis 497

tempt v.

The cookies tempt the boy.
tempts   tempted   tempting

tend v.

I tend to believe he is a fraud.
I am inclined to believe he's a fraud.

ten number: 10

Ten times ten equals 100.

tendency n.

She has a tendency to lose her temper.
She is inclined to lose her temper.

tend v.

I tend the baby.
I take care of the baby.

tender adj.

Her steak is very tender.
Her steak is not tough.

tend v.

She didn't tend to her cooking.
She didn't pay attention to it.

tennis n. game

They like to play tennis.

498   tennis shoe

tennis shoe n.

This is a pair of tennis shoes.
tennis shoe   tennis shoes

terrible adj.
or
The man has a terrible headache.
He has an awful headache.

tent n. cloth shelter
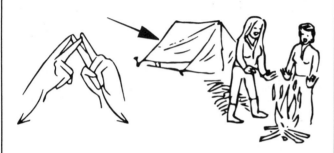
They will sleep in the tent.
tent   tents

terrific adj.
or

They had a terrific time.
They had a wonderful time.

tenth n. 10th
or

His appointment is on the tenth.

terrify v.

Lions terrify me.
terrifies   terrified   terrifying

tepee n. teepee
*

The indian sleeps in a tepee.
tepee   tepees

test n.

He passed the test.
test   tests

that   499

testify v.

She had to <u>testify</u> at the trial.
She had to <u>give evidence</u>.

thank v.

Did the boy thank his father?
thanks   thanked   thanking

testimony n.

Her testimony convinced the jury that the man was guilty.

Thanksgiving n. holiday

Thanksgiving is the fourth Thursday in November.

Texas n. state: TX
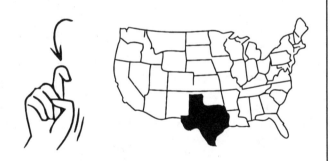
Texas became a state in 1845.

thank you

He forgot to say "thank you."

than conj.

The boy would rather play baseball than mow the lawn.

that adj.

That marble is yours. (adj.)
That is yours. (pron.)

500 the

the definite article

A boy and girl went skating.
The boy fell down.

theirs adj., pron.
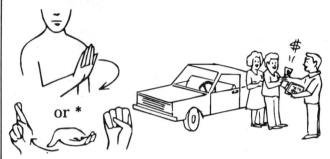
This is their car. (adj.)
This car is theirs. (pron.)

theater n. theatre

They went to the theater.
theater   theaters

them pron.

The marbles belong to them.
The marbles belong to the boys.

theft n.

The burglar admitted the theft.
He admitted stealing the money.

themselves pron.

They made lunch themselves.
No one helped them make lunch.

their adj.

They bought this house.
This is their house.

then adv.

First he got a book to stand on,
then he reached for the cookie jar.

thigh 501

therapist n. worker

The therapist helps him improve his speech.

they pron.

or *

The man and woman own the house.
They own the house.

there adv.

or

There is my home.
I live there.

thick adj. not thin

or

This steak is thick.
thicker   thickest

thermometer n.

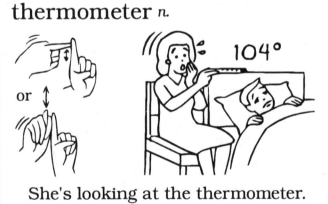

or

She's looking at the thermometer.
thermometer   thermometers

thief n.

or

The thief ran away.
thief   thieves

these adj., pron.

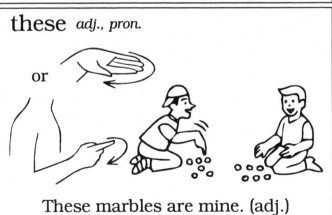

or

These marbles are mine. (adj.)
These are mine. (pron.)

thigh n. body part

*

He patted his thigh.
thigh   thighs

502 thimble

thimble n.

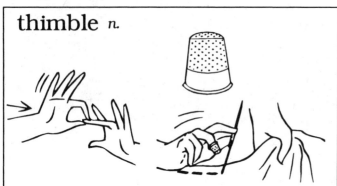

She has a thimble on her finger.
thimble   thimbles

think v.

I have to think about my ball.
thinks   thought   thinking

thin adj. skinny

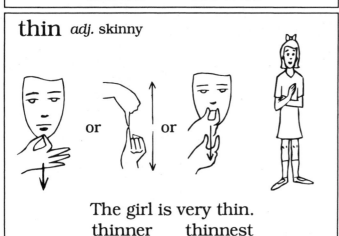

The girl is very thin.
thinner   thinnest

third adj. 3rd

The man wearing the cap is third in line.

thin adj.

This steak is thin.

third n. fraction: 1/3

He ate a third of the pie.

thing n.

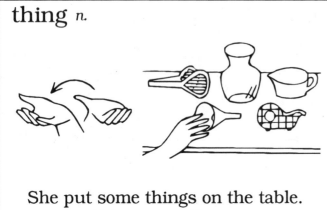

She put some things on the table.
thing   things

thirsty adj.

The man is very thirsty.
thirstier   thirstiest

thoughtless 503

thirteen *number:* 13

The girl is thirteen years old.

those *adj., pron.*

Those marbles are yours. (adj.)
Those are yours. (pron.)

thirty *number:* 30

June has thirty days.
There are thirty days in June.

thought *pt. of* **think**

The boy thought about his future.

this *adj., pron.*

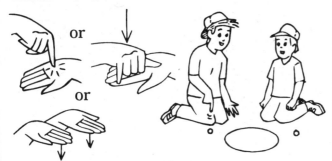

This marble is mine. (adj.)
This is mine. (pron.)

thoughtful *adj.*

He is a thoughtful person.
He shows concern for other people.

thorn *n.*

The thorns have sharp points.
thorn   thorns

thoughtless *adj.*

He is a thoughtless person.
He doesn't care about other people.

504 thousand

thousand *number: 1000*

The boy counted to a thousand.
thousand   thousands

three fourths *fraction: 3/4*

Three fourths of the pie is left.
Three quarters of it is left.

thread *n.*

or *

This is a spool of thread.

threw *pt. of* **throw**

The girl threw the ball.

threaten *v.*

He did threaten to kill me. He said he would kill me if I didn't obey.

thrill *v. excite*

Did winning $1,000,000 thrill her?
thrills   thrilled   thrilling

three *number: 3*

I have three pears.

throat *n. body part*

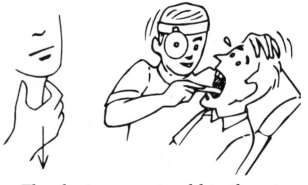

The doctor examined his throat.

throne n.

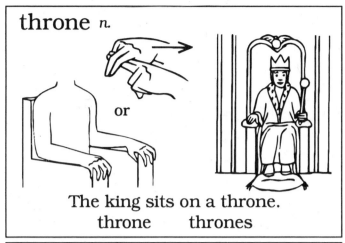

The king sits on a throne.
throne   thrones

throw out v.

He should <u>throw out</u> that junk.
He should <u>get rid of</u> it.

through adj.

She <u>is through with</u> the laundry.
She <u>has finished</u> it.

throw up v.

The boy had to <u>throw up</u>.
He had to <u>vomit</u>.

through prep.

The bird flew through the window.

thrown pp. of **throw**

The man has thrown the spear.

throw v. toss

She likes to throw the ball.
throws   threw   throwing   thrown

thumb n. body part

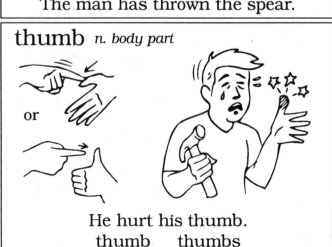

He hurt his thumb.
thumb   thumbs

506 thumbtack

thumbtack n.
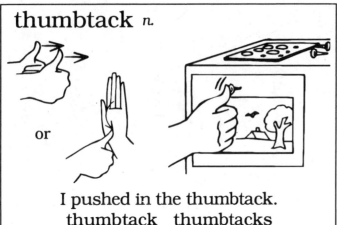
I pushed in the thumbtack.
thumbtack   thumbtacks

ticket n.

He bought tickets for the movie.

thunder n.

We heard the thunder and saw a flash of lightning.

tickle v.
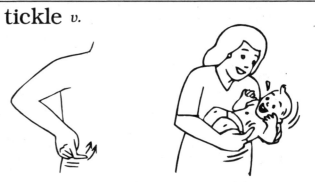
Mother likes to tickle the baby.
tickles   tickled   tickling

Thursday n. day of the week
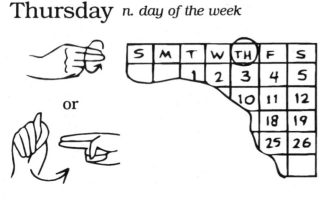
Thursday comes before Friday.

tie n. clothing
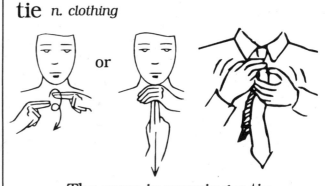
The man is wearing a tie.
He's wearing a necktie.

ticket n.

He got a ticket.
ticket   tickets

tie n.

The game ended in a tie.
Both teams had the same score.

time 507

tie v.

The girl can tie her shoes.
ties　　tied　　tying

tightrope n.
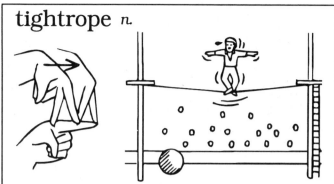
The man is on the tightrope.
tightrope　　tightropes

tiger n. animal

The tiger has stripes.
tiger　　tigers

tights n. clothing

She is wearing tights.

tight adj.

The dress is much too tight.
tighter　　tightest

time n.

It usually snows this time of year.

tighten v.
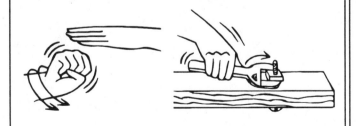
He must tighten the nut.
He must make it tighter.

time n.

He can't tell time so he got to school too early.

508 times

times *prep.*

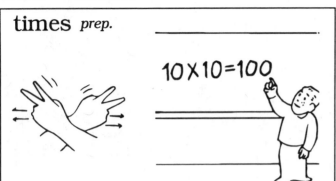

10 times 10 is 100.
10 multipled by 10 is 100.

tip *n.*

It is customary to leave a tip.
tip   tips

timid *adj.*

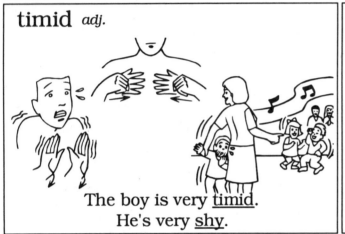

The boy is very timid.
He's very shy.

tip *n.*

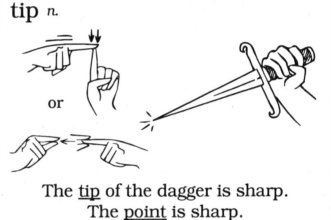

or

The tip of the dagger is sharp.
The point is sharp.

tin *n. metal*

or

The can is made of tin.

tip *n.*

The tip was covered with snow.
The peak was covered with snow.

tiny *adj.*

or

or

One bear is tiny.
One is very small.

tip over

How did I tip over my glass?
How did I upset it?

toaster 509

tiptoe v.

Why did he tiptoe into the room?
tiptoes   tiptoed   tiptoeing

to prep.

He gave a gift to the girl.

tire n.

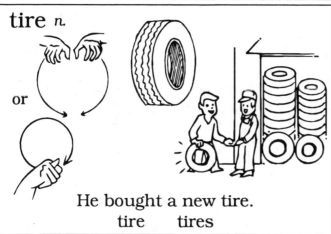

He bought a new tire.
tire   tires

toast n.

He's eating a piece of toast.
one piece   two pieces

tired adj.

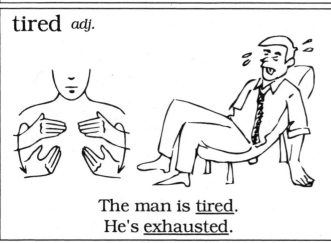

The man is tired.
He's exhausted.

toast v.

I will toast two slices of bread.
toasts   toasted   toasting

title n.

What is the title of the book?
What's the name of the book?

toaster n. electrical appliance

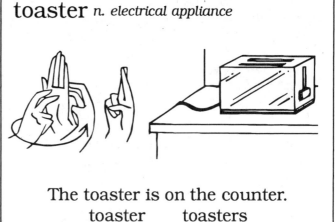

The toaster is on the counter.
toaster   toasters

510 today

today n.
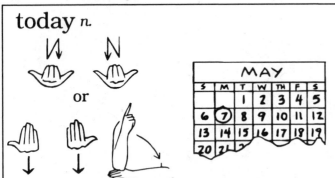
Today is the 7th of May.
Tomorrow will be the 8th of May.

told pt. of tell
The man told the children a story.

toe n. body part
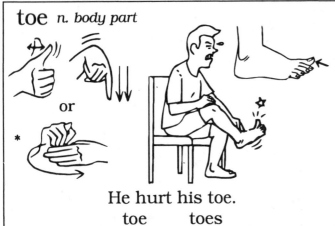
He hurt his toe.
toe   toes

tomato n. vegetable
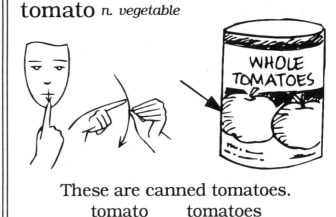
These are canned tomatoes.
tomato   tomatoes

together adv.
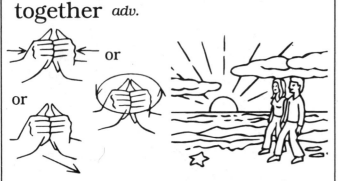
They walked together.
They walked with each other.

tomorrow n.
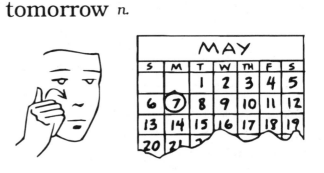
Tomorrow will be May 8.
The day after today will be May 8.

toilet n.

He flushed the toilet.
toilet   toilets

tongue n. body part
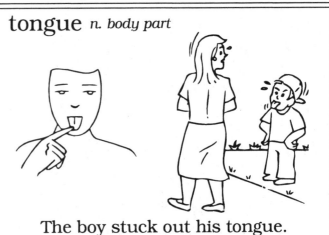
The boy stuck out his tongue.

tooth 511

tonight n.

I will call you tonight.
I'll call you this evening.

took pt. of **take**

The boy took the girl's ball.

tonsils n. body part

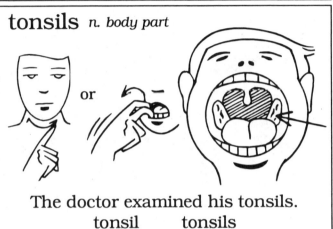

The doctor examined his tonsils.
tonsil   tonsils

tool n.

A carpenter uses many tools.
tool   tools

too adv. also

He got a B in English.
He got a B in reading, too.

toot v.

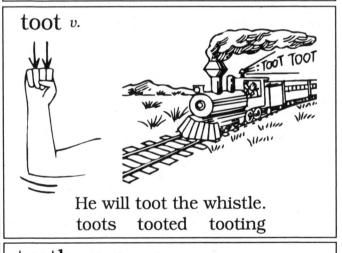

He will toot the whistle.
toots   tooted   tooting

too adv.

That dress is too tight.
It's very tight.

tooth n. body part

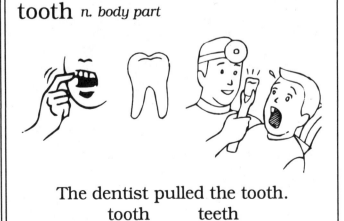

The dentist pulled the tooth.
tooth   teeth

512　toothache

toothache n.

He has a toothache.
toothache　　toothaches

top n.

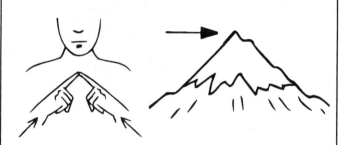

The top was covered with snow.
The peak was covered with snow.

toothbrush n.

She's using a toothbrush.
toothbrush　　toothbrushes

top n. toy

He is playing with the top.
top　　tops

toothpaste n.

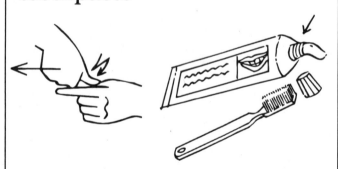

This is a tube of toothpaste.

torch n.

The man is carrying a torch.
torch　　torches

top adj.

The box is on the top shelf.
It's on the highest shelf.

tore pt. of tear

The boy tore the paper.

toss 513

torment *v.*

He should not torment the dog.
He shouldn't make it suffer.

tortilla *n.* food
He bought tortillas to make tacos.
tortilla   tortillas

torn *adj.*

The dress is torn.

tortoise *n.* turtle
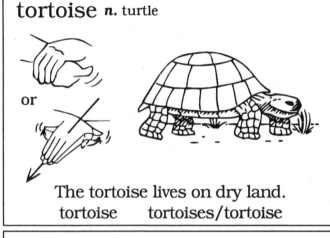
The tortoise lives on dry land.
tortoise   tortoises/tortoise

torn *pp. of* tear
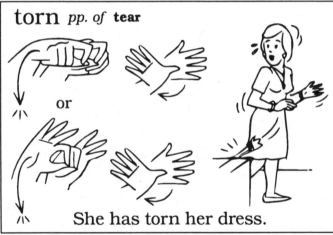
She has torn her dress.

torture *v.*
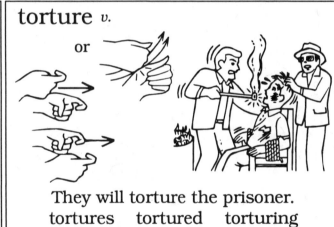
They will torture the prisoner.
tortures   tortured   torturing

tornado *n.*
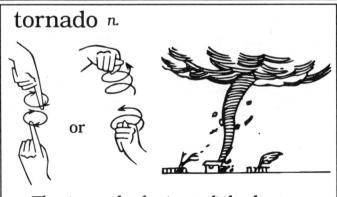
The tornado destroyed the house.
tornado   tornadoes/tornados

toss *v.*

I will <u>toss</u> my coat on the bed.
I'll <u>throw</u> it on the bed.

514 tostada

tostada *n. food*

He ordered a tostada.
tostada   tostadas

tough *adj.*

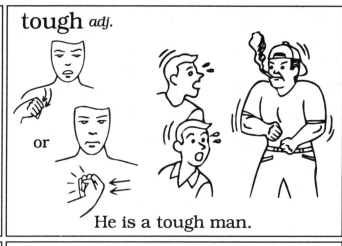

He is a tough man.

total *n.*

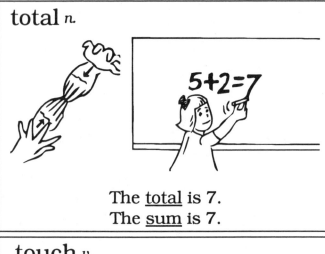

The total is 7.
The sum is 7.

tour *n.*

They took a studio tour.
They were shown around the studio.

touch *v.*

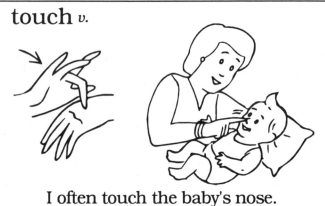

I often touch the baby's nose.
touches   touched   touching

tow *v.*

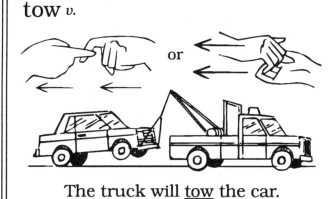

The truck will tow the car.
It will pull the car.

tough *adj.*

His steak is tough.
His steak is hard to cut and chew.

toward *prep.*

Father pointed toward the dog.
He pointed to the dog.

traffic light 515

towel n.
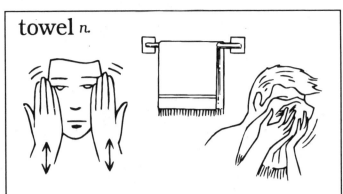
He dried his face with a towel.
towel   towels

tractor n.

The farmer is driving a tractor.
tractor   tractors

town n.

A town is larger than a village.
town   towns

trade n.

He has a good trade.
He is trained for skilled labor.

toy n.

The boy has many toys.
toy   toys

trade v. exchange, switch

They will trade sandwiches.
trades   traded   trading

track n.
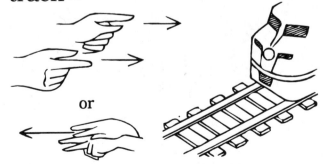
Trains run on tracks.
track   tracks

traffic light n.

You must stop for the traffic light.
traffic light   traffic lights

516 trail

trail n.

He walked along the trail.
He walked along the path.

train v.

He will train the lion.
trains   trained   training

trail v.

or
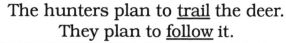
The hunters plan to trail the deer.
They plan to follow it.

trampoline n.

She is jumping on the trampoline.
trampoline   trampolines

trailer n. vehicle

The car is pulling a trailer.
trailer   trailers

transfer v.
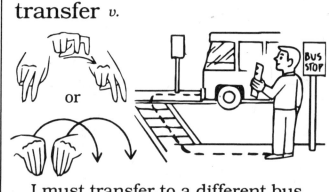
I must transfer to a different bus.
transfers   transferred   transferring

train n.

He is waiting for the train.
train   trains

transfer v.

She'll transfer the cookies
from the pan to the plate.

tray 517

transparent adj.
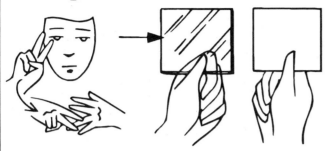
The glass is transparent.
You can see through it.

trapeze n.
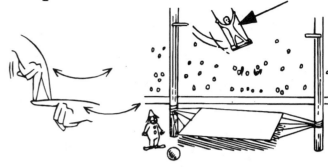
We watched the man on the trapeze.

transportation n.
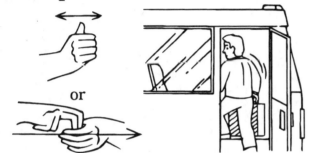
He uses the bus for transportation
- to get to and from his job.

trash can n.
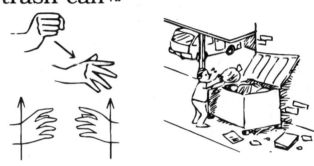
The trash cans are in the alley.
trash can   trash cans

trap n.

We set a trap to catch the mouse.
trap   traps

travel v.

They like to travel.
They like to take trips.

trap v.

They were trapped in the elevator.
They couldn't get out.

tray n.
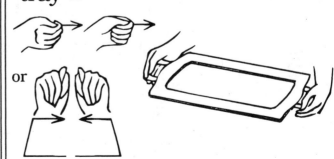
The tray has two handles.
tray   trays

518 treasure

treasure n.

The pirate is burying the treasure.

tree n.
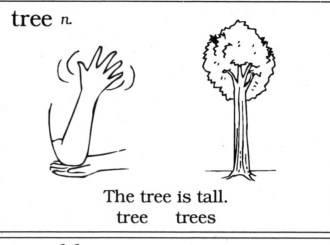
The tree is tall.
tree   trees

treat v.

I treat my husband like a king.
treats   treated   treating

tremble v. shake

The woman began to tremble.
trembles   trembled   trembling

treat v.
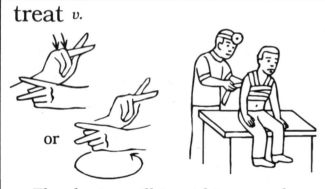
The doctor will <u>treat</u> his wounds.
The doctor will <u>care for</u> his wounds.

triangle n. shape
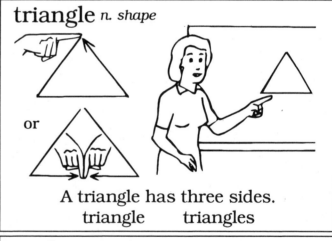
A triangle has three sides.
triangle   triangles

treatment n.
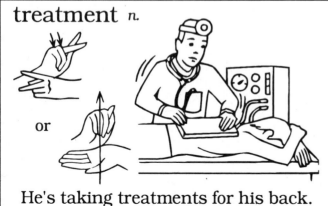
He's taking treatments for his back.
treatment   treatments

trick n.

The boy played a trick on Father.

triple 519

trick v. cheat

The man will trick her.
tricks   tricked   tricking

trim v.

I have to <u>trim</u> this hedge.
I must <u>clip</u> this hedge.

tricycle n. toy

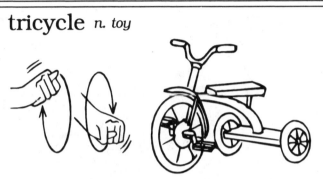

The tricycle has three wheels.
tricycle   tricycles

trip n.

They are leaving on their trip.
trip   trips

tried pt. of **try**

The boy tried to reach the
cookie jar, but he was too short.

trip v.

What caused him to trip and fall?
trips   tripped   tripping

trim v.

They will <u>trim</u> the tree.
They'll <u>decorate</u> the tree.

triple v.

Did the price triple?
Is it three times as much now.

520 trolley car

trolley car n.
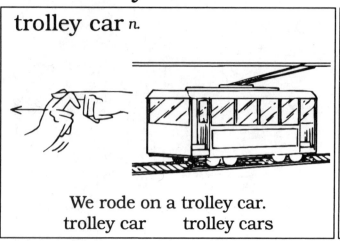
We rode on a trolley car.
trolley car   trolley cars

trousers n. pants

This is a pair of trousers.

trombone n. musical instrument
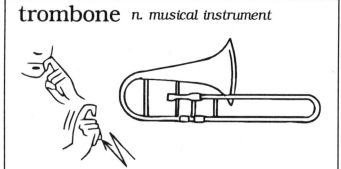
Can you play the trombone?
trombone   trombones

truck n. vehicle
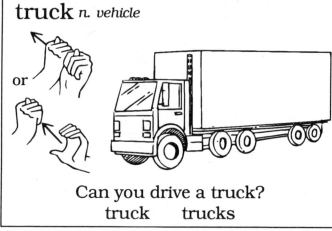
Can you drive a truck?
truck   trucks

trophy n. award

He won the trophy.
trophy   trophies

true adj.

I broke the window.
That is true.

trouble n.

He had trouble with the TV.
He had a problem with it.

trumpet n. musical instrument

He can play the trumpet.
trumpet   trumpets

try 521

trunk *n. animal body part*

The elephant has a long trunk.

trunk *n. chest*

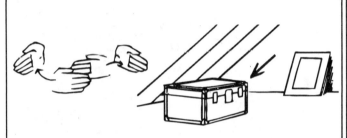

I put the trunk in the attic.
trunk   trunks

trunk *n. car part*

He will put the bags in the trunk.

trust *v.*

or

I just don't trust that man.
I don't believe he's honest.

trust *v.*

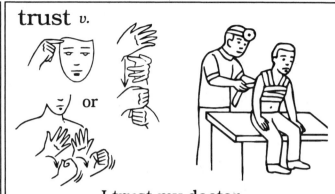

or

I trust my doctor.
I have faith in him.

truth *n.*

or

The boy told the truth.

truthful *adj.*

or

The boy is truthful.
He always tells the truth.

try *v. attempt*

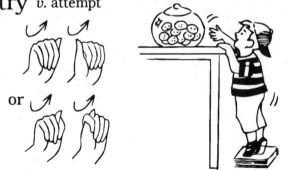

or

He will try to reach the cookies.
tries   tried   trying

522 try on

try on v.
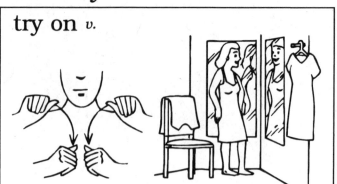
She will try on the dress.
She'll try the dress on.

tuba n. musical instrument

Can you play the tuba?
tuba   tubas

T-shirt n. clothing

The boy is wearing a T-shirt.
T-shirt   T-shirts

Tuesday n. day of the week
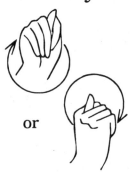 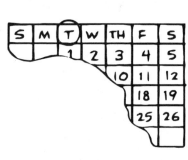
or
Tuesday comes before Wednesday.

TTY n. TDD

He called her on the TTY.
He called her on the TDD.

tug v.

He tried to tug the drawer open.
He tried to pull it open.

tub n.
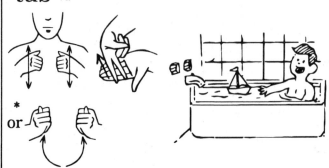
*
or
The boy is in the tub.
The boy is in the bathtub.

tulip n. flower

*
The tulip is very pretty.
tulip   tulips

turn 523

tumble v.

Did some boxes <u>tumble</u> off the cart?
Did some of them <u>fall</u> off the cart?

turn n.

or

The driver is making a right turn.

tuna n. food

She opened a can of tuna.

turn v.

The weather may <u>turn</u> bad.
The weather may <u>become</u> bad.

tunnel n.

or
*

The car drove through the tunnel.
    tunnel   tunnels

turn v.

He will turn the page.
  turns turned turning

turkey n. bird

We had turkey for Thanksgiving.
    turkey   turkeys

take **turns** n.

The children must take turns.
    turn   turns

524 turn down

turn down v.

Please turn down the volume.
Please lower it.

turn off v.

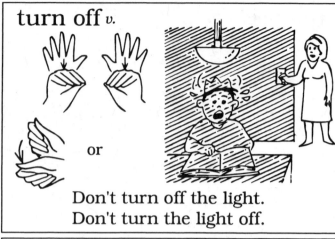

Don't turn off the light.
Don't turn the light off.

turn down v.

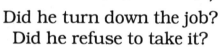

Did he turn down the job?
Did he refuse to take it?

turn on v.

Why did he turn on the light?
Why did he turn it on?

turn in v.

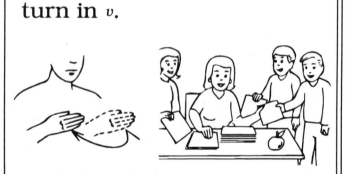

We had to turn in our homework.
We had to hand in our homework.

turn out v.

They turn out thousand of cars.
They produce thousand of them.

turn in v. *informal*

She is ready to turn in.
She's ready to go to bed.

turn out v.

Did Edison's plans turn out well?
Were his ideas successful?

twenty 525

turn over *v.*

He will <u>turn over</u> the pancake.
He'll <u>flip over</u> the pancake.

turtle *n.*

Turtles have hard shells.
turtle   turtles

turn over *v.*

I'll have to turn over your offer in my mind. I'll think about it carefully.

TV *n.*

They like to watch <u>TV</u>.
They like to watch <u>television</u>.

turn over *v.*

What made the car <u>turn over</u>?
What made it <u>overturn</u>?

twelve *number:* 12

Twelve eggs make a dozen.

turnip *n. vegetable*

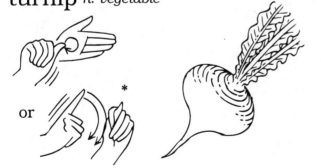

or

Turnips are white inside.
turnip   turnips

twenty *number:* 20

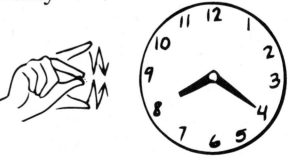

It's twenty minutes after eight.
It's 8:20.

526 twice

twice *adv.*

The phone rang twice.
It rang two times.

type *n. sort*

What type of seeds did you plant?
What kind of seeds did you plant?

twin *n.*

The girls are twins.
twin   twins

type *v.*

The woman can type fast.
types   typed   typing

two *number: 2*

The boy saw two apples.

typewriter *n.*

Typewriters and computers
have many keys.

tying *-ing form of* **tie**

The girl is tying her shoe.

typist *n. worker*

He is a good typist.
typist   typists

U u

ugly *adj.*

The witch is ugly.
uglier   ugliest

unbutton *v.*

I must unbutton my coat.
unbuttons unbuttoned unbuttoning

umbrella *n.*

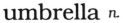

The girl has an umbrella.
umbrella   umbrellas

uncle *n. male relative*

That man is my uncle.
He is my father's brother.

unable *adj.*

or

He is unable to reach the cookies.
He can't reach them.

unclear *adj.*

The directions are unclear.
They're are hard to understand.

unaware *adj.*

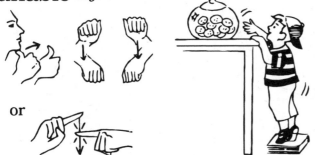

She is unaware of the snake.
She's not aware of it.

unconscious *adj.*

She is unconscious.
She's not conscious.

527

528 undependable

undependable *adj.* unreliable

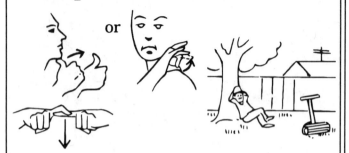

He is undependable. Sometimes he helps - sometimes he doesn't help.

underline *v.*

Please underline the verbs.
Please draw a line under the verbs.

under *prep.*

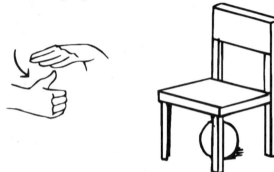

The ball is under the chair.

underneath *prep.*

The clock is underneath the picture.
It's below the picture.

under *prep.*

The cost is under a dollar.
The cost is less than a dollar.

understand *v.*

He doesn't understand that word.
understands   understood   understanding

underclothes *n.* clothing

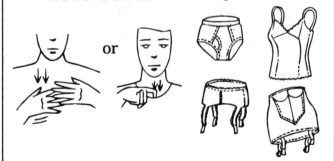

She bought some underclothes.
She bought some underwear.

understood *pt. of* **understand**

The boy understood the question.

university 529

underwear n. clothing

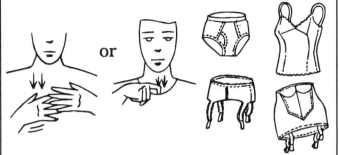

She bought some underwear.
She bought some underclothes.

unhappy adj.

The young woman is unhappy.
She's sad.

undress v.

She had to undress.
She had to take off her clothes.

uniform n. clothing

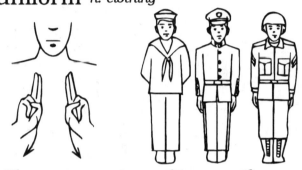

They are wearing military uniforms.
uniform   uniforms

unemployed adj.

He is unemployed. He has no job.

United States n. country

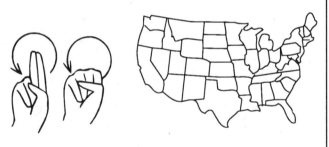

Washington, D.C. is the capital
of the United States.

unfair adj.

Mother was unfair.
She was not fair.

university n.

He graduated from the university.
university   universities

530 unless

unless *conj.*

You can't enter unless you pay.
You can't enter if you don't pay.

until *prep.*

School doesn't start until 9 o'clock.

unlock *v.*

She will unlock the door.
unlocks   unlocked   unlocking

untrue *adj.*

Your accusation is untrue.
It's false.

unsanitary *adj.*

Her kitchen is unsanitary.
Her kitchen is filthy.

unzip *v.*

I must unzip my jacket.
unzips   unzipped   unzipping

untie *v.*

He will untie the ropes.
He'll unfasten them.

up *adj.*

The man is up.
He's out of bed.

upstairs 531

up adv.
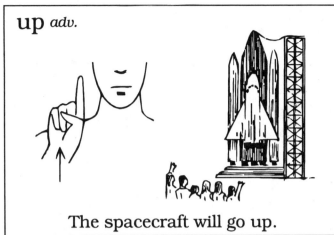
The spacecraft will go up.

upset adj.

Father is upset.
He's worried.

up prep.

He walked up the stairs.

upset v.

How did I upset the glass of milk?
How did I spill it?

upon prep.

He hung the picture upon the wall.
He hung it on the wall.

upside down adv.

He hung the picture upside down.

upset adj.
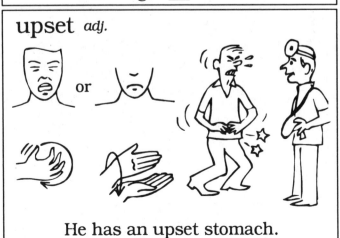
He has an upset stomach.

upstairs adv.

The girl is upstairs.
The boy is downstairs.

532   urge

urge *v.*

I <u>urge</u> you to study.
I <u>encourage</u> you to study.

use up *v.*

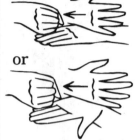 

Did he use up all the milk?
Did he empty the carton?

urinate *v.*

The boy had to urinate.
urinates   urinated   urinating

used to *adv.*

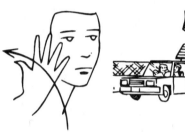 

They <u>used to</u> live in Mexico.
They <u>formerly</u> lived there.

us *pron.*

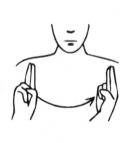 

This is our house.
It belongs to us.

used to

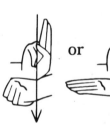 

He is not <u>used to</u> hot weather.
He's not <u>accustomed to</u> hot weather.

use *v.*

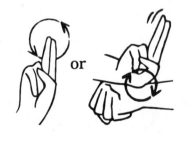 

He had to use a drill.
uses   used   using

usually *adv.*

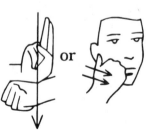 

He <u>usually</u> gets up at 6:30.
He <u>ordinarily</u> gets up then.

V v

vacant *adj.*
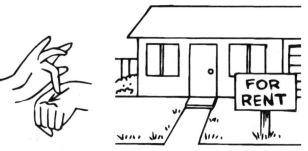
The house is vacant.
No one lives in the house.

valentine *n.*

The boy gave the girl a valentine.
valentine   valentines

vacation *n.*
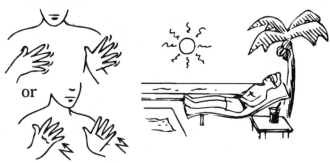
He takes his vacation in August.
vacation   vacations

Valentine's Day *n.*

Valentine's Day is February 14.

vaccinate *v.*
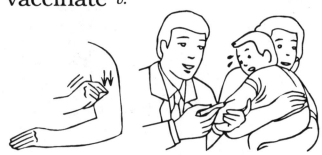
He will vaccinate the baby.
vaccinates   vaccinated   vaccinating

valid *adj.*
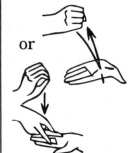
His license is valid until 5-15-98.
It's legal until 5-15-98.

vacuum cleaner *n.*

The woman bought a vaccum cleaner.
vaccum cleaner   vaccum cleaners

validate *v.*

Please validate my ticket so
I won't have to pay for parking.

533

534 valley

valley n.

The cabin is in a small valley.
valley   valleys

van n. *covered truck*

or

He is driving a van.
van   vans

valuable adj.

or

The ring is very valuable.
It's worth a lot of money.

vanilla n. *flavor*

The boy likes vanilla.

value v.

or

We value the bull at $1000.00
values   valued   valuing

vanish v.

The vase will <u>vanish</u>.
It will <u>disappear</u>.

vampire n.

Vampires live on blood.
vampire   vampires

vase n. *flower container*

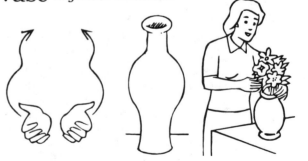

She put the flowers in a vase.
vase   vases

vest 535

Vaseline n.

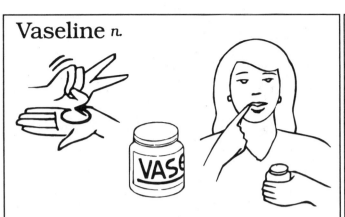

She put Vaseline on her lips.

verb n.

The underlined words are verbs.
verb   verbs

vegetable n. *food*

Vegetables are good for you.
vegetable   vegetables

verdict n. *decision*

The jury brought in a verdict.
verdict   verdicts

vehicle n.

There are four vehicles on the road.
vehicle   vehicles

very adv.

It is very hot today.
It is hotter than usual today.

veil n.

The bride wore a long veil.
veil   veils

vest n. *clothing*

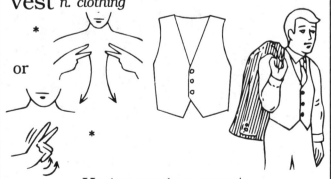

He is wearing a vest.
vest   vests

536 videotape

videotape n.

He wants to watch a videotape.
videotape   videotapes

vinegar n.

Vinegar is sour.

view n.

The view from the window was nice.

violate v.

Some drivers <u>violate</u> the law.
Some drivers <u>break</u> the law.

village n.
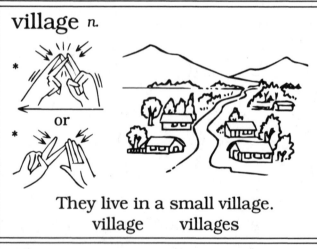
They live in a small village.
village   villages

violet n. *flower*
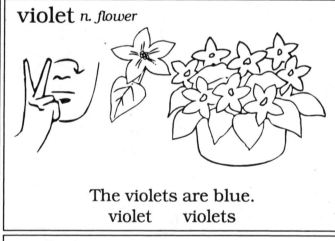
The violets are blue.
violet   violets

vine n.
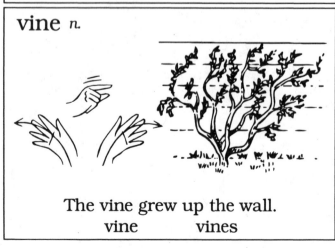
The vine grew up the wall.
vine   vines

violin n. *musical instrument*
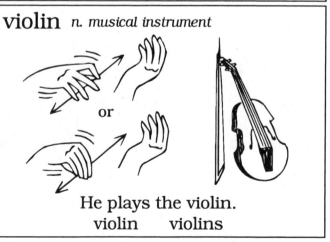
He plays the violin.
violin   violins

vocabulary 537

visible adj.

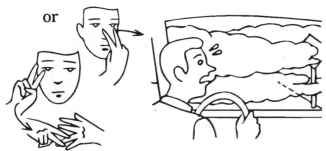

The road was barely visible.
I could barely see the road.

visitor n.

They have visitors for dinner.
They have company for dinner.

vision n.

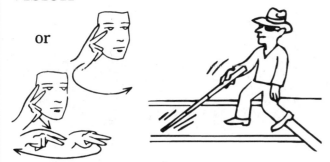

His vision is poor.
His sense of sight is poor.

vital adj.

It is vital that plants have water.
That's very important.

visit n.

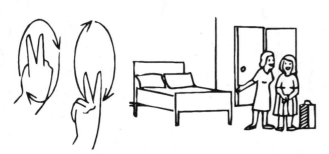

My mother came for a visit.
She stayed with us for a short time.

vitamin n.

 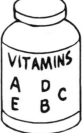 

He takes vitamins every day.
vitamin   vitamins

visit v.

We came to visit him.
We went to see him.

vocabulary n.

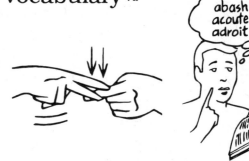

He has a large vocabulary.
He knows and uses many words.

538 voice

voice n.

The girl has a nice voice.
voice   voices

vomit v.

The boy had to <u>vomit</u>.
He had to <u>throw up</u>.

volcano n.

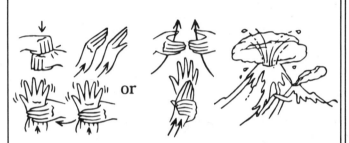

We saw a volcano.
volcano   volcanoes/volcanos

vote v.

I always vote.
votes   voted   voting

volleyball n. game

They are playing volleyball.

vowel n.

These letters are vowels.
vowel   vowels

volunteer v.

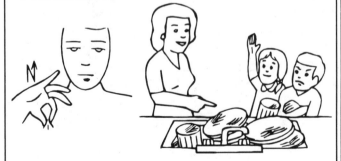

I <u>volunteer</u> to wash the dishes.
I <u>offer</u> to wash them.

vulture n. bird

Vultures eat dead animals.
vulture   vultures

W w

wade v.

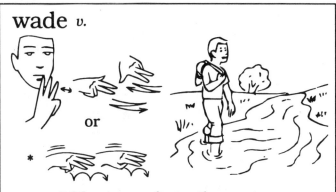

I like to wade in the water.
wades   wading   waded

wagon n. toy

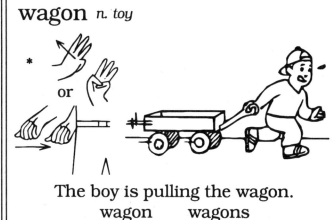

The boy is pulling the wagon.
wagon   wagons

waffle n. food

I made waffles for breakfast.
waffle   waffles

waist n. body part

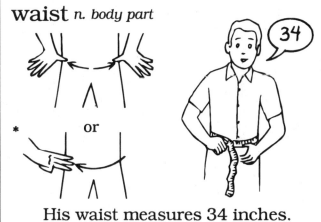

His waist measures 34 inches.

waffle iron n. electrical appliance

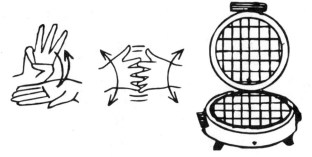

We have a new waffle iron.
waffle iron   waffle irons

wait v.

He had to wait to see the doctor.
waits   waited   waiting

wage n.

He is paid the minimum wage.
He's paid the lowest possible wage.

wait a minute

Please wait a minute.
I'll be right with you.

540 wait on

wait on v.

The clerk must <u>wait on</u> the customer.
She must <u>serve</u> the customer.

walk n.
They took a walk in the park.
walk   walks

waiter n. *male worker*
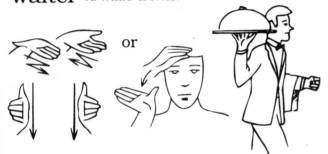
The waiter is carrying our food.
waiter   waiters

walk n.

He is sweeping the <u>walk</u>.
He's sweeping the <u>path</u>.

waitress n. *female worker*

The waitress took my order.
waitress   waitresses

walk v.

They will walk home.
walks   walked   walking

wake up v.

I wake up when the alarm rings.
wakes up   woke up   waking up

walkie-talkie n.
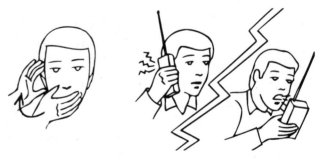
The men are using walkie-talkies.
walkie-talkie   walkie-talkies

want 541

wall n.
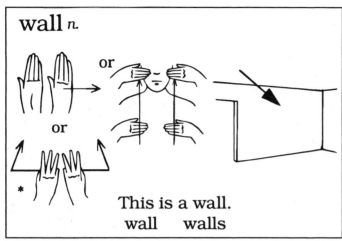
This is a wall.
wall   walls

wand n.
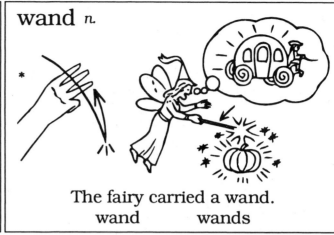
The fairy carried a wand.
wand   wands

wallet n.

He keeps his money in his wallet.
He keeps it in his billfold.

wander v.

The boy likes to wander around.
wanders   wandering   wandered

walnut n. food

The squirrel is holding a walnut.
walnut   walnuts

want v.
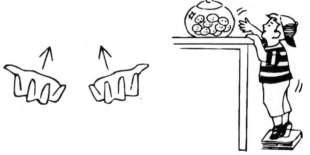
I want a cookie.
wants   wanting   wanted

walrus n. animal
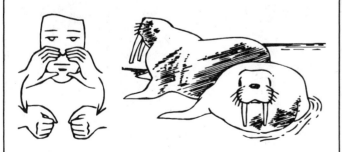
The walrus has long tusks.
walrus   walruses

want v.

I want the picture on that wall.
I wish to have it there.

542 war

war n.

Many people died in the war.
war   wars

warranty n.

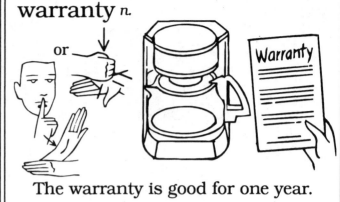

The warranty is good for one year.
warranty   warranties

warehouse n.

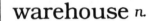

The warehouse is full of boxes.
warehouse   warehouses

was pt. of **am** and **is**

Bill was asleep, but
the alarm woke him up.

warm v.

We must warm our hands.
warms   warmed   warming

wash v.

She has to wash the clothes.
washes   washed   washing

warn v.

Signs warn us of danger.
warns   warned   warning

washcloth n.

She is holding a washcloth.
washcloth   washcloths

watch 543

washer *n. household appliance*

She is using the <u>washer</u>.
She's using the <u>washing machine</u>.

wasp *n. insect*

Wasps can sting you.
wasp   wasps

washing machine *n.*
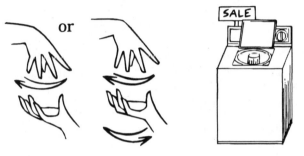
She has a new <u>washing machine</u>.
She has a new <u>washer</u>.

waste *v.*
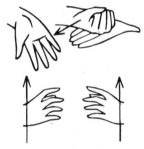
I waste a lot of paper.
wastes   wasted   wasting

Washington *n.*

George Washington was the first president of the United States.

wastebasket *n.*

He emptied the wastebasket.
wastebasket   wastebaskets

Washington, D.C.
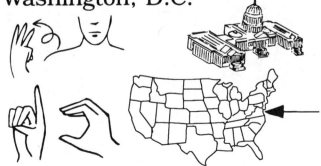
Washington, D.C. is the capital of the United States.

watch *n.*
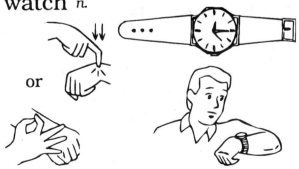
He looked at his watch.
watch   watches

544 watch

watch *v.*

They like to <u>watch</u> TV.
They like to <u>look at</u> TV.

waterfall *n.*

The waterfall is beautiful.
waterfall   waterfalls

watch out *v.*

Mother told her to <u>watch out</u>.
Mother told her to <u>be careful</u>.

watermelon *n. fruit*

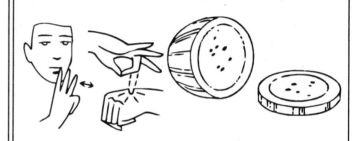

The watermelon is sweet and juicy.
watermelon   watermelons

water *n.*

The boy is drinking
a glass of water.

wave *n.*

A big wave rolled over the boat.
wave   waves

water *v.*

I have to water the lawn.
waters   watered   watering

wave *v.*

I will wave to my friend.
waves   waved   waving

weary 545

wavy *adj.*

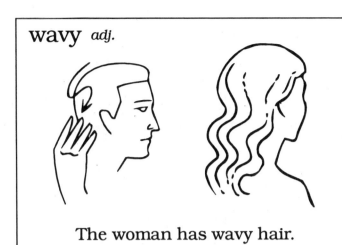

The woman has wavy hair.

weak *adj.*

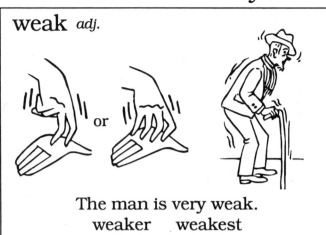

The man is very weak.
weaker   weakest

wax *v.*

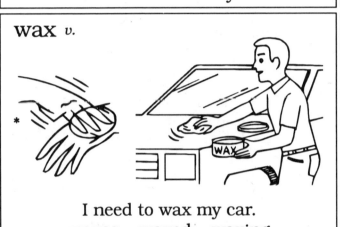

I need to wax my car.
waxes   waxed   waxing

wealthy *adj.*

The woman is wealthy. She is rich.
wealthier   wealthiest

way *n.*

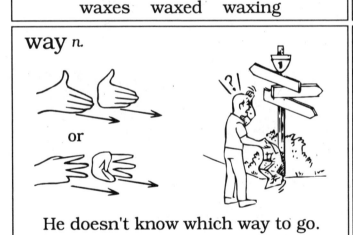

He doesn't know which way to go.
way   ways

wear *v.*

He is wearing a coat.
wears   wore   wearing   worn

we *pron.*

We bought this house.
You and I bought it.

weary *adj.* tired

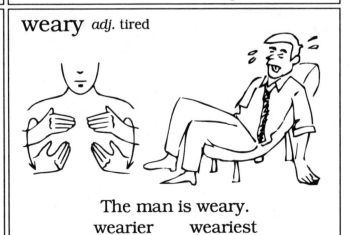

The man is weary.
wearier   weariest

546 weather

weather n.

The weather is fine today.
It's nice and sunny today.

wedding n.

The wedding was beautiful.
wedding   weddings

weave v.
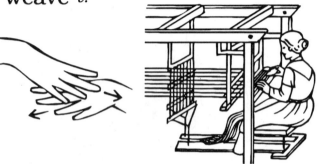
The woman can weave cloth.
weaves wove/weaved weaving woven

Wednesday n. day of the week

Wednesday comes after Tuesday.

weave v.

I saw the car weave in and out.

week n. 7 days
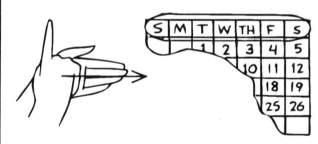
There are seven days in a week.
week   weeks

web n. cobweb, spider web
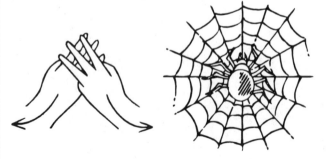
The spider is making a web.
web   webs

weekend n.

It rained all weekend.
It rained Saturday and Sunday.

well 547

weekly adv.

He gets paid weekly.
He gets paid once a week.

weird adj. strange

They heard a weird noise.
weirder   weirdest

weep v.
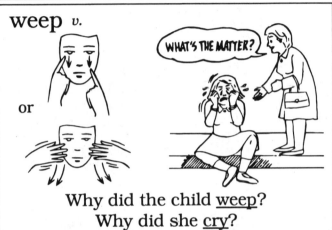
Why did the child weep?
Why did she cry?

welcome v.

We must welcome our guests.
welcomes   welcomed   welcoming

weigh v.
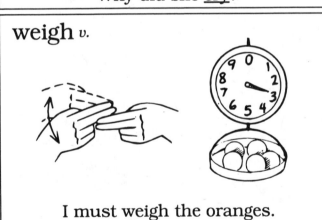
I must weigh the oranges.
weighs   weighed   weighing

weld v.
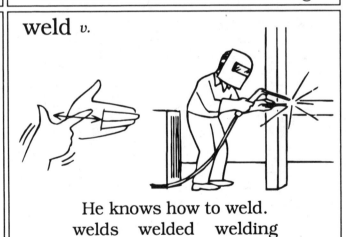
He knows how to weld.
welds   welded   welding

weight n.

Her weight is 160 pounds.

well adj.

He did well in math.
He did good in math.

548 well

well *adj.*

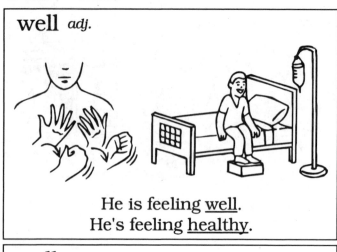

He is feeling well.
He's feeling healthy.

went *pt. of* **go**

The boy went home.

well *interjection*

Well, I just don't know where my ball is.

were *pt. of* **are**

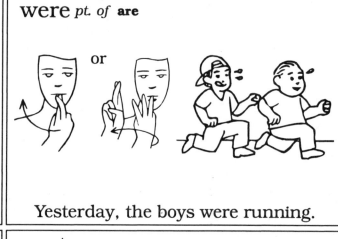

Yesterday, the boys were running.

well *n.*

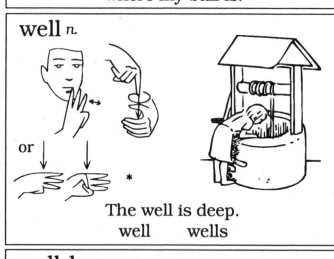

The well is deep.
well   wells

west *adv.*

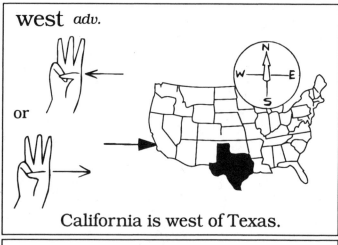

California is west of Texas.

well-known *adj.*

Lincoln's face is well-known.
Lincoln's face is familiar.

wet *adj.*

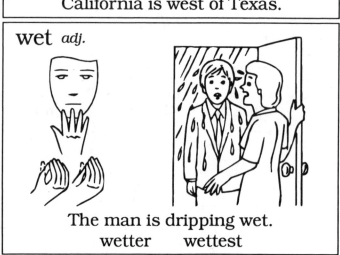

The man is dripping wet.
wetter   wettest

when 549

whale n.

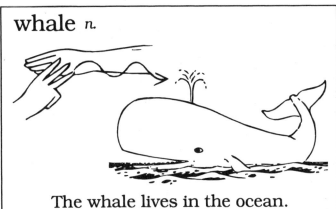

The whale lives in the ocean.
whale   whales

wheel n.

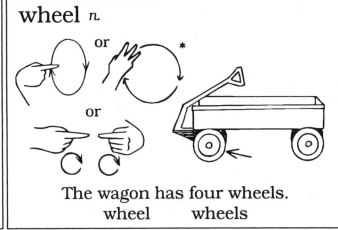

The wagon has four wheels.
wheel   wheels

what pron.

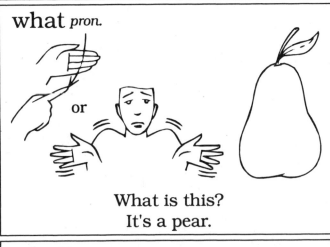

What is this?
It's a pear.

wheelbarrow n.

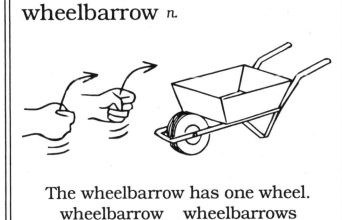

The wheelbarrow has one wheel.
wheelbarrow   wheelbarrows

what's wrong

What's wrong?
What's the matter?

wheelchair n.

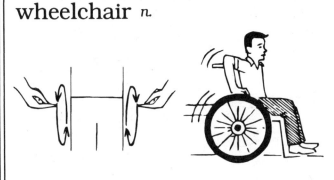

The boy must use a wheelchair.
wheelchair   wheelchairs

wheat n. grain

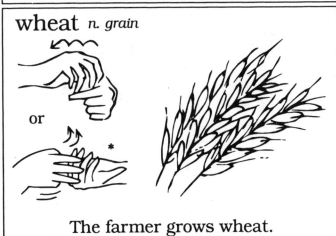

The farmer grows wheat.

when adv.

When did Bill wake up?
What time did he wake up?

550　where

where adv.

Where are the apples?
They're on the box.

whip n.

The trainer has a long whip.
whip　　whips

which pron.

Which do you want?
I want the apple.

whip v.

She is whipping the cream.

while conj.

While I play golf, my
wife has her hair done.

whipped cream

He put whipped cream on his pie.

in a while

I'll call you back <u>in a while</u>.
I'll call you back <u>soon</u>.

whiskers n. body part

The cat has long whiskers.
whisker　　whiskers

whom 551

whisper *v.*

What did she whisper to him?
whispers   whispered   whispering

White House
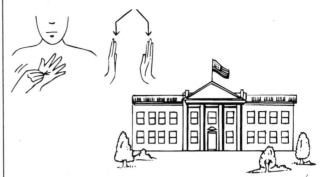
The President lives in the White House.

whistle *n.*

The whistle makes a loud noise.
whistle   whistles

who *pron.*
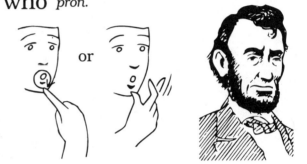
Who is this?
It's Abraham Lincoln.

whistle *v.*
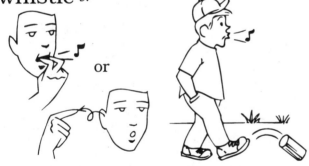
The boy can whistle.
whistles   whistled   whistling

whole *adj.*
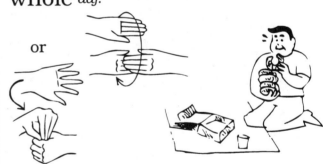
He ate the whole box of donuts.
He ate all of the donuts.

white *adj. color*

The snow is white.
whiter   whitest

whom *pron.*

She does not know whom to blame.
She doesn't know which boy to blame.

552 whose

whose *pron.*

Whose book is this?
It's Mary's book.

width *n.*
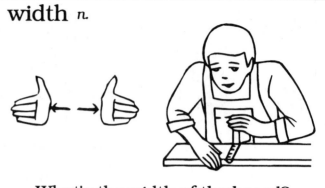
What's the width of the board?
How wide is the board?

why *adv.*
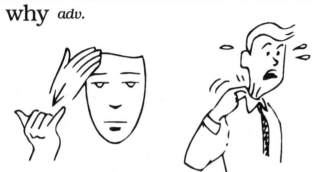
Why is the man uncomfortable?
Because his collar is too tight.

wiener *n. food*
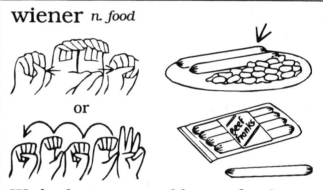
We had <u>wieners</u> and beans for dinner.
We had <u>hot dogs</u> and beans.

wicked *adj. evil*

The wicked man kidnapped the baby.
more wicked   most wicked

wife *n.*
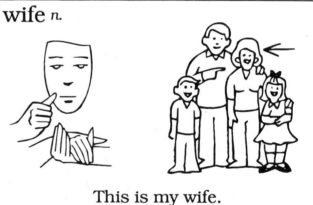
This is my wife.
I am married to this woman.

wide *adj.*
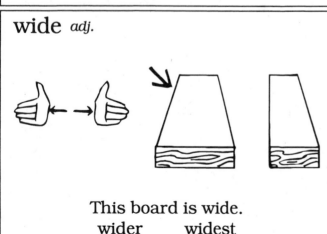
This board is wide.
wider   widest

wig *n.*
*

The woman may buy a wig.
wig   wigs

win 553

wiggle v.

Please don't wiggle.
wiggles   wiggled   wiggling

will n.

He will plant the tree.
He is going to plant the tree.

wigwam n.

The Indians lived in a wigwam.
wigwam   wigwams

willing adj.

He wants to leave, and Mother is willing. Mother is agreeable.

wild adj.
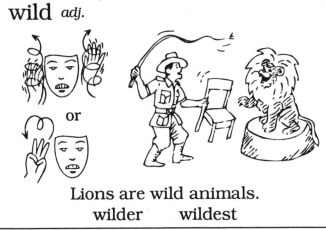
Lions are wild animals.
wilder   wildest

willpower n.

She does not have much willpower.
She doesn't have much determination.

will n.

The lawyer read the will.
will   wills

win v.

Wow! I never thought I would win.
wins   won   winning

554 wind

wind n.

The wind is blowing.
wind   winds

window seat

She has a window seat in her room.

wind v.

I have to wind the clock.
winds   wound   winding

windy adj.

It is windy today.
The wind is blowing today.

windmill n.

The windmill pumps water.
windmill   windmills

wing n. animal body part

The bird has two wings.
wing   wings

window n.

The window is made of glass.
window   windows

wink v.

She blushes when I wink at her.
winks   winked   winking

witch 555

winter *n. season*

It is very cold this winter.
winter   winters

wish *n.*

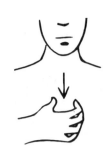 

The boy made a wish.
wish   wishes

wipe *v.*

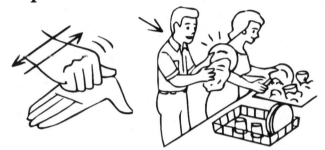

I often wipe the dishes.
wipes   wiped   wiping

wish *v.*

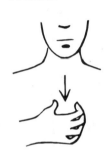 

I wish I could find my ball.
wishes   wished   wishing

wire *n.*

The fence is made of wire.

wishbone *n.*

They will break the wishbone.
wishbone   wishbones

wire *n.*

She received a <u>wire</u>.
She received a <u>telegram</u>.

witch *n.*

The witch is ugly.
witch   witches

556 with

with *prep.*

The boy is walking with his father.
They are walking together.

wives *plural of* **wife**

The husbands enjoy fishing.
Their wives enjoy dancing.

withdraw *v.*

She will withdraw some money.
She'll take some money out of the bank.

woke up *pt. of* **wake up**

Bill woke up at seven o'clock.

without *prep.*

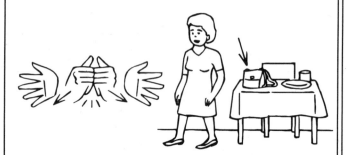

She left without her purse. She
left and forgot to take her purse.

wolf *n. animal*

The wolf is howling at the moon.
wolf   wolves

witness *v.*

I happened to <u>witness</u> the accident.
I happened to <u>see</u> it.

wolves *plural of* **wolf**

We saw a pack of wolves.

wooden 557

woman *n.*

The woman is happy.
woman   women

wonderful *adj.*

The woman feels <u>wonderful</u>.
She feels <u>great</u>.

women *plural. of* **woman**

The <u>women</u> are angry.
The <u>ladies</u> are angry.

won't *contr. of* will not

I <u>won't</u> mow the lawn.
I <u>will not</u> mow it.

won *pt. of* **win**

Our team won the game.
Our team got the most runs.

wood *n.*

The piece of wood is crooked.
The board is crooked.

wonder *v.*

I wonder which way I should go.
wonders   wondered   wondering

wooden *adj.*

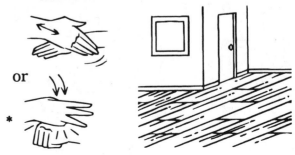

The room has a wooden floor.
The floor is made of wood.

558 woodpecker

woodpecker n. bird

The woodpecker has a pointed bill.
woodpecker   woodpeckers

wore pt. of **wear**

She wore a pretty dress.

woods n.

Tall trees grow in the woods.

work n.

He is looking for <u>work</u>.
He's looking for <u>a job</u>.

wool n.

Wool comes from sheep.

work v.

The men work in a factory.
works   worked   working

word n.

The boy spelled the word.
word   words

work v.

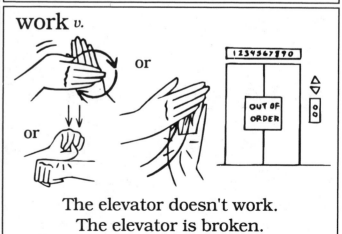

The elevator doesn't work.
The elevator is broken.

worse 559

worker n.
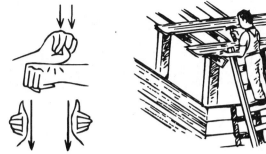
He is a good worker.
worker   workers

worn-out adj.

The car is completely worn-out.
It needs many new parts.

world n. the planet Earth

The world is round.

worn-out adj.
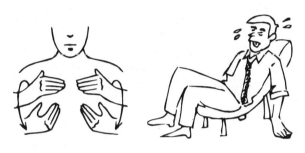
The man is completely worn-out.
He's exhausted.

worm n.
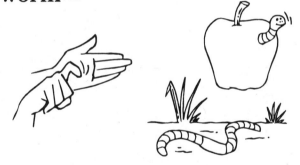
There is a worm in the apple.
worm   worms

worry v.

I worry about paying my bills.
worries   worried   worrying

worn pp. of wear
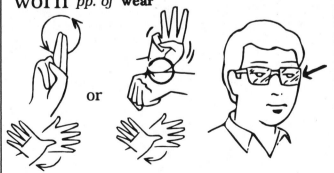
He has worn glasses since he was a child.

worse adj.

He did worse in art than he did in English and reading.

560 worst

worst adj.

His worst grade was in art.

would like
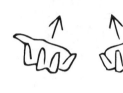 
I would like a cookie.
I want a cookie.

worth adj.

The bull is worth $1000.
The bull is valued at $1000.

wound pt. of wind

The man wound the clock.

worthless adj.

The car is worthless.
It has no value.

wound v. injure

Did the bomb wound the soldier?
wounds   wounded   wounding

would v.

Would you please hang
the picture on that wall.

wow interjection

The boy shouted "wow" when
he saw all the gifts.

wrist 561

wrap v.
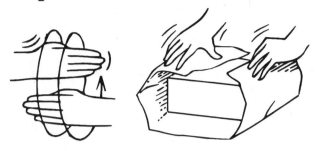
I have to wrap this package.
wraps   wrapped   wrapping

wrestle v.
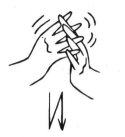 
The men like to wrestle.
wrestles   wrestled   wrestling

wreath n.
 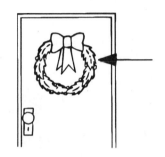
They hung a wreath on the door.
wreath   wreaths

wring out v.

I must wring out the towel.
wrings   wrung/wringed   wringing

wreck v. damage
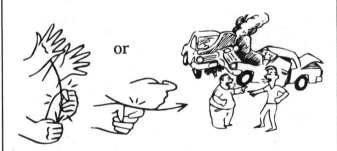
Did the accident wreck the cars?
wrecks   wrecked   wrecking

wrinkle v.

Why did you wrinkle the paper?
wrinkles   wrinkled   wrinkling

wrench n. tool
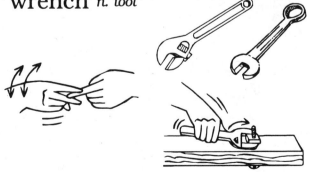
The man is using a wrench.
wrench   wrenches

wrist n. body part
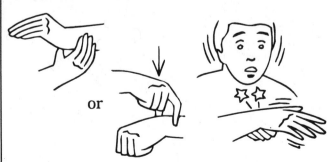
He sprained his wrist.
wrist   wrists

562 wristwatch

wristwatch *n.* watch

He looked at his wristwatch.
wristwatch   wristwatches

wrong *adj.*

Both answers are wrong.
The answers are not correct.

write *v.*

I will write a letter to my friend.
writes   wrote   writing   written

wrote *pt. of* **write**

Daniel Defoe wrote this book.

writer *n.*

Daniel Defoe was a writer.
Daniel Defoe was an author.

wrung *pt. of* **wring**

He wrung my hand.
He grasped it firmly.

written *pp. of* **write**

He has written a letter.

wrung out *pp. of* **wring out**

She has wrung out two towels.

Xx Yy Zz

Xerox *n.*

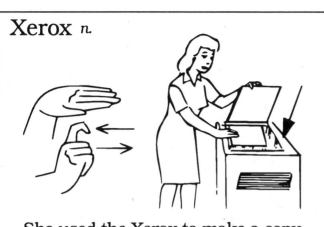

She used the Xerox to make a copy.

yank *v.*

Don't <u>yank</u> my hair.
Don't <u>pull</u> my hair.

x ray *n.*

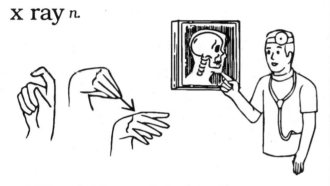

The doctor pointed to the x ray.
x ray   x rays

yard *n. 36 inches*

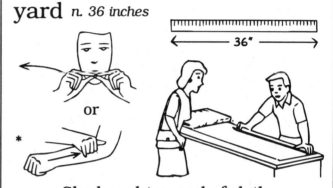

She bought a yard of cloth.
yard   yards

xylophone *n.*

He plays the xylophone.
xylophone   xylophones

yard *n.*

The yard is behind the house.

yam *n. vegetable*

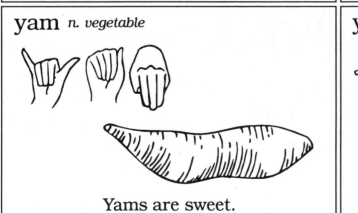

Yams are sweet.
yam   yams

yardstick *n.*

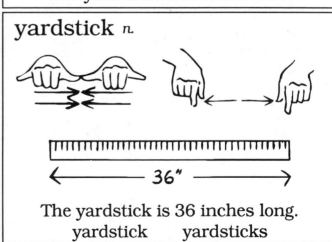

The yardstick is 36 inches long.
yardstick   yardsticks

564 yarn

yarn n.

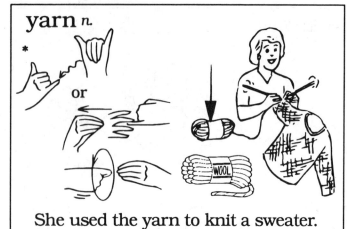

She used the yarn to knit a sweater.

yellow adj. color

The banana is yellow.

yawn v.

He had to yawn.
yawns   yawned   yawning

yes adv.

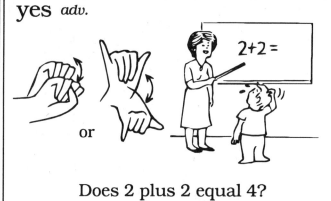

Does 2 plus 2 equal 4?
Yes, it does.

year n.

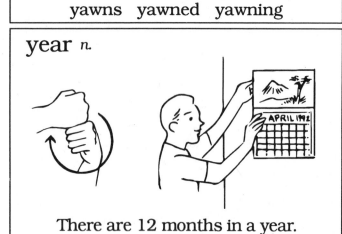

There are 12 months in a year.
year   years

yesterday n.

Today is November 7.
Yesterday was November 6.

yell v. holler

I will yell for help.
yells   yelled   yelling

yet adv.

You can't play yet.
You can't play now.

youngster 565

yield *v.* give up
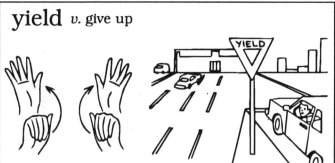
He must yield the right of way.
He must let other cars go first.

you *pron., singular*

I want you to behave.

yogurt *n.* food

Yogurt is made from milk.

you *pron., plural*

I want you to behave.

yoke *v.*
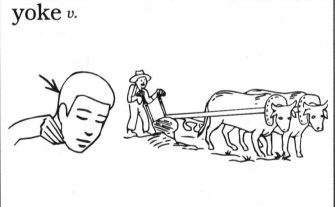
I yoke the oxen together.

young *adj.*

She is a young woman.
She is not old.

yolk *n.*

The yolk of the egg is yellow.
yolk   yolks

youngster *n.* child

They have two youngsters.
They have two children.

566 your

your pron., singular  Those are your marbles.	**yourself** pron.  Help yourself to the cookies.
your pron., plural  You must improve your behavior.	**yourselves** pron.  Help yourselves to the cookies.
you're welcome  I said, "Thank you." Father said, "You're welcome."	**yo-yo** n. toy  The boy played with his yo-yo. yo-yo yo-yos
yours pron.  That is your marble. That marble is yours.	**Yugoslavia** n. country 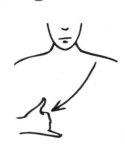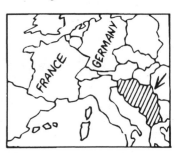 Belgrade is the capital of Yugoslavia.

zoo 567

zebra n. animal

Zebras have black and white stripes.
zebra   zebras

zipper n.

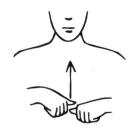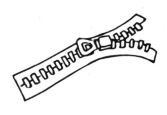

This is a zipper.
zipper   zippers

zero n. 0

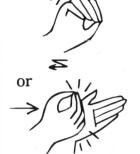

Subtract 5 from 5 and you have zero.

zombie n.

They saw a <u>zombie</u>.
They saw a <u>walking corpse</u>.

zip v.

I will zip the sweater.
zips   zipped   zipping

zone n. area

You can't park in a loading zone.
zone   zones

Zip Code n.

His Zip Code is 90044.

zoo n.

We saw many animals at the zoo.
zoo   zoos

Appendix

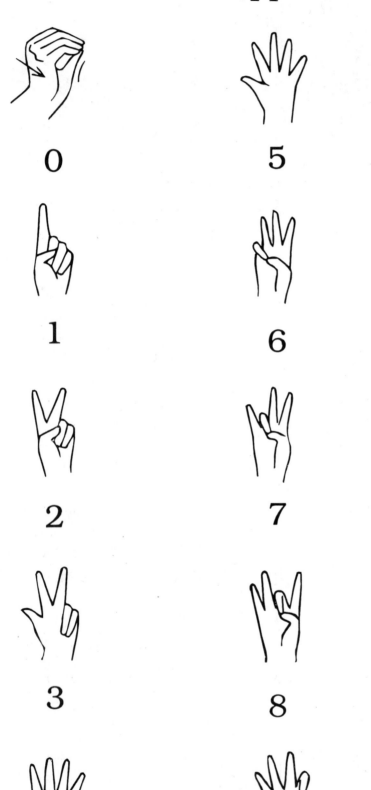
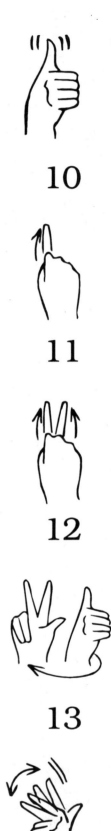

0

5

10

1

6

11

2

7

12

3

8

13

4

9

13

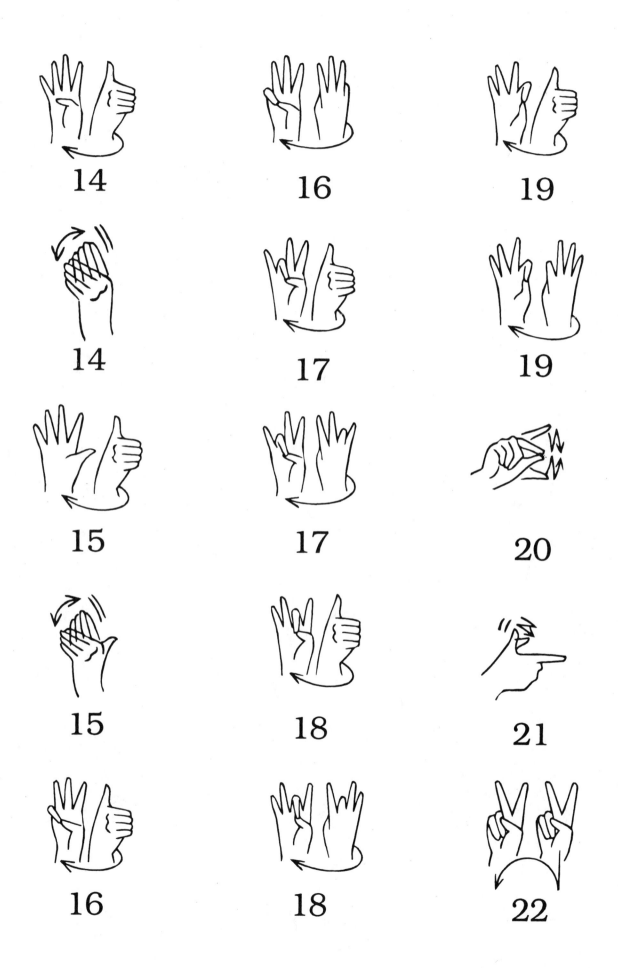

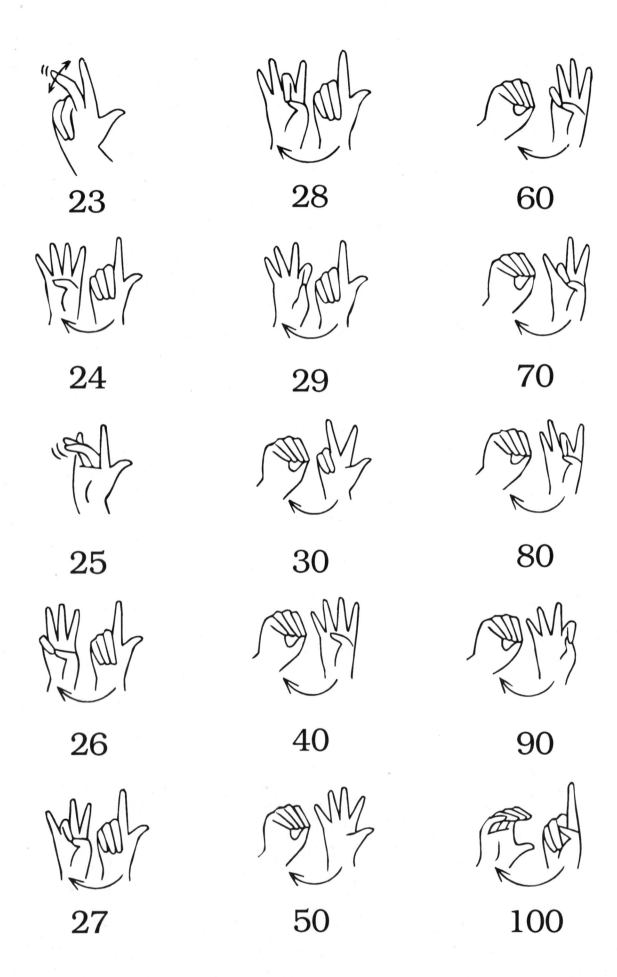